CU00925533

Praise for
Song of the Cardinal

"*Song of the Cardinal* is one of the most beautiful and captivating books I have ever read. It is a 360-page *Chicken Soup for the Soul*® story."
— JACK CANFIELD, coauthor of
the *Chicken Soup for the Soul*® series

"I am thrilled to share with you a book that will undoubtedly touch your soul. It's been such an honor to walk alongside Cynthia on her journey of healing and self-discovery, and now you have the chance to join her on this transformative path.

In this book, Cynthia invites you into her world, where she went from having everything she could ever wish for to experiencing the profound loss of Harry, the love of her life. This pivotal moment became the catalyst for a powerful spiritual awakening and true transformation.

Cynthia's story is a testament to the human spirit's ability to rise from the ashes and embrace a higher purpose. Her journey is a mirror reflecting our own potential for growth and enlightenment. If you're ready to be inspired and awakened, this book is a must-read. Dive into Cynthia's journey, and let it ignite the transformative fire within you."
— KYLE CEASE, transformational comedian and
New York Times bestselling author

"If I had been able to read *Song of the Cardinal* after my precious Jack died, I would not have shut down for three years."
— BETTY HEERY, retired lower school administrator,
Memorial Day School

"Cynthia Waine Brandt has invited us into the most vulnerable of places. Her epic journey after the indescribably devastating loss of the love of her life takes us to the depths of agony and elevates us to the cutting edge of emotional and spiritual evolution. *Song of the Cardinal* is a landmark writing that teaches us how to truly grieve and leaves us with the most profound understanding of how nothing loved is ever lost."

—BEDFORD COMBS, LMFT, clinical director,
Heartstream Journeys

"In *Song of the Cardinal*, author Cynthia Brandt weaves a captivating tale of love, loss, and the enduring human spirit. After losing the love of her life, she goes on a transformative journey to rediscover purpose and joy. Through heartache and healing, Cynthia unearths the miraculous messages of life that remind us all of our inner strength and capacity for renewal. This poignant narrative not only offers solace to those grieving, but also inspires a renewed sense of hope and connection to the beauty that life holds."

—SUSAN GRAU, author of *Infinite Life, Infinite Lessons*

"*Song of the Cardinal* is a deeply moving and profoundly life-altering story of love, heartbreak and transformation. It is an inspirational read for those seeking understanding and meaning after the loss of a loved one."

—JULIE DOSS, author, artist and spiritual guide

"Beautifully written and unbelievably inspiring for those in the darkness of grief or any other suffering. Peacefully, emotionally and painfully intense."

—DONNA PARRIS MARTINEAU

"I was entertained, I was broken-hearted, I laughed, and I still wish I had met Harry."

—Ida Eliason, retired controller,
Sitka Community Hospital

"Cynthia Brandt eloquently narrates her experience of a significant loss, illustrating how loved ones continue to live on in our memories, guiding present and future decisions. She beautifully describes how continuing bonds that are formed by the bereft may be projected, in her case onto the song of a cardinal. Beyond her grief, Cynthia Brandt exemplifies the ways in which survivor guilt and living a life of apology can influence us, limiting our capacity to make choices in our best interest."

—Mary Lamia, PhD, author of *Grief Isn't*
Something to Get Over: Finding a Home for
Memories and Emotions After Losing a Loved One

"Cynthia is undoubtedly one of the most talented authors I have ever had the pleasure of reading. For years, I have eagerly awaited the release of her book, knowing it would be nothing short of captivating. Cynthia did not disappoint. This book vividly brings to life the larger-than-life Harry and delves deeply into Cynthia's own experiences of grief and self-discovery amidst the pain. It is a poignant and compelling read for anyone who has experienced loss and is searching for themselves amidst the sadness. It is one of those rare books that you simply cannot put down."

—Reverend Jeannette Paxia,
empowerment speaker and coach

"Cynthia's writing style is riveting. Every few pages, I have to stop reading just to feel all the emotions. It's that real. It's that powerful. It's love captured in every word."

—David Greer, CEO, Story Road Marketing

"Cynthia Brandt's words are a balm for the heart and soul."
—SHERRY ROMANSKY SPENCER, Starbucks barista

"If you have ever known grief, this book will inspire you to see that, even after a heart-wrenching loss, you can have not only a life, but an exceptional, inspiring life."
—SANDI ATKINSON, retired, American Football Coaches Association

"In *Song of the Cardinal*, author Cynthia Brandt demonstrates that peace can reign supreme regardless of external circumstances and provides assurance that we can find a renewed sense of purpose and joy in life, even from the depth of sorrow. A willingness to share her spiritual journey as she transforms personally and professionally provides a comforting perspective that our loved ones are never, ever "lost." A thought-provoking and inspiring read!"
—TANYA THOMAS SCOTT, PhD, results coach

"We all want to know that the spark is within us. That feeling of an internal core light, never extinguished and just waiting to be ignited. In *Song of the Cardinal*, Cynthia Brandt demonstrates an indomitable faith in her ability to reflect on and respond to both an internal spark and external cues from the universe to guide her. Through masterful storytelling and raw honesty, she prompts us to ask and answer bigger, harder questions in our own lives. Most importantly, her righteous portrayal of darkness, despair and renewal reminds us that life does not happen to us, it happens for us. Prepare to dive into the light. Your cosmic cues await"
—KRISTEN JONES JOHNSON, nurse practitioner

SONG
OF THE
CARDINAL

SONG

OF THE

CARDINAL

*A true story of miracles and magic
after heartbreaking loss*

CYNTHIA WAINE BRANDT

STARFISH PUBLISHING

Many publishers and individuals provided permission to reprint copyrighted materials. Please see pages 346-347 for a listing of these permissions.

For information about special discounts for bulk purchases, please contact Starfish Publishing at info@starfishpublishing.com

For information on booking the author for a speaking engagement or consulting services, please visit www.cynthiabrandt.com

Starfish Publishing, LLC
Anchorage, Alaska

Cover Design by 99designs.com
Cover Art (feather) by Adobe Stock; (cardinal) by Shutterstock;
Cover Art (stylus) by IrongateArmory.com

Interior design by Tabitha Lahr
Interior art (feather) by Shutterstock; (section divider) by Adobe Stock

Printed in the United States of America

Library of Congress Control Number: 2024917495

ISBN 979-8-9905407-1-2 (hdcvr)
ISBN 979-8-9905407-0-5 (pbk)
ISBN 979-8-9905407-2-9 (ebook)
ISBN 979-8-9905407-3-6 (audiobk)

To Harry

A bird does not sing
        because he has an answer.

He sings
        because he has a song.

—Joan Walsh Anglund

Chapter 1

This just may do me in.

Seconds before those eerily matter-of-fact words echoed in my mind, I stood up, walked around the large steel desk in my hospital client's office in Juneau, Alaska, and unplugged my laptop cord. I was calmly and meticulously wrapping it around the power pack when those words came through—a veritable death sentence for my heart and soul.

Moments later, I slung on my backpack, stood as straight as I could, and positioned it squarely between my shoulders. With the weight of the world now riding inside, along with my laptop, makeup and meds, I turned off the light, closed the door, and walked out of that office and into a life without Harry.

While driving to the client-provided condo to collect my things before heading to the airport, I replayed the previous hour of my life. When I answered the last call, after anxiously awaiting updates from Atlanta, the worst I expected to hear was that doctors at the hospital were going to be putting Humpty Dumpty Harry back together again while I flew across the country to be with him.

Never in a million years would I have expected Death to be on the other end of that call.

Even though I knew that Harry had collapsed at a business dinner forty-five minutes earlier, it never occurred to me that my larger-than-life Prince Charming would die. After hearing the horrifying words, I sat in stunned silence for several seconds. And then I did what any normal, rational human being would do, having just learned that the love of her life had died 4,000 miles away.

I hung up.

Without uttering a single word, I hung up on Death.

And then I sat staring at the piece of paper in front of me on which I had written the caller's name. And *Harry*. I shook my head, whispering "No," over and over again. Each new "no" was louder and longer than the one before, until I unleashed a blood-curdling "NOOOOOO!" that should have shattered every window in the building.

But no glass fell. No one came running. It was dead silent, because that blood-curdling cry was actually me screaming on the inside. The only thing that shattered was my heart.

January 21, 2014 started out like any other day. I was in Alaska, where we lived full time. My husband had traveled to Georgia for business, to check on our house in Braselton, and to await an appointment with a cardiologist. By the time I woke up four time zones away, Harry had enjoyed a tasty breakfast at Papa Jack's—our favorite country-cooking diner—made a gazillion phone calls, ran a few errands, prepared for a business meeting, and sent emails to keep me updated on his day and check in on mine.

Later, he sent me a picture taken from the glass elevator at the Hyatt in downtown Atlanta. His message was, *Here's George Jetson!* Next came a picture of his hotel room. Harry was doing one of the things that he did best: simple gestures to keep us connected, no matter how far apart we were.

I replied, *It's missing one thing!* and then took a selfie. Before I could send it, Harry completed my thought with, *The Baby!*, one of his nicknames for me. I laughed as I sent the selfie to him and then turned my attention back to work with a smile on my face.

Harry reveled in the closeness we shared. "We're psychically connected!" he often exclaimed. Our exchange that afternoon was an example of that, and of the fun we had—like little-kid playmates—adding sparkle to an otherwise ordinary day.

Around midday Alaska time, while I sat in a noisy hospital cafeteria having lunch, we messaged back and forth with our usual inside jokes and rapid-fire dialog. Late in my afternoon, I had just returned to the office after a meeting, when I received yet another picture. This time, it was a photo of Harry and his dear friend and colleague Henry. It was around 8:00 p.m. Eastern time, 4:00 p.m. in Alaska.

I loved that Harry was with Henry. They had met professionally and became close over the next twenty years, calling each other "brother" to signify their deep connection. Harry was especially excited about this visit, as he had not seen his Puerto Rican brother in nearly five years. I was sure they would have a festive evening.

As I was wrapping up a meeting about thirty minutes later, I smiled when I heard the sound signaling another message from Harry, and wondered what he was up to this time. But I became concerned when I saw the message: *Cynthia, can you call me?* As I pressed and held the H on my phone, I thought, *Harry never calls me "Cynthia."*

My concern was well-founded, because it was not my mischievous, adorable Harry who answered. It was Henry, and he was noticeably concerned. I could tell he was doing his best to convey a sense of calm as he informed me that Harry had collapsed while they were waiting for their table, and that he had been transported to the hospital via ambulance. Though Henry didn't have any details on Harry's condition, he said that he would call back right away with any updates.

I fought back tears after hanging up. My thoughts raced, and I felt panic surge from deep within. But just as suddenly as the festive afternoon had darkened, the shields came up, and I went into crisis-management mode. I'm not sure exactly when I became an expert at turning off emotions and calmly swinging into action during emergent situations, but it served me well in that moment. I needed to get myself to Atlanta and rally a team to support Harry until I arrived.

Finding reinforcements wouldn't be difficult, since we had an extensive network of friends and family in Georgia. I was born in Savannah, and had lived there for 41 years until I moved with Harry to Braselton, which was an hour northeast of Atlanta. Harry was from Wisconsin, but had lived most of his life in the Atlanta area, and the last 13 years in a close-knit neighborhood in Braselton, less than an hour from the hospital.

After turning to the computer and taking a deep breath to focus on the task at hand, I logged into my Alaska Airlines account. I had one shot to get out of Juneau that night. The last flight was nearly full. I noted that there was one first-class seat available. Immediately, I heard Harry's voice in my head: *The Punkin doesn't fly coach.* It was his tease whenever I was booking business travel in coach, and his way of letting me know he thought I was worthy of first class at all times.

The first-class seat was 1F, my favorite when flying with Harry. Tucked away in the front-right corner of the plane by the window, with the bulkhead in front and Harry to my left, I couldn't have been more comfortable. The same seat was available for the Seattle to Atlanta leg the next morning, so I purchased the first-class ticket. It was going to be a long trip to Georgia, and I wanted to walk into Harry's hospital room feeling as rested as possible and looking like a ray of sunshine.

I sat back to think about the news I'd just received. I was horribly concerned, and my heart was already breaking because I wasn't there with him. But oddly enough, I was also relieved.

For a few weeks, we had been trying to reschedule Harry's mid-February appointment with a cardiologist. Just over a month before, while we were in Georgia for Christmas, Harry had an ultrasound after our doctor in Braselton detected a heart murmur during a routine examination. By the time the results came back, we had returned to Alaska, and I was about to depart for a new engagement as interim chief financial officer (CFO) for the community hospital in Juneau.

The news was sobering. The report showed that Harry had aortic stenosis, and the radiologist recommended that he have a more comprehensive test to determine the extent of it.

Immediately, we both researched and spoke to people in the healthcare community. It was alarming to learn that the condition may require surgery to replace a valve in Harry's heart someday. But the consensus across the board was the same: since he was feeling great and having no symptoms, we should monitor the condition. Surgery would only be required if the condition worsened and Harry became symptomatic.

But I was uneasy, especially since I was going to spend a significant amount of time away from home on the new project in Juneau. And I couldn't stop wondering what else might be wrong.

After a couple of days digesting the news, we sat down in the dining nook in our condo that looked out on downtown Anchorage, the Cook Inlet, and the snow-covered Chugach Mountains. Over morning coffee, we hatched a plan. I would head to Juneau to kick off the new client engagement. Harry would return to Georgia to handle some business and personal affairs and await an appointment with his newly selected cardiologist. I would join him a couple of weeks later. This seemed the best way for us to manage the unexpected development, and for me to uphold my professional commitment.

Almost ten years earlier, I had started a CPA firm to provide financial management and advisory services to hospitals. My third client was in Nome, Alaska, and the first in what would become a niche for me: remote community hospitals in Alaska. While I had a small team during my first project in Nome, by the time I took on the Juneau engagement, I was a sole practitioner. So, I didn't have anyone who could step in, even for a week or so. It was a very busy time for the client and important for me to be there as promised. Our large group of friends in Braselton made it easier to decide. Even so, I couldn't shake my apprehension.

In fact, at the last minute, I changed my plans. Just as I was leaving for my flight to Juneau, I sat down at my desk and whipped out my laptop.

"What are you doing, Punkin?" Harry asked, standing at the front door with my luggage.

"I'm going with you," I said as I logged into Alaska Air. "Until we know the extent of the stenosis, I don't want to let you out of my sight."

Harry said nothing as he stepped away from the door and sat down across the desk from me. When I looked up and saw the slight smile on his face, I knew I'd made the right decision. "Thank you, Punkin. But what about Juneau?" he asked.

"I'm certain they'll understand if I defer for a few days. Hopefully, we can get your appointment moved up while I'm there."

But despite daily calls to the cardiologist, we could not change the appointment. The schedule was completely full; Harry was a new patient and asymptomatic. Though I suggested we try someone else, he was unwilling to do so, because the specialist came highly recommended. When it became clear that an earlier appointment was not happening, he insisted I head to Juneau. "I've never felt better. I promise I wouldn't let you go if I thought something was wrong."

Now, after the initial shock of learning Harry had collapsed, I felt a sense of relief. He was at one of the best hospitals in the state. I was certain that he would receive excellent care, and we'd finally have the more comprehensive assessment we were anxiously awaiting.

When I called our dear friends Paula and Broughton, Paula told me that her mother also had had aortic stenosis, and one of her first symptoms was a fainting spell. After hanging up, I felt a bit better. *A fainting spell. That's exactly what Henry described. Okay, we can deal with that.*

But by the time the next phone call came, my sense of relief had waned. Too much time had passed since Henry called. A fainting spell should have been long over by then. The caller was an admission representative, looking for information to register Harry as a patient. I responded to her initial questions calmly, but as they continued, it suddenly became unbearable for me.

"Listen," I said, "I work in healthcare finance, and I know you are simply doing your job. But right now, I'm in Alaska, 4,000 miles away, while my husband is there in your ER. I'm completely in the dark here, so the only person I want to talk to is someone who can update me on his condition. If you can't do that, then I suggest you find someone who can."

After a brief pause, she responded, "Yes ma'am, I understand."

I hung up with the admissions rep and then made several more calls to Georgia. By the time I finished, Paula and Broughton, Harry's sister Heidi, and my sister Deborah were on the way to the hospital.

The next call came, seeming to confirm that the admissions rep had granted my request. It was a female paramedic who had been in the ambulance with Harry. When I asked her to please tell me what she could, she responded, "All I can tell you is that they are working on him very aggressively right now." I realized then that we were dealing with much more than a fainting spell.

I sat for a moment, imagining the "aggressive" scene in the ER. I felt an overwhelming regret that I had ignored my instincts to stay with Harry. My entire body shook. I felt sure that the serious surgery we'd anticipated had arrived much sooner than expected. I desperately wanted to be there. I wanted my smile to be the first thing Harry saw when he woke up, and to tease him with a playful, "So, what happened to 'I've never felt better'?" I wanted to tell him how much I loved him, that I would take excellent care of him, and that an even more beautiful life awaited us on the other side of his recovery.

As usual, I was looking on the bright side of things, searching for light in the darkness. At that moment, I had no idea just how dark it was about to become, or how long it would take to see the light once more.

The phone rang again. I wrote down the caller's name.

"I was one of the doctors working on Harry," he said.

Noting the past tense, I took a deep breath. The pause gave me just enough time to feel a sense of relief that the crisis was over. But then he continued.

"I'm afraid I have some very bad news for you."

While I have total recall of that sentence, I'm not quite positive what he said immediately afterward.

And that's when I hung up on Death.

Immediately, I felt searing pain and a cauldron of anger and guilt bubbling up inside. I wanted to scream and never stop. I wanted to hurl the heavy steel desk in front of me, and everything on it, clear across the room.

But as I shook my head and quietly whispered "No," over and over again, I somehow knew that what I did next was going to set the course for the rest of my life. Instead of screaming, I sat quietly. And I couldn't believe what went through my mind.

There's no way that Harry would be gone so soon, unless there was a very good reason for it. This must mean I am destined to do something significant without him.

Even now, it seems unfathomable that, of all thoughts I could have had in that moment, I had that one. But I had switched from crisis mode to survival mode. Grasping for a lifeline of meaning distracted me from the worst feeling of all bubbling up from that cauldron of emotion: Harry was dead, and because I had not followed my instincts, it was my fault. Had I allowed that belief and the overwhelming guilt to boil over, I would have melted into nothingness.

After taking another deep breath, I made several phone calls. I don't remember many of them, but I'll never forget the call with my sister Tanya. After I broke the news and she confirmed I was as okay as I could be, she simply asked, "What do you need me to do?"

"Come to Braselton."

"I'll be there tomorrow."

Asking for help had never been easy for me, so Tanya's reply was a pinpoint of light in the darkest night of my life.

Finally, it was time to go. I stood up, and my entire life flashed before me. It had been a long haul, and Harry was my reward for all the struggle and hard work. But now he was gone because I had failed to protect my most treasured love. That's when the death sentence came through: *This just may do me in.*

But after putting on my backpack, I felt a sudden shift from resignation to determination as I thought, *But it won't.*

In that split second, I decided that there was no way I was going to dishonor the memory of the most beautiful person I had ever known, or tarnish the uncommon love we'd shared by letting Harry's death do me in. No matter the pain. No matter the guilt. No matter what.

Years later, I would realize that in this decisive moment, a doorway to miracles had cracked open ever so slightly, and I had indeed set the course for the rest of my life.

With my newfound resolve, though shaky at best, I drove to the condo, hyper-focused on what I needed to do. I climbed the narrow stairs with cement blocks for legs. At the top, a man with a smile on his face appeared, eager to greet his new "neighbor."

"Not now," I said, waving him off as I brushed past, having decided that I couldn't bear to say it out loud to a stranger. *My husband just died.* Once inside, I felt the stifled scream again as I packed, noting that my favorite dress and blazer had just become my funeral attire.

Less than thirty minutes later, I was driving to the airport through dense fog and heavy rain with a vice-like grip on the steering wheel, fulfilling my need to be in control of something, even if it was just the rental car. I was focusing on the road, not daring to allow myself to think about Harry's last moments—whether he was in pain, whether he was scared—or the enormity of what had happened. When my phone rang, I knew better than to answer it because of the conditions—both mine and the weather.

I pulled into the rental car lot, grabbed my luggage, and made my way inside. I was relieved to see a familiar face at the counter, and greeted her with a weary smile and an, "I need your help."

I had a long-term rental, so after I explained what happened and we discussed my estimated return date, she held out her hand. "Give me the keys, Cynthia. The car will be right here for you when you get back."

Next, I walked up to the Alaska Air ticket counter and said it again: "I need your help." Looking back on that night, I realize I defaulted to a line that I had heard Harry use hundreds of times to open many types of conversations or requests for help. I always marveled at how it worked for him. Apparently, I had learned well, because now it was working for me when I needed it the most.

My stop at the counter confirmed that the incoming flight, and my ride to Seattle, might not land because of the heavy fog. I needed that jet to land. I needed to keep moving.

After requesting priority rebooking if they canceled my flight, I remembered that a call had come through while I was driving to the airport. It was Paula, now at the hospital in Atlanta. I was certain she was calling to check on me after receiving the devastating news. But as I listened to her message, in which she explained they had received no updates about Harry's condition, I realized with horror that the hospital had not informed the group of friends and family that Harry had passed away.

I found a quiet place, sat down with a thud of resignation, and braced myself, waiting for Paula to answer. In a brutally ironic twist of fate, from 4,000 miles away in Alaska, I now had to deliver the devastating news to those who had gathered to support Harry.

Paula's "Hello, love!" was almost more than I could bear. Oozing comfort and concern, she immediately asked how I was doing, and if I had any updates. Paula adored Harry; I hated what I was about to say, knowing what it would do to her.

"He's gone, Paula," I said in a trembling voice. It was agonizing to hear her cry out in disbelief. I felt her overwhelming sense of despair and knew that everyone else in the room was soon to feel the same.

I remember little after our initial exchange, but I do recall feeling that Harry's death had suddenly become more real. After we hung up, I wearily stood and gathered my things.

Once through security, I made my way to the closed coffee shop, the quietest spot I could find. After catching my breath, I sent a text to Max, one of my professional connections in Juneau. *I've just received the worst possible news about Harry.* Seconds later, my phone rang. After confirming the meaning of my text, Max immediately took charge.

"Cynthia, where are you?"

"At the airport."

"Where at the airport?"

"In the coffee shop."

"Okay, tell me exactly where you are sitting."

My voice started shaking. "I'm sitting at the counter that faces the window."

"Okay, good. Now, tell me what happened."

It was a cold, foggy, and rainy night in Juneau. My best friend and the love of my life had just died, and not a single person on the planet who was part of my life knew exactly where I was until Max called.

For over ten years, that was something I never had to worry about. Harry always made a point of knowing where I was, the weather, and noteworthy events. He even knew the daily special at Airport Pizza in Nome, Alaska, before I did.

One night, I missed my exit on the way to a hotel outside of Washington, D.C., while talking to him on the phone. In a time before Google Maps, he had asked me to provide a landmark. When I casually responded, "Will the Washington Monument do?" he burst out laughing, and then gave me turn-by-turn directions back to the hotel ten miles away. Two days later, I received a special delivery—a TomTom Go navigation device. It was just like Harry to make sure I could find my way, even when he wasn't around.

On that foggy January night in 2014, I didn't have Harry or a TomTom Go. But I had Max.

Originally from Texas, Max had been in Alaska for over 20 years. He was a hard-charging mover and shaker in Juneau and throughout the state. Our paths had crossed because his CPA firm performed the annual financial audit for a few of my clients, including the one in Juneau. We had developed an excellent professional relationship over the six years I had been providing service in Alaska. His take-charge demeanor provided much-needed calm and comfort.

"Cynthia, can you see the trees across the runway?"

"It's solid gray."

Max, who was also a pilot, launched into pilot-speak, relaying what he was seeing on the Flight Aware tracking website.

I had Flight Aware up as well. Harry had taught me its value, especially when traveling in Alaska. I could see that the jet had already made one attempt to land. Max and I talked as it circled again before going into its third loop. Max gently cautioned me that the pilots would only make one more attempt to land before continuing on to Seattle.

For the first time in over six years, I felt the remoteness of Alaska. I stared out the window into the pitch-black night, losing hope that I would soon be on my way. But seconds later, the pilots punched through an opening in the seemingly impenetrable gray. The jet emerged as if by magic, touching down right in front of me.

Max said he would monitor my journey to Atlanta and suggested I check in with him as I traveled. Next, I called the Marriott at the Seattle Airport, and asked to speak with Jennifer in the concierge room. When she answered, I defaulted to my line of the night and asked for her help.

I'd met Jennifer a year and a half earlier. I had returned to her hotel from a business meeting to find Harry in the concierge room where he had been all afternoon, working on plans for his new business. Harry had been an entrepreneurial Renaissance man. He had a real estate license, had co-owned a company that made cigarette boats (think *Miami Vice*), and spent many years working in the demolition industry. These endeavors had one thing in common: sales. And he was very good at it, because he didn't see himself as a "salesman." He saw himself as a guide. A mentor. A resource. He knew that selling was about relationship and trust, not about closing the deal. He was starting a new business to teach and train others on the principles that had guided his very successful career.

That afternoon at the Seattle Airport Marriott, using his engaging personality and colorful storytelling, Harry made a friend in Jennifer. By the time I arrived, he had laid the groundwork for me to have a new friend as well.

So, on that bleak night in January 2014, I explained to her what had happened, and asked if she could hold a room for me. After recovering from her initial shock and sorrow, Jennifer said she would take care of things.

When I hung up, Henry called. We had a short but beautiful conversation. He assured me that Harry did not appear to be in pain before collapsing, that someone started CPR immediately, and that the paramedics arrived in just over five minutes. I was so grateful that Henry had been there and told him so while also acknowledging how shocking it must have been for him. Henry became emotional as he said, "Cynthia, my sister, God blessed me with such a gift to be with my brother during his last moments on earth. I will cherish that always, as I will Harry."

After our call, it was time to board the jet. As I stepped onboard, it occurred to me that I wasn't sure what would happen when they closed the hatch. Having gone into survival mode, I was faring pretty well under the circumstances, but I knew that could change once we were airborne. So, after most everyone had boarded, I stepped into the galley and spoke to the flight attendant.

I returned to my seat, appreciative of her concern and relieved that someone on board was aware of my situation. Shortly afterward, she closed the boarding door. It was then that I realized, despite my having bought the only available first-class seat, there was now an empty one. And it was Harry's seat . . . the one to my left.

After the flight attendant finished the beverage service, she sat down next to me. With concern, she asked how I was doing, and if I had a photo of Harry. I showed her one of my favorites. After confirming with me that we often flew to Seattle, she smiled. "I remember him. And you always sat here, didn't you?"

It was my turn to smile. "Yes. These were *our* seats."

She commented as she stood up, "Isn't it interesting that Harry's seat is open tonight? We don't usually have empty seats in first class."

I admitted being surprised, since I thought I had snagged the last first-class seat. But after she walked away, I thought about it more. Things had lined up as well as they could have: my favorite seats for both flights, pilots who punched through the fog, friends stepping in to help, and an empty seat next to me on the first leg of the journey. I felt protected somehow. I was also very grateful to have the front-right corner of the plane to myself, with no one there to hear me weeping in the dark cabin, or to ask the inevitable question, "So are you heading home?"

Moments before we landed, my airplane angel appeared again. This time, she handed me a plastic trash bag filled with packages of pretzels. "It's not much, but the hotel won't have any snacks or food available when you get there. These may tide you over until breakfast." She also gave me two bottles of water.

We landed in the wee hours of the morning. In a daze, I walked through the deserted Seattle airport. After boarding the plane train, I clung to a pole, resting my head on its cool steel, already weary from the grief that would consume me over the months and years ahead.

And so, a day that started out like many ended like no other. I walked into the hotel room, wearily dropped my backpack on a bed I knew would see no sleep, and opened a card on the desk that read, *Cynthia, I am so sorry for your loss of Harry.* Knowing I would get in long after her night was over, Jennifer had left a virtual hug: the card and two bottles of my favorite sparkling water.

I sat at the desk in the hotel room, making phone calls to some of our truest friends as the sun rose in each time zone and brought "mourning" to our world. At 6:00 a.m. I left for the airport and the flight to Atlanta.

Before that morning, I had not been very active on social media. So, I had posted nothing on Facebook about Harry's collapse or his death. Just after sitting down in seat 1F, I saw that Harry's sister Heidi had written a post, informing friends that he had passed away, and that I was on my way back from Alaska.

Initially I winced, worried that close friends were going to learn of Harry's death on social media. But almost immediately, I dismissed the concern as compassion for Heidi flooded my heart. Harry was her big brother and only sibling. Both of their parents were deceased. I suspected that, despite her own feelings of devastation, she had gotten the word out to help in our collective moment of despair. Not only did it help, but Heidi's instinct to write a post actually became a gift beyond measure that day.

By the time I saw it, the comments had exploded with messages of disbelief, horror, and sadness. But there was also something else. Soothing to my weary eyes were words of faith, hope, and love for Harry. And for me. I felt an unexpected comfort, and a little less alone for the five-hour flight to Atlanta.

I was still reading comments and emails as the plane sprinted down the runway and took off into the dreary morning. The gray sky was a perfect match for my now colorless world. As we climbed higher, the engines groaned, and the cabin shook fiercely. I continued to look at emails, but noted that the plane was fighting more than usual.

Suddenly, the cabin calmed. I felt intense heat on my face. Startled, I glanced out of the window. With wide-eyed wonder, I gazed at the majestic sight before me. Cotton ball clouds carpeted the sky, while Mount Rainier peeked above them in the distance. The sky was the deepest blue I could ever remember seeing, and the sun blazed through a long sliver of wispy clouds right into my window.

Despite the heat from the sun, chills coursed through my entire body. Tears glazed my eyes, and I felt an unexpected fullness in my heart. I couldn't believe how quickly the gray day had turned into a sparkling blue.

Breathlessly, I began taking photos, hungrily trying to capture what I knew was a miraculous moment. And then I sat back to catch my breath. As I stared directly into the sun, I felt the chills intensify as an amazing energy surged through my body. It felt like a moment of ultimate truth as Harry seemed to exclaim:

Death is no match for me, Punkin! I'm right here and always will be. This morning, I've brought you a brilliant sun to dry your tears and keep you warm. And cotton candy clouds to make you smile. I will always be close, keeping an eye on you!

I had no doubt that Harry had orchestrated this incredible moment. I felt him with me. In me. All around me. Filling me up and surrounding me with his spirit and essence. But there was more. For a few glorious seconds, I didn't know where I ended and the Divine began. I just closed my eyes and let the sun have its way with me.

Harry bursting into my sorrow that morning was exactly the way he had burst into my life: with light, love and laughter. In the years before I met him, I was plagued by depression, anxiety, workaholism, and the feeling of being an impostor in my own life. But I had healed in many ways, and learned to look for happiness no further than myself. Meeting Harry had been my reward.

The seeds I planted to outgrow my old self found a green-thumb gardener who provided the unconditional love, steadfast friendship and abundant laughter that I needed. His greatest enjoyment seemed to be watching me blossom. We met when I was 38 and he was 44. We got married almost exactly two years later, on my 40th birthday. For another eight and a half years, we had our own little fairytale. He was my Prince Charming, and I was his Cyntharella. It was the first time in my life that I felt loved, protected, and safe to be myself.

And now, without understanding how it was possible, I was feeling his love and protection again. As I basked in the warmth of his presence, I was reminded of the empty seat on the flight out of Juneau the previous night. I didn't know what it all meant, but a short time later, I felt nudged to write a post and share a photo I had taken that morning:

> Hello everyone. I just want to let you know that Harry is already at work. This is the brilliant "good morning" he arranged for me on takeoff from Seattle. As if to say, "I'm here Punkin, please don't cry." The sun has been shining on me the entire way. One of the most beautiful flights ever. It's nice being up here in heaven with him.

Even many years later, I would distinctly remember the sense of peace I felt as I wrote that short post. On some level, it was important to me that others hear from me. I wanted my sense of calm to come through, not just for me, but for them as well. I wanted everyone to be okay. I wanted me to be okay. I wanted Harry to be okay. But there was something else. In the midst of incredible sorrow, I had experienced an amazing feeling of love and light, and I wanted to share that with others.

As I continued to wing my way across the country, responses to my post flooded in. I was overwhelmed and amazed by the encouraging and comforting words the comments contained.

I also thought about our departure from Alaska in December. We were torn about going to Georgia for Christmas. After spending a blissful nine months together, with neither of us on the road for the first time in our marriage, we thought that a festive white Christmas in Anchorage would be a perfect grand finale before we hit the road again in the new year. But my mother was in her eighties, and seeing her had won out over the plan to stay in Anchorage.

When we got into the cab on the morning of our flight, we were like two kids who were homesick before we even left the house. It was unusually quiet during the short ride.

Just as we approached the airport, I felt Harry shift next to me. When I glanced over, I saw him lower his head slightly to look out of the window at the winter wonderland. And then, with a gentle wave at the snow-covered fir trees, and a voice laden with little-boy poignancy, he softly called out, "Goodbye, white Christmas."

Harry rarely expressed sadness or disappointment, so it hurt my heart to feel both emanating from him that morning. Unbelievably, thirty days later, it was me, with my heart now seemingly broken beyond repair, on my way to wave goodbye to so much more.

I touched down in Atlanta to a heartfelt text from Max, who had indeed been following my flights. I was beyond grateful for his kindness and watchful eye. He was one of many angels who made it possible for me to survive the worst twenty hours of my life. At the top of a very long escalator ride to Atlanta's main terminal, I found two more of them in Paula and Broughton, who were waiting for me with smiles, tears, and hugs.

While I'd made it to Atlanta in one piece, I now faced monumental challenges an hour away in Braselton. I was on my way to pull together a memorial service while keeping myself from falling apart. And I was returning to the first place that had ever felt like home, knowing that it was now missing the very reason it had.

I knew I was heading into the most difficult days of my life—perhaps months or years. I *didn't* know that the miracles and magic I had already experienced would continue. Even on my darkest days, they would infuse me with light and love, and change my heart and my life in ways I never could have imagined.

Chapter 2

I don't remember much about getting to the house that afternoon, but I do remember how it smelled. Like home. Like Harry. Just like the first time I walked into the house over ten years earlier.

I had arrived after a four-and-a-half-hour drive from Savannah. Harry provided turn-by-turn directions by phone during the last few minutes of the journey. As I eased down the driveway, I found him standing by the garage, barefoot, and wearing an untucked blue polo shirt, khaki shorts and his sly smile. He looked totally confident, comfortable, and at ease. It felt like the first of countless times Harry would welcome me home. This surprised me, because I had been wondering why someone as worldly and sophisticated as Harry would be interested in me. But there he was, waiting with a smile that promised fun and festivities. So, I hopped out of my Mustang convertible, leaned into a hug that fit me like a glove, and bounded up the garage stairs after he motioned with a flourish and a gentlemanly, "After you . . . "

When I opened the door, I noticed two things right away: the gladiolas and the scent. Flowers were everywhere! Perfectly arranged and placed, they seemed to bring the house to life. But the scent wasn't from the flowers. It seemed to emanate from every nook and cranny—like a comfortable elegance that was as much a part of the house as the honey-colored flooring and matching kitchen cabinets.

That night, smooth jazz played in the background on the porch as we enjoyed a meal, expertly prepared by Harry, and a glass (or three) of perfectly paired pinot noir. A delightful weekend followed, and by early the next week, when back in Savannah, I experienced my first case of being homesick. Every time I had returned, I always enjoyed that first scent of being home with Harry.

This time, I was arriving from Alaska instead of Savannah. There was no hug from Harry in the driveway. No gladiolas. No anticipation of a glorious weekend. There was only that beautifully familiar, comforting, elegant scent. A scent that, in less than 24 hours, had gone from signaling the joy of being home with Harry to emphasizing the harsh reality of being home without him.

Not only was Harry not home, I didn't know where he was. The body, that is. I had not even asked. I suppose it was because, though my whole life had instantly turned into one big question mark, there was one thing I had no doubt about: Harry wasn't in that body any longer. I didn't feel the need to see it, as I wanted my last memory of him to be the hug and kiss we exchanged in the driveway ten days earlier. He had cut up an apple and wrapped it in a paper towel, insisting I take it "in case the Punkin got hungry" on the ride to the airport. I was indeed glad to have the apple on the ride, but even more glad to have the paper towel. As soon as we were out of Harry's sight, the big, hot, salty tears rolled down my face. And they didn't stop until we neared the airport almost an hour later.

I had not wanted to leave Harry and return to Alaska. At all. I wasn't worried about what we knew. I was worried about what we didn't know. My default, especially during uncertain times, is to be assertive and in charge. We were having to wait over a month for an initial appointment with a specialist. I had suggested to Harry that he should simply go to the doctor's office each day and sit in the waiting room. I was quite positive that they would quickly find an appointment for the 6'4" Robert De Niro look-alike. "They'll take one look at you and think, *I better work him in, or I'm gonna end up in a sack in the river!*"

Harry had joked back, "It's your job to go be a rockstar and bring home the bacon. It's my job to stay here and be sickly."

We had both laughed at the time, but now it felt like the joke was on us.

So, there I was, with his oversized, blue leather chair wrapped around me, reading the information that Paula and Broughton had gently passed along before they left. The hospital social worker had provided it the night before. When I finished reading, I picked up my phone and dialed the handwritten number on the back of the pamphlet.

"Fulton County Coroner's Office, this is Richard. How can I help you?"

So, now I knew where Harry's body was, but I didn't understand how or why someone working at the county morgue could sound so pleasant.

I was struck by how comforting it was to listen to a total stranger tell me why they did an autopsy, why I could take my time deciding on arrangements, and why the morgue was the best place for the body until then. But the biggest "why" was yet to come.

"Cynthia, has anyone shared Harry's cause of death with you?"

I inhaled sharply. In less than twenty-four hours, the Universe was delivering the worst kind of one-two punch. First Harry's death. And now I was about to face the ugliest truth I had ever known, the one I had been trying to avoid since the previous night.

Harry's cause of death was my carelessness. My not following my instinct. My not taking a stand. My not protecting the most precious and cherished gift I had ever been given.

As these thoughts raced through my mind, I responded, "No one has told me, but I assume it was aortic stenosis?"

Richard paused for a second and then continued, more softly than he had spoken before, "Actually, it wasn't. Have you ever heard of the widow maker?"

"I have."

"And I'm assuming that Harry had had no symptoms?"

"None that I was aware of."

"Not surprised. Usually, the first symptom is the last one. Cynthia, Harry had atherosclerotic cardiovascular disease, and died from a massive heart attack."

"So, aortic stenosis wasn't the cause?"

"It didn't help matters, but no, it was not the primary cause of death."

Over the coming years I would be consumed with a pervasive, debilitating guilt. With an iron grip, I would hold on to the belief that I should have been aware. I should have known better. And because I wasn't, and I didn't, it was my fault that Harry had died. But for a moment that afternoon, the man at the morgue, who must have seen he could be a light in the darkness for others, had provided a momentary respite from the guilt.

I may have received a temporary break from the guilt, but there was no relief from the reality that I now had a funeral to plan, and friends and family to receive. I had not yet learned that the sooner I let myself fall apart, the sooner I would be able to put myself back together again. And so, as I had the night before, I let shock and adrenaline be my suit of armor. But in the light of a new day, I also had reinforcements. Within hours of my landing in Atlanta, Tanya pulled into the driveway making good on her promise, and Brian, one of my dearest friends, arrived from South Florida.

In the years before Harry, each had "done time" as my very best friend. And though they barely knew one another, they had an instant rapport. Like old friends, they bantered and teased and laughed easily—all the while keeping an eye on me. Wisely, they let me be in charge as much as I wanted to, but quickly stepped in to take the lead whenever they saw the need to do so. The next day, they were by my side as we headed out for breakfast and to make arrangements for Harry's service.

Our first stop was Papa Jack's. Admittedly, I was in search of something much more filling than bacon and eggs, and I found it waiting for me just inside the door. The love, hugs, tears, and smiles came from every direction. And though I felt comfort and drew strength from the outpouring, I also instantly felt something else. Every single hug landed my broken heart next to another one as I felt their pain and sorrow.

For years, I had watched and listened to Harry engage with the owner, Bill, and his crew. He instantly homed in on what made their hearts sing and never failed to point the conversation in that direction. He teased and taunted with his playful sense of humor, even on his last day. That morning, Harry had breakfast at Papa Jack's while enjoying a lively exchange with one of his favorites, Cindy. It brought me much comfort to know that he started his last day with people he loved and who loved him back.

After breakfast and another round of hugs, we headed for The Inn at Chateau Elan. On the flight across the country, I had decided that we weren't going to have a funeral. We were going to have a party. One of Harry's best friends had reached out to the owner of Chateau Elan—also a very good friend of Harry's—to share the news and set up a time for me to meet with him.

When we pulled up to the hotel, they were expecting us. Two bellmen, perfectly synchronized, pulled the doors wide for us to enter. A small team was waiting inside. Our dear friend Koray, who was the concierge manager, greeted me with a hug and tears in his eyes. Dawn, the event planner, was bearing a clipboard and a sympathetic smile. Henk, the owner of the Chateau, was quick to arrive with his usual swirl of energy. He guided us out of the lobby and to a quiet seating area in the atrium.

After expressing his condolences and own sense of loss, Henk recalled how the three of us had sat together, only a few weeks before, and chatted while Harry and I had breakfast. Eventually the two began talking about the best place to "park" a sail boat. After covering options up and down the East Coast, Harry had stressed that a sailboat be docked in a location that provided for easy and frequent access. Henk remembered exactly what Harry had said: "A sailboat is meant to be sailed, Henk. It's a great way to enjoy life."

I remembered that day vividly. Harry's description of the recommended marinas and the list of "things to consider" mesmerized me. He had lived on a sailboat for a bit after his father passed away, and, in his words, was "living life like a Jimmy Buffett song" when his best friend Paolo tossed him a lifeline and pulled him back to shore.

"Harry, you cannot live the rest of your life on a sailboat. I know a company that needs you. You can do the job with your eyes closed."

Paolo has given me many gifts in the years I've known him, but I suppose this was the greatest gift of all—bestowed upon me before we even met. Harry came to shore, and eventually I became his bride. He sold the sailboat many years before my arrival, but he had a model of a beautiful one in his home office as a reminder of a significant time in his life.

"So, Cynthia, I understand you might like to have the service here. What did you have in mind?"

I explained that I wanted to have something to represent how Harry had lived. "Festive" and "elegant" were two of the words I used. Henk, who had known Harry for 20 years, seemed to understand completely, and asked us to follow him.

We headed down the hallway of the conference center and into one of the first rooms. As Henk gently explained how they would transform the room into a beautiful venue, my eyes filled with tears. It had become exponentially real that I was standing inside the Chateau, where we had enjoyed so many festive times and where I'd secretly hoped to have a vow renewal ceremony for my 50th birthday and our 10th-year anniversary in just over a year. I could dress it up with plans to celebrate, but Harry was dead. I was planning his funeral, and we were just a nod away from having his service in a hotel

conference room. For a moment I could barely see for the pool of
tears that filled my eyes.

And then it happened again. Just like that moment in the CFO
office in Juneau. A flicker of light. A refusal to accept the darkness.
I glanced over at Tanya, who had glanced over at me. My sister's face
said what was in my head. Harry's voice pretending to be king.

Heavens no. This simply will not do! And then a bellow, *We
MUST have a proper venue for the festivities!*

In that moment, I decided I didn't want to "settle" on any detail
related to Harry's service, even if it meant I ruffled a few feathers.
There was no do-over here. I took a breath and smiled.

"Henk, I have no doubt that your team can make this room
beautiful. I'm thinking it's a little . . . "

"Small."

Startled, I glanced to my left. My hesitation had provided Tanya
the perfect opportunity to save me.

Taking her cue, I continued. "Exactly. I know you picked this
based on what I said earlier, but now that I see it, I'm thinking I was
off on the count. I think we'll easily have double the people. Do you
have something larger with a little more . . . atmosphere?"

Henk looked over at Dawn. "What else do we have?"

"What about the Cask Room?"

"The Cask Room is available?!" Henk asked.

Dawn nodded. "I know it's hard to believe. It never is. Especially
not on a Saturday evening."

Henk suddenly shifted into a higher gear. He actually seemed
excited.

"Wanna take a ride?" he asked.

"Absolutely!" I said with a huge sense of relief. I didn't know what
the Cask Room was, but if it wasn't that conference room and had
anything to do with wine, then it was probably perfect.

By the time we left the Chateau that afternoon, I was in a stupor. Just like that, we had secured the venue for a "Very Harry" memorial service and reception. Henk's team would decorate the pavilion next to the winery for an elegant memorial service and convert the Cask Room from a dark cave of barrels into a candlelit reception of wine and hors d'oeuvres. Carol Albert, the pianist Harry and I had met just weeks before at the hotel restaurant, would play during the service. Henk's team, many of whom had known Harry for years, would be on hand to ensure that everything went smoothly.

The only detail we did not confirm was someone to perform the service. Just before we left, Dawn gave me a list of the officiants who might be available, and said she would call me later in the day to confirm if my first choice was free. She was not optimistic because the popular chaplain was typically booked for weddings on Saturdays.

As we rode back to the house, I was less concerned about the officiant because something significant was happening. I could feel it. While we marveled out loud about the long odds for everything to come together so perfectly, I was quietly amazed. As on the previous morning's takeoff from Seattle, I was certain that another divine moment had just occurred. When I walked into Harry's office just moments later, I received a sign of confirmation.

It was dark because the shutters were closed, but one tiny beam of light had landed squarely on the key that was dead center of Harry's keyboard. I stood in the dimly lit room and stared at the H shining back at me. I shivered. It wasn't just that H was his first initial. It is what I called him. And it's what he and my mother Hilda called each other.

I ran to the kitchen and returned with my cell phone. The light had moved just a tad while I was gone, but it was still mostly shining on the H. I took a photo, walked back into the great room, showed my phone to Tanya and shared my interpretation.

"I think Harry approves of our plans."

When Dawn called me later that afternoon, I hung up with a smile. We already had the Cask Room and Carol Albert live on the piano. And now we had Jeremiah O'Keefe-West, an Irish chaplain and popular wedding officiant, to lead the memorial service just steps from Paddy's Irish Pub.

Paddy's Pub is an authentic Irish pub that the original owner of Chateau Elan had purchased in Ireland. The pub had been taken apart, shipped and reassembled just a very short walk from the hotel. It had been the scene of many a raucous night with Harry and a variety of friends and customers over the years. I never grew tired of hearing the entertaining stories, and over the years, I had accumulated a few of my own.

Now we were going to make a few more. Harry always loved a party, and on Saturday night, we were going to have a big one, in his honor. Some of his out-of-town friends were already on their way. And Paolo, his best and dearest one, was winging his way from Italy.

Tanya and Brian had provided me with unbelievable comfort and support since their arrival. I couldn't have survived the first day without them. But Paolo arrived with something that neither of them could provide. He was the friend who had known and loved Harry longer and more deeply than any other I knew. The three of us had spent a lot of time together over the years. We had memories and inside jokes. As the days, weeks, and months unfolded, it was apparent that Paolo and I were uniquely bonded in our profound grief of losing Harry. His own experiences of hardship, including the tragic loss of his youngest son and a devastating earthquake that severely damaged his family's factory, had qualified him to provide wise counsel and guidance.

So, when he asked me on Thursday morning what we needed to do that day, I replied as if he were my mafia partner in crime, "We have to decide what to do with the body."

We both burst out laughing, but it was true. The time for my next big decision had arrived: Was I going to bury Harry's body or cremate it? As I consulted my team and a few others, I remembered a dinner conversation from a few years before.

We had just raised our glasses in honor of the mother of one of our friends. She had recently passed, and they cremated her body. I remember Harry researching cremation at the time. Surprisingly, the dinner conversation turned to that very topic. But when things became predictably heavy, Harry swooped in with the perfect antidote.

"Did you know you can actually have your ashes put in a rocket and shot into space? You can even have jewelry made out of them these days." Glancing my way, he continued, "That's what you need to do, Punkin. When the time comes, cremate my big-ass body and get yourself a pair of diamond earbobs!" The mood lifted as we erupted in laughter.

I polished off the moment with, "Just earbobs? I'm thinking there would be enough for a matching pendant, too!"

What seemed to be hilariously funny just a couple of years earlier, had now become my horrific reality. And I was worried about the ramifications of cremation. I knew some believed that a person whose body had been cremated didn't fare as well "afterward" as those who were buried. But what about the people who pass away and aren't able to be buried for one reason or another? Why wouldn't they have the same eternal privileges as anyone else?

And then, I heard Harry's voice in my head saying the perfect thing at the perfect time: *Make it easy on yourself, Punkin.*

We hadn't purchased grave sites. And because I had always said, "Home is where Harry is," the question of where exactly home was or would be had become very complicated. Open or closed casket? A burial service? But where? I was quickly seeing what "easy" was going to be. Then I heard the voice again. Only this time it was, *Whatever The Baby wants.*

And that did the trick.

"The Baby wants earbobs," I replied as I picked up my phone. And while I waited for the funeral home to answer, I added, "And a pendant."

Chapter 3

I've been blessed with many things in my life, including a sense of humor. It's one of the many things that Harry and I had in common. He used to say, "Punkin, we laugh more in a day than most people laugh in a year."

No doubt when the thought crossed my mind to add his ashes to my jewelry collection, Harry was hooting in heaven. And though I had no intention of carrying through with that idea, I had indeed decided to cremate his body. But I wasn't sure if one dresses a body for cremation, so I found one of his suits and took it to the dry cleaners just in case. After all, if we were going to dress the body, we had to do so properly.

The next decision wasn't even on my radar until Paolo asked, "Cynthia, are we going to attend the cremation?"

Surprised, I replied, "I hadn't even considered that. Of course we should. I'll check in with the funeral home."

"Yes," he said taking in a sharp, deep breath. "We should be there."

My team of Tanya and Brian had expanded when Paolo arrived. And it now had another member. Bud, or as Harry called him, "The Bud Man," was Harry's close pal and colleague of twenty years. He arrived from New Jersey just in time to join us at the funeral home. The Bud Man and Paolo were also long-time friends. It felt good to have them with me.

When we all arrived at the funeral home, the funeral director, Mike, was there to greet us. He escorted us to a typical-looking conference room—big table, lots of chairs. He took a seat at the head of the table. I sat to his right with my back to the wall with Tanya next to me. The others sat across from me.

As Mike organized the papers, I looked across the table, meeting Paolo's beautifully sad brown eyes and Bud's sky-blue ones shimmering with tears. In many ways, the two men could not have appeared more different. One was a dark, somewhat reserved Italian, and the other an outgoing, fair-skinned man from Jersey. But they shared a deep bond, having known and loved Harry longer than I had. Both had dropped everything to be there. Even with their sad expressions, they also had the trace of a smile on their faces, sending me love, strength, and encouragement.

I tried to stem the tears that were falling, as I realized that the conference room was anything but typical. Shelving ran high on all four walls, displaying urns of various shapes, sizes, and colors. I knew that another decision lay before me: choosing one of them for Harry's ashes.

After handling the paperwork, I couldn't hold the tears any longer as I thought, *How did we go from chasing rainbows and planning our future to Harry becoming ashes and me choosing a container to put them in?*

"Do you know yet what you plan to do with Harry's ashes?" Mike asked, gently leading me back from the abyss. "It may help you decide on the style." Mike was doing a fantastic job in a tough situation. I probably made it even tougher by injecting my sense of humor as I replied with a totally straight face.

"I'd like to shoot them into space. Or wait—how about a pair of earbobs? And a pendant. Please."

Mike responded with a blank stare until Tanya rescued him with, "She's only kidding."

But the humor gave me enough time to decide. Even if it was going into a vault or the ground eventually, until then, I wanted the container to be "Very Harry." And nothing on the shelves fit the bill.

"What about something like a cigar humidor?" I asked.

Not only had I raised an interesting question, I'd also raised the mood in the room, especially for my two brothers across the table. They knew the answer to that question. Harry was an aficionado of many things, including cigars. They smiled and nodded in approval.

Mike began flipping through a catalog. "How about something like this?" he asked, pushing the book toward me.

I quickly scanned the description, and seeing the word "veneer," asked if it was solid wood.

"Well, it has a coating—" he began.

"Oh no, it has to be solid wood," I interrupted. I could just hear Harry saying, *You put me in particle board?!*

I explained that I wanted something traditional and elegant. "Classic," Paolo offered.

When Mike showed us his next idea, we all loved it immediately. Made of maple with a hand-rubbed cherry finish, the oversized urn had a flat, hinged lid and then cascaded in a series of boxed edges and curves to its molded base. A large rectangle cut into the lid framed a perfect spot for Harry's initials, and beneath it was a tray for keepsakes. It was indeed classic. Elegant. Masculine. As I nodded my approval, I thought, *If Harry were a box, this would be him.*

Thinking we were done, I sat back with a sense of accomplishment and relief. But we weren't done. Mike was asking again what I planned to do with the ashes, as it impacted how they would be stored inside the "humidor." This time I gave a straight answer. "I would like to sprinkle his ashes around the world, at all of his favorite places."

"So, here's what we can do, Cynthia. We have stainless steel tubes." Mike slid the catalog to me, opened to another page. "Each comes with its own velvet pouch. We can put Harry's ashes in the tubes, store them in the box, and then you can just take a tube with you for each trip."

I could tell he liked the idea. So did I. "Tubes it is!"

"Uh, well, it will be about twenty tubes."

I stared.

He continued, "Harry was a big guy."

I burst out laughing, and the others joined in.

We came up with a cost-effective alternative: I would purchase ten tubes and leave the rest of the ashes in a plastic container.

"The tubes can go on one side of the box. The container can go on the other," Mike said. "The tubes are totally reusable, so you can simply bring them back and we'll transfer the ashes as needed, or you can do it yourself."

Now I had an urn that looked like a humidor and steel cigars to boot. Despite the circumstances, I couldn't help but be pleased. It was "Very Harry."

With the logistics out of the way, it was time for Paolo and Bud to see the body. It was very important to them, and so I scheduled the cremation to allow both to arrive in time for a viewing. I still felt no need to see the body. Brian sensed that I was wilting a bit and offered to grab some lunch for me. I gave him an appreciative nod and looked to Mike for the game plan.

That's when I learned that Harry's body had been behind me, on the other side of the wall, the entire time we were meeting. Mike explained that he was going to take Bud and Paolo into the back room, and suggested that Tanya and I step outside to get some fresh air.

So, this was it. Suddenly, I felt so tired. So deflated. Tanya and I sat down on a bench just outside the door. Mike came out shortly thereafter, allowing Paolo and Bud to be alone with Harry.

I'm not sure how much time passed, but eventually they came outside. They did not seem to be the same two men who had walked into that back room. I looked at them, not knowing what to say or do.

"He's beautiful, Cynthia," Paolo started. "Like he's sleeping."

I glanced at Bud, who had a dreamy, peaceful look on his face.

"You should see him," Paolo continued. I looked back at Bud, who was nodding slightly with raised eyebrows that seemed to say, *You really should, Cynthia.*

"He looks like he's about to have a massage," Paolo added with a gentle smile.

With those words, Paolo not only provided me with a comforting image, he also provoked a burst of memories. Harry loved telling the story of how he and Paolo padded through the Chateau Elan spa in their robes, the place entirely to themselves when it was first built. They wandered from the sauna to the heated pool to the hot tub at all hours of the night, simply because they could. They had massages by day. Years later, he insisted on scheduling massages at the house for all three of us any time Paolo came to visit. "We will luxuriate when the Mad Italian arrives!" he'd proclaim. A creature of comfort, Harry loved to encourage the rest of us to follow suit.

My firm stance on not seeing the body was wavering. I looked at Tanya, who shrugged.

"You're no help," I teased.

I still didn't feel a need to see the body, but sensed this moment was presenting itself for a reason. I looked up at Bud and Paolo, my trust in them complete.

"Okay, then," I said as I stood up. "And you'll come with me?" I asked.

"Absolutely."

"Of course."

The body was facing away from the door, so I didn't get my first real peek until I walked alongside the table and turned. When I did, I understood instantly why Paolo and Bud felt so strongly that I should see him. He did indeed look as if he were about to have a massage, covered with a sheet, only his head and very upper torso exposed. He looked totally natural. I had decided to forego "dressing" the body, and was now glad that I had. Smiling inside, I heard Harry's voice: *Why ruin a perfectly good suit, Punkin?* I was also smiling inside because there was a completely pleasant surprise waiting for me.

Harry was smiling back at me!

Oh, it was slight and subtle. It probably would have escaped most, but I had seen it a thousand times. And then I knew why I was there.

Harry carried deep emotional pain. Some of it he shared with me; some he did not. He certainly never passed any of it along to me. He was the most consistently pleasant person I had ever met. So quick to laugh. So caring and attentive. But I knew it was there. I also knew there wasn't a single thing I could do to extract it from him. So, I had decided to do the only thing I really had control over. I would simply love him as totally and completely as I could.

But now, it was gone. I traced the curve of his face with my fingers. I touched his bare shoulder. His arm. There was only peace. I had seen it in Paolo and Bud, and now felt it in the room. Maybe the gentle push I felt to see the body was Harry nudging me, knowing that seeing and feeling his peace would help me feel it, too.

I ran my fingers lightly over his close-cropped hair, and I smiled, a few tears trickling out. The previous year, Harry had gone all Alaskan with a thicker beard and longer hair. I called it his *Braveheart* look. After seeing a photo of him on social media, his friend Kirk had teased, "Are there no barbers in Alaska?"

Just before Thanksgiving, Harry began contemplating a more coiffed look. One night, after we enjoyed a three-martini dinner, he announced it was time.

Alaska did indeed have barbers, and if Harry had his way, it was about to have one more.

"I am *not* cutting your hair."

"Yes, you are."

"Nope."

We were sitting at my desk, a U-shaped executive setup that we had assembled a year or so before. It took two days, two bottles of Veuve, and one Phillips head screwdriver, but we had gotten it done. I was sitting inside the U and facing him across the desk.

"Harry . . . no. Your barber, Charlie, is one block away."

"Charlie is a jackass."

This caught me off-guard, because Harry really liked Charlie. I burst out laughing. There was a lot to love about Harry, including his many personas. One minute he could be the benevolent king, the next minute the little-kid playmate or the mafia man who "knew people."

And then, there was the cranky curmudgeon.

"Besides," he continued with a trace of indignation while delicately primping his hair with both hands, "I can't trust these gorgeous locks to just anyone!"

It was below freezing outside, but I suddenly felt flushed. And shaky—most likely a combination of the three martinis and the realization that I was about to cut Harry's hair for the first time. It was right before we were going to visit our niece in Fairbanks, and then travel to Georgia for Christmas. There was no margin for error.

"Fine," I said, whirling around in my chair and grabbing the red-handled scissors out of a coffee mug on my credenza.

"What are you doing?" he cried out.

"You want your hair cut, don't you?"

"Not with *those*!"

"Shall I get a knife from the kitchen?" I asked sarcastically, hoping that might change his mind.

He cackled and with catlike quickness, popped up, returning almost instantly with a towel, his beard trimmer and a triumphant smile.

Harry had beautiful hair. When I met him, it was short, dark, and very thick. Now it was shoulder-length, salted with gray, but still thick and luxurious. I was nervous. He changed the attachment on the trimmer, handed it to me, and draped the towel over his shoulders. I started to sweat.

I turned on the trimmer and reached toward the top of his head. He must have sensed my motion because he leaned away, saying, "No, no, no," like a parent who was about to redirect the behavior of a child and teach a gentle lesson at the same time.

"It's like shearing sheep, Punkin."

I stood there, not believing what I'd just heard. It wasn't exactly the lesson I was expecting.

"Thanks for clearing that up for me." I was now not only sweating, but I was also irritated.

Harry turned slightly and said, "Here, give me your hand."

With the trimmer still clenched in it, I did. He guided my hand to his head, rested it gently and pushed upward. And just like that,

I was shearing sheep. I did it next by myself. Then again and again. Harry's long, luxurious hair began to cascade to the floor. Before long, the deed was done.

I sat down in my chair. My nerves were shot. I picked up the scissors I'd left on my desk and turned around to put them back into the coffee cup. When I turned back around, I burst out laughing. Harry had used some of his hair to create a Fu Manchu mustache that was somehow staying in place.

He reached down to the floor, grabbed more hair and spread it on the desk between us. We laughed and giggled, making mustaches, eyebrows, and beards using Harry's fallen locks.

The next morning, I brushed my hand over his short-cropped hair, admiring my handiwork. "It feels like carpet," I said teasingly, to which Harry responded, "It's quite possibly the best haircut I've ever had!"

Standing in that viewing room, barely 60 days after the haircut, I ran my fingers over his hair again. I was so thankful that Harry had insisted I "shear sheep" that night. It provided his brothers Paolo and Bud a final glimpse of the Harry they had known and loved. Plus, our "drinking with scissors" extravaganza provided me with a cherished memory, and the comfort of knowing that the first and best haircut I ever gave Harry was the last one he ever had.

Mike was waiting for us when we stepped back into the conference room and announced they were ready to start the cremation, unless anyone needed more time.

A part of me wanted to beg Mike for more time. To ask him for another hour. Another week. Another year. To plead with him for that lifetime Harry and I were supposed to have together. But how could I possibly bargain for more time when I had been luckier than most? Harry and I had loved abundantly in our short time together. Who was I to ask for more? Besides, I knew the time I wanted was not the kind of time Mike had to give.

I gave the nod for the cremation to begin. And at that moment, Tanya returned to the conference room with Brian, back from the lunch run, right behind her.

I had known Brian since I was 12 years old. Though only two years older than me, he had been like a mentor, seeing potential in me long before I did. He enlisted in the Navy after graduating high school, and we had no contact for almost 20 years. Then on Thanksgiving in 2001, my brother ran into Brian while visiting his brother in Florida, and put us on the phone together. From that moment until I met Harry, Brian and I were joined at the hip.

He was the friend to sit up in my living room all night when he thought I was in danger, or drive six hours straight, when I had emergency surgery, just so he could be there to take me home from the hospital, or become the best of friends with the love of my life. After I got to Seattle in the wee hours of the morning after Harry passed away, Brian stayed on the line with me for hours, neither of us talking for long stretches of time. Just knowing he was there was enough.

Earlier in the week, he had come to my rescue by dropping everything to be by my side. He of all people knew how devastating Harry's death was for me. And on this day, he came to my rescue once more.

When he put the bottle on the table, I recognized the orange label immediately. Harry and I had popped many a cork of Veuve Clicquot, so I was pleasantly surprised that Brian had just walked in with a bottle of our favorite champagne.

Paolo and Bud erupted with, "Oh nice!" and "Now we're talking!" Tanya smiled. I glanced at Mike, but I could tell that if there were any rules against alcohol in the crematory, they were going to be waived that day. He gracefully declined our invitation to join in and excused himself without saying a word about the booze.

And so, with only the thin wall of the conference room separating us, we cried, laughed and toasted champagne while Harry's body was cremated. Raising our glasses in his honor, as we'd do often over the coming years, we toasted the man who showed us how to live, to love, and to laugh—to transform the ordinary into extraordinary and find the festive in just about every possible thing.

Brian rescued me that day, not because I needed to drink and cry, but because toasting champagne during his cremation was exactly what Harry would have ordered up for us, had he been able to. It gave me what I had thought impossible just an hour before, and exactly what I needed at that moment—a little more time, after all.

Chapter 4

Brian may have provided us with a bit more time that afternoon, but when we returned to the house, I became acutely aware that time was running out to complete the last item of preparation for the memorial service—to plan the service itself. No amount of champagne could change that.

As I sat down in the dining room to take the call with the chaplain, Jeremiah, I knew once again there'd be no do-over for my decisions. The two I had been most concerned about were the music and the tribute to Harry—a.k.a. the eulogy. But as I had with the urn decision, I let my intuition lead the way, even if it came in the middle of the night.

I had no clue how exhausted I was. While I knew that the gut-wrenching sobs I allowed in private were wearing me out, I didn't realize that my struggle to maintain composure, keep a smile on my face and quarterback the arrangements were taking a greater toll. I crawled into bed each night and fell fast asleep. However, shortly afterwards I would begin tossing and turning, continuing until it was once again time to wake up into the nightmare of a life without Harry.

During one of those nights, I opened Facebook. The first post in my feed was Harry's New Year's post from three weeks earlier. It was a photo of a brilliant sun from the cockpit of a plane with a heartfelt message of wishes for a fantastic New Year. The featured comment from one of his high school friends was *Here comes the sun, and I say it's alright.*

I drew a sharp breath as time seemed to stand still. The lyrics looked huge on the screen of my phone.

Harry loved the sun. He often snuck over to the shutters in our bedroom and opened the east-facing slats so that the sun would shine directly on my waking face. Then he would bellow, "The SUUUUUN!" I'd giggle and burrow further under the covers.

That night as I lay in that same but now much-too-empty bed, I allowed myself to wonder for the first time, *Are these just coincidences, or something more?* I was definitely seeing a pattern. The brilliant sun the morning after Harry passed. The illuminated H on the keyboard. And now, Harry's last post and a comment with words from "Here Comes the Sun."

I pulled the lyrics up on my phone and played the iconic Beatles song. I cried as I heard Harry singing to me. It felt like a little beam of sunlight had penetrated the darkness, as if he were telling me the *long, cold, lonely winter* was over. Not just beginning. As if in some horrifically beautiful mystical message, he was assuring me that this was a time of rebirth for both of us, though in dramatically different ways.

In that moment, I knew I had to use the song in Harry's service. And I surrendered more to the possibility that Harry was sending me messages. After all, he had lined up a few powerful ones to get my attention. With this last one, as if to really drive home his point, he enlisted the help of an accomplice with the perfect name.

Sonny.

Smiling, I put the phone away, pulled up the covers and burrowed back in. I knew I might be using far-fetched ideas of eternal connection to comfort me in my grief. But these happenings didn't feel like random coincidences. They felt familiar, laced with Harry's playfulness and sense of humor. I was thankful for the latest one—a comforting night light casting a soft glow as I drifted back to sleep.

During our call to plan the service, Jeremiah and I first talked about music. I wanted Carol to play "All I Ask of You" and "Music of the Night" from *The Phantom of the Opera*—two of my and Harry's favorites—before the service. We also found spots for them during the service. But the newest addition to the playlist, "Here Comes the Sun," had a more prominent place in the lineup. Carol would play it right before the eulogy. I thought it would give everyone a mood boost, including the person I had chosen to speak. I felt certain that a little sunshine to light the way would be perfect. I knew this because the person I had chosen to deliver the main tribute to Harry was the person whose heart was likely the most broken.

And I was going to need all the help I could get.

I knew that my giving the eulogy was risky. I could tell that Jeremiah thought it was as well. But he didn't know I *was* going to get all the help that I needed, and that it had already started to arrive—the first of which came from a most unlikely source and just in the nick of time.

Kendall and I had crossed paths in Alaska several years before. We were members of a team of professionals assisting the health system in Nome with two large construction projects—a hospital and a nursing home to replace their existing facilities. He was one of several engineers on the project and I was providing financial management services. We had spent a lot of time working together during the multi-year project and had an excellent professional relationship. He and three others from that team had sent me a collective condolence. And then Kendall sent his own.

As I read his message, I felt affirmed. He had no way of knowing what I was contemplating, but there it was in black and white:

I've heard you talk about Harry in a variety of situations. It seemed your eyes always lit up accompanied by a laugh or a smile.

As I read his words, I couldn't deny the truth of them or the impeccable timing of their arrival, just before my call with Jeremiah.

I didn't have to worry about falling apart or not knowing what to say. I had just been reminded that talking about Harry was one of my favorite things to do. I could feel the light and love swirling inside. I could see myself smiling. I could hear my friends laughing. And that's when I said it out loud.

"I just need to get to the podium."

When I spoke with Jeremiah a short time later, I had no doubt that I needed to do it. And I wanted to do it. It was killing me that I had not been with Harry the night he died. I wanted to speak at his service because it would give me a chance to do what I couldn't do that night. To hold him. To say, "I love you." And "thank you." To wave goodbye.

This was a gift of opportunity. Since Harry was one of the most incredibly talented people at giving the perfect gift, I felt like he was still at it somehow.

I could feel him gently pushing me to the edge of my comfort zone, and then see him handing me a box with that slight, mischievous smile. Pieces of wrapping paper that didn't match. Corners of the box not covered completely. Shipping tape wound around and around and around. "I wrapped it myself," he would say as I looked at him with feigned horror. But I knew that something fun, or festive, or beautiful was always waiting inside.

And that's what this felt like—Harry handing me a treasure once again. Only this time, it was disguised by the horrifying wrapping of his memorial service, and I had to get to the podium to accept this divine gift. To peel back the shipping tape, tear off the ugly paper, and throw open the box.

As I spoke with Jeremiah, my conviction grew. Even so, we had developed a plan to accommodate the unexpected. After "Here Comes the Sun," Jeremiah would return to the podium. If he didn't get the "I'm good" nod from me, he would continue with his own version of a eulogy. No one would be the wiser. If I changed my mind, I could always join in at the end, when others were going to speak.

We had a plan for the service, but I had no plan for the tribute. How would I start? What would I say?

It seemed like only yesterday when I had posed similar questions to Harry. We were about to meet in person for the first time, and I had wondered out loud what I was going to say or do. Harry's response had immediately set my mind at ease.

"A proper greeting may be a smile. Perhaps a spoken word. Maybe a handshake or even a hug. I'm very much looking forward to seeing what the moment brings."

I was thinking of that moment the next afternoon as I got dressed for the service. I was deep in thought—pondering how to start my remarks. The service was now only a few hours away, and I had not yet written anything down. Even though I was constantly repeating my newfound mantra, "I just have to get to the podium," I still didn't know what I was going to say when I got there.

Harry's words from 11 years before suggested that I didn't have to know. I could relax. I could trust that the moment would provide. But this moment was quite different. It wasn't me saying hello to him for the first time in a romantic riverside restaurant in Savannah on a sunny July afternoon. It was me saying good-bye to him, around the corner from our Braselton home, in front of friends and family on a cold January evening. Summer had become winter.

I needed more than the moment: I needed an opening. I knew that time was short, so I decided to compose my opening remarks while dressing. Upon arrival, I'd find a quiet place and write it all out. I just needed a "start." I wanted to tell a story, but there were so many, and I just didn't know which one.

That's when it happened.

Rocks and beads crashed to the floor in a cataclysmic eruption. I looked in the mirror and saw a bewildered me looking back. When I looked down, silver beads of varying sizes were still bouncing. The larger black-polished, rock-like pieces were scattered over the tile. Remnants of my necklace dangled from my hand.

I had been holding on by a thread, and it appeared as if my necklace had been, too. Seeing it shattered on the bathroom floor triggered a fear that I may be right behind it.

But then I blurted out, "Harry hated this necklace." I started laughing. I now had my opening.

I may have had my opening, but I was far from being in the clear. I didn't realize how little time I'd have to myself after arriving at the Chateau. I made the rounds, overwhelmed with relief and gratitude. Henk's team had transformed the pavilion into a beautiful garden. It looked more like a wedding venue than a memorial service, with white wooden chairs arranged in a V spreading out from the front where the podium, flowers and photos were arranged perfectly.

The Cask Room could have been right out of *The Phantom of the Opera* with sconces lit, candles and flowers adorning linen-draped tables, oaken barrels lining the walls, cozy chairs and settees placed for intimate conversations. I had provided elegantly framed photos of Harry and our life together. Henk's team had made good use of them. They were a perfect complement to the room.

I sat down to prepare my remarks, but found myself looking at the photos instead. Harry as a baby. Our wedding. Me, Harry and Paolo, in our chef coats, cooking dinner at home. The final photo of Henry and Harry right before he collapsed. Everything had come together so beautifully, and I was filled with an unexpected peace.

It was very similar to that hot July afternoon 11 years before. I had smiled and felt an inner peace the moment I saw him. And then, as I leaned into a hug custom made for me, I had said, "Hello Harry," as if greeting a long-lost friend.

The arrival of that memory was perfectly timed. It felt like Harry was there, wrapping me in a comforting hug once again. My fear and anxiety slipped away as I realized that the tribute to Harry wasn't what I said at the memorial service, or what I served at the reception. It was what I did and how I chose to live from that night forward.

I looked down at the blank 8 ½ x 11 sheets on my lap. I folded them in half and on one side at the top I wrote *Necklace Story* and a few bullet points.

I flipped the paper over, and on the back, I wrote in very large and thick letters the word *LAUGH*. Now I just had to get to the podium.

I sat for a minute longer and let the feelings flood through me. Then, I stepped from the dark comfort of the Cask Room into the open pavilion that was filling with family and friends. Anticipating Harry's gift, I took a deep breath and whispered to my love, "This better be a good one, H."

I'm not sure why I doubted it would be. Harry had never let me down. Ever. His gifts were always perfectly fun or functional. Most often, he addressed my needs before I even knew I had them. On the rare occasion that I actually asked for his help, he often responded with, "My feet have wings!" Now that he had a pair of angel wings to match and new special powers, there was no telling what he could do.

I didn't have to wait long to find out.

When I stepped from the Cask Room into the pavilion, I stepped out of darkness into light. From lingering doubt to absolute faith. From unanswered questions to the ultimate truth. In an instant, anxiety, exhaustion and heartbreak disappeared. In its place, resting gently in my heart and soul, was a feeling—so sweet, so tender, so warm, so strong. I saw the shipping tape slip away and the ugly paper drop to the floor and there, in the bittersweet box of the Chateau Elan Pavilion, I found the gift.

I felt it in the hugs, kisses, squeezes of the hand, and tearful smiles. I heard it in Carol's lovely piano playing, and in the laughter when

Jeremiah, the Irish minister, glanced over his shoulder at the door to Paddy's Irish Pub and suggested that if he went missing, we might know where to find him. I saw it in the hotel staff, standing ready to assist if needed. I saw it in my mother's eyes. It was inside me and everywhere I turned. It started the moment I stepped through the pavilion door, and has never been in short supply since.

When I placed the folded paper on the podium and looked up into the faces of those who had gathered, I knew that while I was busy trying to arrange a tribute to Harry, he had been busy wrapping a present for me. It was the perfect size and color, and the most beautiful one yet. My own little miracle.

The gift of eternal love.

Undeniable, unwavering and unconditional.

A love that transcends all time and space, finding its way from one heart to another, no matter what. I didn't know that night just how often or in how many ways this love would manifest in the years to come. But I knew it was there. Always giving with a generosity beyond measure. And though I initially felt that it started that night at the Chateau, I would realize eventually that it actually never started. And it certainly hadn't ended. It just simply had always been, and always would be.

As I stood at the podium and felt the love radiating from every person sitting in front of me, I tried to explain it.

"It wasn't love at first sight. It was forever at first sight."

Even the hostess at the Chart House in Savannah seemed to know that, 11 years earlier.

I had entered the restaurant and, not seeing Harry waiting, I scurried into the restroom to freshen up. Moments later, I approached the hostess stand. "Good evening. I'm meeting someone . . ."

"Oh yes," she interrupted. "Your husband is already here. He's out on the balcony. Right this way."

I fell in behind her while smiling inside: *Does she know something I don't know?*

He must have caught our activity out of the corner of his eye, because we hadn't gone very far when he stepped through the balcony doorway. Immediately, I was struck by his presence as the details of everything else around me faded away. He was an impressively large man, dressed in black from head to toe. He had dark skin, dark hair, and dark eyes. Yet there was nothing dark about him at all. Exuding a curious swirl of confidence and gentleness, he graciously thanked the hostess for her help, and then turned his full attention to me.

And he didn't let up for the next six hours.

We closed the Chart House that night after martinis and dinner on the balcony and coffee inside at the bar. The next day, he called me at work and invited me to lunch.

And so it began.

There's no doubt in my mind that Harry and I were destined to meet. To this day, I wonder how that might have happened, had I not expanded my horizons and my search criteria to 250 miles. To give myself a very special 38th birthday present.

Just three months before, I didn't know what Match.com was. But I had a rogue employee who was overusing the internet at work, and his inordinate amount of time on that website piqued my curiosity. The next month, while completing my status report, I smiled at one of the objectives: Use Technology as a Tool, as I thought, *Well, why not make that a pillar of my own strategic plan?*

So, I created a profile—describing myself as a fun-loving, giggly mess who enjoyed driving my Mustang convertible around the coastal roads of Savannah, top down, baseball hat on, music playing loud. I could slip out of my jeans into a little black dress and be equally comfortable in both. I had a fairly big job that I loved (the "love" part not entirely true), had accomplished much at a young age, and was generally very good at anything I set my mind to. I acknowledged that I was still a work in progress—a diamond in the rough. With a list of many things I had not yet experienced—riding a Ferris wheel, learning piano, riding in a hot-air balloon, writing a book . . . to name a few—I was hoping to find someone to be my friend, my confidant and my cheerleader, and who would let me be the same for him. I also confessed to being a hopeless romantic in search of her own love story.

Initial results were mostly underwhelming. But I was having fun, especially since I knew that most of my friends would be horrified to know I was shopping for a man on Match.com. This was in 2003, and online dating had not yet become mainstream. It still felt a bit "seedy"—like I had been sitting in my house with the blinds drawn, trolling internet chat rooms.

I didn't use a photo in my profile. I had a fairly big job—as controller of a nearly billion-dollar health system—and I wanted to do my shopping in a cloak of darkness.

When I was just about to give up and relegate my Friday nights to watering flowers and cutting grass, I decided to cast a wider net. So, I expanded my search to 250 miles and my timeline to another few weeks. If I had no luck by then, I would take my shopping elsewhere. Or not shop at all.

Almost immediately, an intriguing profile showed at the top of my matches. He had gone swimming with dolphins in the waters off of Maui, enjoyed a coffee in the Italian town of Sirmione, and knew which end of the spatula to hold. He had taken up residence on a sailboat for a while, living his life like a Jimmy Buffett song. Said he didn't have any baggage—you could find that at carousel nine at the Atlanta airport. A self-described Renaissance man with a wicked sense of humor and a great spirit, he was in search of his female counterpart and someone to spoil.

For weeks, I did my expanded search. For weeks, his profile topped my matches. I was intrigued, but I was also certain that this worldly and sophisticated man would not be interested in me. My internal skeptic was hard at work, as usual, not letting me be true to myself. It had kept me in a career that did not make my heart sing.

It had kept me in unhealthy relationships for far too long. It had delayed repair of a debilitating knee injury for 20 years.

When I allowed my heart and soul to speak, all I ever heard was, *Follow your heart. Believe in the fairytale. True love is real.*

When my skeptic had the floor, it simply laughed and said, *Life is supposed to be hard. Be grateful for what you have.*

But I had been working hard on myself, and the skeptic was getting the floor less and less.

And so, on the night of my 38th birthday, after a beautiful dinner with dear friends, I returned home, walked straight up the stairs to my office, and reviewed that intriguing profile again. I listed every quality he was seeking. He had snuck 18 of them into his "searching for" section. His write-up concluded with an invitation to reach out if interested, so that *we may endeavor to know one another better.*

I hit 18 out of 18 by stretching a couple of them. So, I crafted an elegantly playful message that included: *I'm sure you would agree that 17 out of 18 is pretty good for any endeavor.* I was hoping to connect by using his own word "endeavor," and to pique his curiosity about which quality I'd missed.

So, there I was, about to give myself one of the best birthday presents ever. But the present wasn't the response or the person on the other end of it. At least I didn't think so at the time. The gift was the "send." It was not just wishing for the fairytale; it was taking a step toward it. Even if this message came up short, I finally believed that I was worth the effort.

And so, with a click of the mouse, I fired off the message, sat back and said out loud, "Happy Birthday to me!"

Oooohhhh . . . is it Cynthia or Cindy? And what about this job of yours? Are you a tugboat captain or maybe the one who dyes the river green on St. Patrick's Day? Perhaps a cook at Waffle House or a test pilot for Gulfstream? So many questions . . .

Harry's response to my message had come the next day. After another exchange, he suggested that we "endeavor" to know one another over the phone. After a week of conversations each night that invariably stretched into the next morning, I asked about "next steps." He had responded most enthusiastically, "I think I'd better head down to Savannah and take you to dinner before someone swoops you away!"

As I look back now on Harry's response to my question, I can see how this one sentence encapsulated the essence of what it felt like to be loved by him. At that moment and for the first time in my life, I felt like a cherished treasure. A rare jewel. Not just a diamond in the rough, but one that was polished and shining brightly for all the world to see.

While I know that I eventually held the enviable position of being the love of his life, as we were married almost exactly two years later on my 40th birthday, the truth is that Harry did this naturally with most everyone. He had a unique ability to connect. To be present. To be interested. To make us feel as if we mattered and were special.

He was also a gifted storyteller. Recounting tales that were so outrageous they were suspect, Harry used his voice, a melodic smooth jazz with a dash of vermouth, for perfect comedic or dramatic effect. Since I accompanied him on quite a few business trips and shared many other social gatherings with him, I had heard most of his stories more than once. But I never grew tired of hearing them, or of seeing the joy and laughter they brought to others.

Standing at the podium to begin my remarks, I hoped that my stories were about to do the same.

The room erupted in laughter when I told the necklace story and suggested that Harry had caused the explosion to help get things started.

I shared the basis of our magical relationship: genuine friendship, mutual respect, and our willingness to say "please" and "thank you." Giving examples, I talked about Harry's ability to find the extraordinary in the ordinary, and his passion for bringing ceremony and celebration to everyday life.

Instead of following the bullets, I followed my heart. Weaving my way through memories and examples, I could tell I was connecting. My loved ones were smiling and laughing. I had found another way to pay tribute. By bringing comfort, laughter, and joy. Exactly what Harry had brought to all of these people who had loved him so.

Of course, I acknowledged our own love story, but I emphasized that our love story wasn't *just* about me and Harry.

"It is about all of us," I said as my hand swept over the room.

I wasn't sure exactly what I meant by that, but it had a lot to do with my experience of walking into the pavilion and feeling the gift of eternal love. It was as if we were now all connected in ways not previously. Later that night, as others came forward and shared "Very Harry" stories, the picture became clearer.

We heard how Harry used to protect his young cousin by walking on the outside of the sidewalk. How his high school classmate "Shorty" was picked on and stuffed into trashcans by football players until Harry "had a word" with the team. Grant explained that Harry had the unique ability to take a very complicated subject, break it down and explain it in simple terms, often with a splash of humor. One of my colleagues, Bill, relayed how, on an unforgettable afternoon on the porch when he met Harry for the first time, "Harry knew things about me I didn't even know myself."

One of my favorite stories, read during the service, came from John, a colleague in Nome, Alaska.

I have never met anyone quite like Harry. He walked in and filled the room completely, and was very intimidating just by physical appearance. But somehow almost immediately after we were introduced, he had a way of putting me completely at ease. There was no subject I ever brought up with Harry that he could not engage in intelligently and thoughtfully. He knew amazing details about everything from wine to Harley Davidsons, and everything in between! I still suspect he must have been in the CIA or some other secret government agency at some point. What I found so wonderful about Harry . . . his sense of humor, his ability to connect, and a sharp yet graciously subtle intelligence woven into everything that he did and said.

Harry was indeed an incredible mixture of brilliance, emotional intelligence, humor, and compassion. He was confident without being arrogant. He was a mentor to many, and a friend to all.

From the moment I read his Match.com profile, Harry seemed too good to be true. Early on, I looked for a fatal flaw. As time went on, I looked for *any* flaw. Of course, he was not perfect. But he couldn't have been more perfect for me. Even the things he did that irritated me, like bugging me to have coffee when I was working on a deadline or buying me presents I didn't think I needed, only made him seem more amazing.

Harry was known to "cut a wide swath" wherever he went. And that he did indeed do—during his countless lifetimes lived in a mere 54 years. In his wake, he left something incredible and amazing for us all: a legacy of love.

I could have chosen to believe that the world became a darker place because Harry left us too soon and without warning. Instead, I've chosen to believe that the world became even brighter, because his brilliance of spirit was released to shine on us in ways not possible before.

Chapter 5

In the days after the memorial service, I saw how Harry's light was shining as my team peeled away. The Bud Man was the first to leave the next afternoon. During a tender, heartfelt chat just prior to his departure, Bud told me he intended to use Harry's death as a catalyst to turn his professional career in a different direction. He also assured me that he was only a phone call away, and that I could always count on him. I'll never forget the conviction in his eyes. It was the first of countless times over the years to come when I would be the benefactor of more gifts from Harry—the love and friendship of those who had been his closest and dearest friends.

Tanya, my little sister angel, headed back to Savannah that same day. But she returned often over the next couple of years whenever I was in Braselton, keeping a watchful eye on me and lending a shoulder and sympathetic ear when I needed them the most.

By Tuesday, it was time for Paolo to return to Italy. His departure was particularly difficult for me. We had been great comrades from the time we met, and eventually called each other brother and sister. In the days between the service and when he left for the airport, we became exponentially closer during the only real time we had spent together without Harry—on the porch talking into the wee hours of the morning, sharing memories and bottles of his "brother's" best wine, and crying as we hugged goodbye—perhaps each feeling as if we were losing a little bit of Harry all over again.

Brian stayed for several days more, doing what he did best: being in charge and getting things done. A retired and decorated Naval master chief who had spent his career on and around nuclear submarines, he was calm under pressure and able to prioritize what had to be done, which was exactly what I needed during that week.

On the day he left, our masseuse and a dear friend phoned to check on me. Just days before, as I continued to marvel at how the gestures of love, care, and concern continued to flow, I had written a short post:

> *As I go to sleep tonight, I give thanks for all of my angels who are performing a perfectly orchestrated symphony of love to keep me safe and comforted.*

And now it seemed another angel had appeared, offering to spend the night with me when she realized I was home alone. During a night that I'll never forget, we talked about everything under the sun. Eventually, after she told me about having keepsakes made from her mother's clothing, I confessed through sobs that, earlier in the day, someone had discarded the clothes Harry was wearing the night he passed away. I wanted to keep them. To touch them. To hold them. Secretly hoping they still had his scent; anything that would connect me to him in his final moments.

Before I knew it, Cindy and I were "dumpster diving" in the wee hours of a cold February morning—one of us holding the lantern and the other almost upside down digging under the dead flowers in the garbage can just outside the garage. I finally pulled the black bag from the refuse and asked Cindy to look at the clothes first. She bravely did so—telling me that she could tell where the clothes had been cut, likely while the paramedics were trying to save Harry's life.

We went back inside, and together we took the clothes out of the bag. Unfortunately, the bag had not protected the clothes from the smell of the dead flowers, so any scent of Harry was long gone.

Yet I couldn't bear to throw them away. Instead, I loaded them into the washer, and after they tumbled dry, I lovingly folded them neatly and placed them on top of the dryer, where they sat for days. I suppose that my need to launder those clothes was a feeble attempt to wash away what had happened. To cleanse. The stack on the dryer, showing no evidence of the trauma they'd clothed, seemed to be just waiting for Harry's return.

But Harry wasn't coming back. At least not in the form in which I had last seen him. Instead, the next day, after Cindy departed, I stopped by the funeral home to collect his ashes. The cigar humidor, specially ordered the day of the cremation, was ready.

In an odd sort of way, it was nice to see Mike, the funeral director, again. He seemed rather proud of how the urn had turned out. I had chosen a design for Harry's initials that closely matched the design he had chosen for his stationery. His initials were burned into the top of the box, and the black lettering and real wood gave the humidor the elegantly classic look I had been hoping for.

I had brought a long, puffy winter parka Harry had given me to cushion him for the ride home. Mike gently placed the box on the coat on the passenger side as I got into the driver's side. And then he reached over, grabbed the seat belt, and stretched it across the box. "Let's fasten him in for the ride," he suggested as he clicked the end into the buckle.

It was a very nice touch, and I appreciated it greatly. I was smiling as I backed out of the parking space, but as I shifted into drive, my emotions suddenly shifted into an entirely different gear as well. I had not made it out of the parking lot when the tears started. They came fast and furious, and I felt as if I had to fight for every breath. Barely able to see, I somehow turned the car around. When I came to a stop, I slammed the gear shift into park, wrapped my arms around the steering wheel and rested my head on top, sobbing as if there were no tomorrow.

Still crying, I picked up my phone and pressed the P.

"Aaahhh . . . Buongiorno . . . ah?"

Not even trying to say hello, I simply continued to cry.

"Cynthia. My sister. What's wrong?" Paolo's voice was filled with care and concern.

After I explained, he asked, "Are you sad? Or, maybe relieved?"

Paolo's voice was soothing, but it was his question, "Are you relieved?" that wrapped around me like a warm blanket of comfort. My tears slowed. And then I knew—I was actually crying tears of relief.

"Yes, I know. It is the same as when I picked up Sebastiano. My brother is with you now."

For a few minutes, I sat in the parking lot of the funeral home, with Harry's ashes riding shotgun while Paolo shared the memory of picking up his precious five-year-old son's ashes just a few years previously. It was extremely comforting to hear his voice—to know that he could understand so well. But it also reminded me that I was not the only one with sorrow in my heart.

"Cynthia, now drive my brother home. On the way, take him by his favorite places. Drive by Papa Jack's. Maybe by the hotel. Drive him through the neighborhood. Take it slow. And if you get upset, just pull over and call me. I will be here."

When I finished talking with Paolo, and because I was not entirely sure of the best route home, I put the address in my phone, selected a route and headed out. It wasn't long before I realized the route I chose was "the back way" home—across the Buford Dam and along Lake Lanier. It is one of the most scenic drives in the area, and a drive that Harry had taken me on during one of those first weekend visits to his house.

It was a gray, drizzly day, which seemed appropriate for the occasion. The speed limit is 25 miles per hour in many places and, I'm sure much to the chagrin of the drivers behind me, I adhered to the limit that day. At one point, I looked in the rearview mirror and saw cars lined up behind me for quite a distance as we snaked along the winding route.

I wondered how many of them were irritated, not knowing I was transporting precious cargo. "Looks like we are having your funeral procession, H!" I joked at one point. My route took me by Papa Jack's. I pulled into a space and unfastened my seat belt.

"I'll just be gone for a minute. You behave yourself," I instructed as I slipped out of the car.

Donna came out from around the serving line and gave me a big hug before she asked, "Whatcha gonna have tonight?"

"I'm going to get mine to go this evening." I smiled and tilted my head toward the door as I lowered my voice. "Harry's out in the car."

Donna burst out laughing. And then, with a Styrofoam container in her hand and a twinkle in her eye, she said, "Would you like one breast or two?"

"I think two would be in order this evening," I twinkled back.

And so, with dinner for two in hand, I returned to the car with Donna close behind me. She had wanted to come out and "say hello."

Later that night as I readied for bed, I thought about the coincidence—the first night with Harry's ashes was the first night without any company. "I see what you did there," I said as I slipped under the covers. And then I laid there, expecting the tears and sorrow to well up inside me again. Instead, I felt an odd sort of peace, and that deep sense of relief I had experienced in the funeral home parking lot after talking to Paolo. I fell asleep that night under the watchful eye of the HCB–inscribed humidor and an oddly comforting feeling that I wasn't "home alone," after all.

Despite the feeling of comfort that had tucked me in the night before, I woke up the next morning in a house without Harry, or anyone else for that matter. After two weeks of being surrounded by friends and family who loved and comforted me more than one person deserved, I was now on my own.

It was an important morning for me. I knew that. A foreshadowing of how I would face each day going forward without Harry. So,

I was determined to "make it a great day," as Harry would say every morning. I was sure that it would be, since one of my best friends from middle school was coming to spend the afternoon with me. But first I had to get through the morning of solitude that now stretched out in front of me.

I knew better than to languish in bed. It was a prime time for depression and sorrow to slip in and take up residency. I had battled depression many years before, and I wanted no part of that again. Especially not now. So, I had made myself a promise to rise each morning, get dressed and apply makeup. Yes . . . makeup. I was acutely aware that I was in the battle of my life. A battle *for* my life. And since no warrior would go into battle without his war paint, mine was applied that morning before I went downstairs.

It was fairly early for me, just after seven. I pressed the espresso machine into service and prepared a small plate of fruit. As I placed the coffee mug, a bottle of Pellegrino and the fruit plate on the kitchen island, I glanced longingly toward the porch.

About a week before, I had stolen a couple of magical moments there and written:

Some of our most special times at home were on our back porch— talking, laughing, solving the problems of the world or sharing times with special friends. Harry loved flowers and always had a child-like excitement for snow. Today, our porch is adorned with flowers from many who loved Harry, and snow has begun to fall softly. So here we are again—taking a coffee. I cannot see you, my love, but I know you are here with me.

I imagined the snowflakes covering me with a light dusting of Harry's love. I fancied he had arranged the unusual snowfall, certain that I would connect the dots and know he was close.

Even though the flowers had been discarded and the snow had long since melted, the memory of that moment was pushing me to the porch. So, I gathered up the breakfast items and stepped out into the brisk February morning.

With a heavy heart, I sat down in my usual spot which had been the scene of so many moments of joy over the years. Our first dinner "at home." Chocolate martinis on Halloween, cigars and port with Paolo. Thanksgiving with Wise Old Al and Nanette. And the very simplest of times. Having coffee. Talking. Laughing.

Suddenly, the sorrow that I had expected the night before was upon me. Insatiable sorrow that felt as if it would swallow me whole if I allowed it to. My throat tightened and my chest began to heave. To keep the inevitable tears from spilling onto my blueberries and into my coffee, I took a deep breath, lifted my chin slightly and tried to blink them away.

And that's when it happened.

My entire world slipped into slow motion and then came to a beautifully, breathtaking, grinding halt.

If a dog barked, I never heard it. If a car drove past on the alley behind the house, I didn't see it. My only awareness was an all-consuming physical and spiritual feeling that I was in the middle of my own little miracle.

"Good morning, love," I whispered with a shaky voice. A tear escaped and trickled down my face. "You sure look good in red today."

He was across the back yard, in a thicket of winter's dull, gray branches, sitting with his gaze fixed upon me. And though he was so small, his presence dwarfed everything around him and filled the backyard from corner to corner.

I felt an overwhelming rush of incredible love and certainty wash over me and through me. Like that morning on the takeoff from Seattle, I didn't know where I ended and the Divine began. It felt as if a window had been opened and the breeze of eternity brushed back the curtains for me to see and feel a magical shower of sparkling light and love.

The blazing red cardinal continued to sit and stare. I cried softly, feeling Harry's love, protection, and presence. But I felt even more. It was as if a red-feathered messenger had swooped into my backyard and transformed the green leyland and cypress trees into sentries standing guard to my broken heart and sorrowful soul. I could hear the message loud and clear, as if Harry were saying:

We've carved out this moment of perfection just for you, my little Cynthee. My Punkin Princess! I know your heart is broken, but it is going to mend and be stronger and more full of love than ever before. And I'll be here watching. Keeping an eye on you. Always . . . and forever.

It was indeed a moment of perfection, and I didn't want it to end. I reached for my phone, thinking a photo would preserve the moment without realizing that the moment had already been captured—imprinted on my heart and soul forever.

Nonetheless, I took three photos. The first and last were five minutes apart. Later I would laugh as I remembered Harry saying, "Nothing ever takes five minutes."

But that morning, five minutes was all it took for me to see and feel limitless love and light. And to believe in the promise that even on the darkest days, the sun continues to shine—just as the cardinal was shining his brilliant red from the gray, wintry branches of the crabapple tree.

I sat on the porch for a while that morning, once again feeling that I was not "home alone." Even so, I didn't think that Harry was hanging out in the backyard sporting a set of new red feathers. I did believe that he somehow had something to do with it, and I was not surprised. Harry was larger than life and reveled that we were "psychically connected." So, there was no telling what he could pull off without physical limitations and a new boss who gave him free rein.

"So, C, have you had any dreams about Harry? Or felt his presence?"

I blinked and took a deep breath. I had a feeling that I was about to have another life-changing moment.

It had been nearly 30 years since I had seen her when she pulled into my driveway just a few hours after the cardinal sighting. As is often the case with lifelong friends, we picked up right where we left off. But we had a bit of a head start on the reconnection. About nine months before, we had started an email conversation.

During that reconnection, Denise had demonstrated an uncanny ability to ask a very profound and thought-provoking question at the most perfect time. This day was no different.

Suddenly we were 12 years old again. I answered by showing one of the pictures I had taken just hours before. And then, with the same schoolgirl dreamy excitement that I might have used to confide, "You'll never *believe* who talked to me today!" I described the cardinal experience that had taken place that morning. It felt as if something significant had happened, but I wasn't sure what it meant.

In many ways, we are always those two little-kid playmates when we are together. For I believe we are already who we are meant to be, even at 12 years old. The challenge is to stay true to that, despite the static and the distractions that prevent us from hearing the whispers and seeing the signs that point us to the road we are destined to travel. Or to hear the messages we are meant to hear.

That afternoon, Denise responded to my story exactly as I expected her to: interested, supportive, and non-judgmental.

But the power was perhaps in what she didn't say.

About a week later, she shared a Facebook post with me. It was a photo of a tree filled with cardinals. The caption read:

A cardinal is a representative of a loved one who has passed. When you see one, it means they are visiting you. They usually show up when you most need them or miss them. They also make an appearance during times of celebration as well as despair to let you know they will always be with you. Look for them, they'll appear.

—Author Unknown

I was stunned. When I asked why she hadn't said anything that afternoon, she told me she knew the experience was very fresh for me, and that she thought it was important that I figure out on my own what it meant for me. "But you already knew it, C," she concluded.

Once again, she was right.

There was no way that I could deny the "coincidences" that had occurred or the physical sensation that came along with them. The swelling of my heart, the full-body chills, the feeling of ultimate truth and unconditional love.

A few weeks later, my little sister, Tanya, returned. And she seemed to have brought someone with her. It was a particularly difficult afternoon; I had been crying and Tanya had been listening.

This time, he swooped in with a flourish and made a hard landing in a nearby cypress tree, the branch continuing to bob after he touched down. Tanya smiled at me with her impish grin.

It's The Baby . . . Tanya! he seemed to say with his raucous arrival. *Thank you so much for taking care of Little Cynthee!*

My heart had leapt when I saw the red bird, but I was careful not to make a big deal about it. I knew that those who loved me the most were watching me closely, knowing how devastated I was. I didn't want them to think I was going off the deep end. But I was on the porch again, feeling a huge sense of loss, and the cardinal had appeared at the perfect time.

A week later, I was heading out to the porch again. As I fumbled with the door while balancing my breakfast and coffee, I heard the loud singing.

I stepped onto the porch, put my breakfast on the table, and looked across the yard toward the crabapple tree.

This time he was a little farther back in the tree. I had to strain to make him out, but he continued to sing and chirp as he edged forward. I just sat there and took it all in. I didn't even reach for the

BlackBerry . . . After all, he was singing to me this time, and I didn't want to spoil it. My mind was racing as I wondered what to say. There was so much I wanted him to know.

It was a moment of truth for me. I was a logical, rational CPA. But I was also trained to recognize trends and patterns. A pattern had definitely formed, and I couldn't discount the divine feelings that came with each encounter.

The truth is, I *wanted* to believe that Harry's larger-than-life spirit had lived beyond his physical body. After all, he had promised me that we would always be together, in those conversations we'd had after a couple of martinis. Would you still love me if I lost my legs? Would you run into a burning building to rescue me? Would you never stop searching for me if I went missing?

He had promised.

If there was one thing at which Harry had batted a thousand, it was always being true to his word. I cannot remember a single time that he didn't do exactly what he said he was going to do. He had made a point of saying that his sole purpose in life was to take care of me. That it was extra important for him to keep an eye on me. And so, in that moment, with the cardinal also batting a thousand—appearing each time I had been on the porch—I believed it was happening.

Even though there could have been so much to say, in the end, I could only muster, "I miss you," as big, hot tears rolled down my face and I opened my heart to the possibility that Harry had made good on his promise to never leave me. The backyard bird fluttered around a bit, still chirping as if to say, *I'm right here! I'm right here!* And then, as he did that very first morning, he made his way to the top of the tree and took flight.

Two days before the cardinal appeared for the first time, I had experienced a different type of divine presence and had written a post about it. The comments had been quite enthusiastic. Some friends had acknowledged that they believed in messages from heaven.

Others commented on the great love that Harry and I had shared. One of my dearest friends suggested I write a book about that great love, which spurred others to encourage me to do the same. And my most favorite teacher from middle and high school chimed in, *Well, my dear, you certainly haven't lost your touch with words. Brilliant and touching. Keep writing things like this and keep them some place special. Proud of you.*

In less than two weeks since Harry had passed away, I was receiving messages from him and encouragement to write about them. The compliments and expressions of gratitude were humbling, and provided me with a glimpse of something not unlike what I had felt at the podium—a realization that in the midst of my sorrow, I was somehow providing comfort, hope, and inspiration to others.

Now weeks later, I had experienced three more divine moments that flew into my life on the wings of a red bird. While I felt called to share the experiences, I was scared. But on the one-month anniversary of Harry's death, I wrote a post about the three cardinal visits. I took a deep breath, and I posted it.

On the next morning, I breathed a sigh of relief.

Clearly, I had sparked something in my friends. One hundred of them liked the post and nearly half of them commented—providing expressions of gratitude, acknowledgments of God's grace, and belief in messages from heaven. Some sent loving words of care and comfort. Some shared their own cardinal stories. Many others complimented my writing, and, the suggestions that I write a book continued.

Harry had also encouraged me to write. With his death and the extraordinary happenings, he seemed to have flung the door wide open as if to say, *And now I've given you even more material! So, get busy with it, sister!*

I cannot deny that the compliments felt wonderful, and my social media posting had been therapeutic. But there was something more.

Suddenly I felt an undeniable connection to so many people, and I loved hearing that my words were providing comfort and hope. I felt stirrings of a divine purpose—that my story of love and loss could have meaning for others, and that Harry's death could be the catalyst for making a career change—something that I had longed to do for most of my adult life.

When I woke the next morning, the feeling was stronger than ever. But I had client obligations. I was in Harry's office at his desk trying to work on financial statements and budgets when the tears fell again. Not only was my heart hurting from missing Harry, but I had the familiar feeling of being a professional misfit.

At that very moment, our dear friend Bill, who I also called "Papa Jack," stopped by the house. No doubt he could tell that I had been crying. He followed me into Harry's office, sat down across the desk from me and said, "Okay. Tell me exactly what you are feeling right this minute."

I'm not sure if he knew what he was getting into, but I knew that another one of my angels had arrived. Crying and talking at the same time, I told Bill that even though I was in so much pain, I was also experiencing something amazingly beautiful. I was afraid that if I went back to Alaska, I would use my work to cover up the pain, and miss an opportunity to experience the depth of the grief I knew I needed to. It felt like I was turning my back on myself and on Harry's memory. I had long felt that I was destined for something other than accounting. The divine moments and the response to my sharing about them had led me to consider moving in a different direction professionally. But I had given my word that I would return.

Papa Jack provided the encouragement I needed. "You and I both know that this is not what you are here for," he said as he motioned to the desk covered with financial reports. "But you are really great at it, and you help your clients tremendously. I know that's important to you. Remember that *you* are still here. You have so much to offer this world. Don't be afraid to follow your heart."

That afternoon, I returned to the porch for lunch. I had fixed a little plate of salami, hummus, celery and blueberries. I felt better after my chat with Papa Jack, but felt guilty for considering a change in course. Admittedly, I was doing my best not to be on the lookout. If a cardinal didn't appear, I didn't want to feel as if I had lost Harry all over again.

The gray, twiggy tree was extra barren. No cardinal in sight. I ate silently for a bit and then the big, salty tears started again, not because the cardinal wasn't there, but because my larger-than-life, in-the-flesh Harry wasn't. I felt silly because on some level, I *did* want that red bird to be in the back yard.

For a minute, I let the pain and despair wash over me. It was not just *my* loss that I felt—Harry was a guiding light for so many other people. I felt like putting my head down and sobbing forever, but I stopped short of that. I couldn't let myself go there. "You're still here," Papa Jack had reminded me earlier. I knew I had to carry on. I had so many people that loved and supported me. I had to find a way to rebuild myself . . . rebuild my life . . . with Harry playing a role, albeit a different one, this go-round.

So, I took a deep breath, released a heavy sigh and glanced up, focusing on nothing in particular. Then I looked to the right, and gasped. In a perfect spot for me to see him through an opening in the trees, he was silently watching.

And then, perhaps because of my movement and exclamation, there was a spastic flurry of red as he dove out of sight—like a kid getting his hand caught in the cookie jar.

It was just like Harry to let me test the waters, thinking he wasn't there . . . helping me to move on just a little more that day, but staying close enough, just in case. Always protecting, always keeping an eye on me.

The cardinal and I had a perfect record now, with the four times on the porch. I had no doubt that our games of peek-a-boo would continue. In fact, I fancied that a feeder, well stocked with barbeque-flavored birdseed and a bird bath flowing with champagne, might be in order.

I also decided that I would not be returning to Alaska or serving my client remotely. It was time to take a break. To allow myself to experience the loss of Harry as fully as possible. To grieve deeply. To grow. And to take steps—even if only baby steps—in the direction of the life that was waiting for me on the other side of it all.

Chapter 6

In the end, it seemed that I wasn't the only one thinking about a bird feeder.

A few days later, I returned from running errands to find a beautiful, wrought-iron feeder and a huge bag of Wagner's cardinal seed waiting for me at the end of the driveway. As I sat in my car smiling, the phone rang.

"Hello Papa Jack!"

"Whaaaaaaat's happenin'?!" Bill was calling to see if I had found "it." As I hung up from our call and made my way into the house, I was thinking how lucky I was to have so many incredible people in my life.

Bill was one of Harry's dearest friends. We met after Harry and I started dating in 2003. One morning Harry asked, "Hey, wanna check out a new place for breakfast? My very good friend has opened up a biscuit joint close by."

The biscuit joint was (and still is) Papa Jack's Country Kitchen, named after Bill's dearly departed father. I could easily imagine that Harry was really saying that morning in 2003, "Hey, I'm going to take you to Papa Jack's this morning so that you can meet my friend and his team—they are going to take such good care of you when I'm not here to do it myself."

Papa Jack's was much more than a "biscuit joint," and over the years we ate there often when in town. Eventually, a lone booth against the back wall of the homey dining room became "our" table. Harry always sat facing the open room, which meant that my view was spectacular: the love of my life and a placard on the wall that read, COUNT YOUR BLESSINGS. RECOUNTS OK.

Sometimes we shuffled in at six in the morning, sleepyheads with hair askew. Harry had a lot more confidence and a lot less hair than I, so he didn't care. Eventually, I didn't either.

On those early mornings, we'd grab our trays and present ourselves in the cafeteria line. When asked by the lively Papa Jack's crew, "What in the world are you two doing up so early?" Harry would simply say, "Whew! What a night. Just posted bail. Is Bill up yet?"

He would invariably send his eggs back to be cooked more and when asked, "More coffee?" he would gladly slide his mug forward with a jovial, "Why yes, since you came all this way."

But what I enjoyed most of all was watching my husband engage in lively conversation with those on Papa Jack's team. I never grew tired of seeing how he remembered tiny details from the previous conversation, even if it had been months. How he asked questions about their lives, their dreams, their families. How he encouraged, and teased, and made them laugh.

And Harry was always kindheartedly busting Bill's chops about changing the bacon or the brand of ketchup, or the fact that he was too busy to sit down and join us.

On that first morning in 2003, I made the mistake of asking about the ho cakes on the menu. For sure, the definition Harry provided was a bit more "colorful" than the one provided by Bill.

On Harry's last morning in 2014, he teased Cindy relentlessly, insisting that he step into the kitchen and "have a word" with the health inspector, to hasten completion of the annual review. So many laughs. Such great conversation. So much coffee. A veritable all-you-can-eat of fun.

After flying back to Atlanta and into a life without Harry, it didn't take me long to return to Papa Jack's, where "our" table had become "my" table.

Some mornings, I would sneak in and cry my way through breakfast before the doors opened. Other mornings I would arrive to find my table adorned with flowers or balloons or a "reserved" note.

On some mornings, when I didn't make it in, Bill would drop by the house with encouraging notes or smiley faces drawn on a Styrofoam container filled with a tasty breakfast. Sometimes, I would arrive at lunch, feigning a craving for fried chicken and green beans, when I was really after a hug and a smile. I'm still convinced that, no matter the time of day that I appeared, my Papa Jack's family took intentional turns to make sure that the seat across from me was never, ever empty.

So, I shouldn't have been surprised that, despite owning a thriving restaurant and catering business, Bill had taken time to deliver a bird feeder just two days before he went into the hospital for surgery.

I was touched, but nervous. I didn't want to depend on the cardinal being in the backyard. I felt like putting up the feeder was an admission that the cardinal was Harry. Even I thought that to be a bit creepy. I knew it was a gift of love, Bill's way of saying, *Let's be sure the cardinal comes to see you, because I'll be laid up for a while and won't be able to.* Even so, I decided to put the bird feeder in the garage, and find a place for it when I felt more comfortable to do so.

As soon as Bill left the hospital, he stopped by the house with his sister Kathy and daughter Brooke. After greetings, he immediately excused himself and, moments later, I saw him place the feeder in a perfect spot in the backyard. Later, we were in the great room chatting when his sister Kathy stood up and turned toward the window.

"Oh my goodness! What a *beautiful* cardinal!" she exclaimed.

This time he was back in the crabapple tree that spring had transformed from a twisted mangle of gray to a powder puff of white. His feathers blazed red against the background of blossoms.

To this day, I'm disappointed that I didn't have my phone handy to take a photo. But truth be told, no picture could have adequately captured the majesty of that moment.

He was looking at the great room and speaking right to my heart, as if to say: *I was here when the wintry limbs were barren, and I'm here in the midst of spring blossoms. I'll be here in the green leaves of summer, and when they turn orange in the autumn and fall. Seasons will come and seasons will go, but I'll be with you . . . always and forever.*

Bill started crying. He was sitting in Harry's chair, as he always did, and I was close by on a red leather sofa. Seeing Bill's reaction, I felt Harry's message expand to one of gratitude to Bill for taking such good care of me, and to assure him that he had been with Bill during his very challenging hospital stay. And probably to say, *Thanks for the feeder, Billy!* Overwhelmed with emotion, I escaped upstairs to my bedroom.

As I sat in my room, I couldn't help but think that the cardinal was demonstrating a boldness and sense of confidence that was eerily familiar. His timing was impeccable. Could it have been just a coincidence? Or was it a continuation of an unmistakable pattern? Part of me wanted to attribute it to coincidence. But the rest of me, my heart and soul, knew that it wasn't. Eventually I would come to believe that sometimes a cardinal is just a cardinal. But so far, the cardinal showing up in the backyard seemed to be so much more.

A week or so later, I came home to find one on the porch. This time it was an artificial cardinal stuck into a bouquet of flowers. A beautiful journal, with quotes on both covers, was leaning against the vase. One of the quotes said, *It is here where she begins to tell her story.* But the quote that meant the most was in the handwritten note Bill had left inside the journal, to let me know that he hoped his gift would *help to get that writing thing of yours started.*

Over the coming weeks, the number of cardinal sightings mounted. I continued writing about them. Friends shared their stories with me privately. Harry's high school classmates sent me friend requests. Cardinal gifts arrived in the mail, including a delicate linen hand towel, embroidered with a beautiful cardinal from Kathy, who had since learned why Bill and I had such emotional reactions that day.

I noticed that people were stirred emotionally. Something magical happened as I shared my experiences with others. The interest level was quite high, and I sensed that a lot of it had nothing at all to do with me. It seemed that my stories were giving others permission to believe what they already felt in their hearts.

Despite the inspiration and excitement around the "happenings," I continued to be out of sorts in a big way. On top of the profound grief, I was not working for the first time in my life. After notifying my client that I was not returning to Alaska right away, I helped them transition to another professional. And then I found myself with unstructured days and evenings. Unstructured except for my daily wake-up call.

"Aaahhh . . . Buongiorno . . . ah?" he would exclaim each morning when I answered. Sometimes I would still be in bed—my "horizontal office," as Harry had called it. Other times, I would already be on the porch taking a coffee. Sometimes, I'd be in my booth at Papa Jack's. But always, I was appreciative that Paolo was taking time every day to check on me.

Sometimes we cried. Other times we laughed at inside jokes we had shared with Harry, and new ones that were now our own. It was rare for a call to end without Paolo's, "Good, my sister. Keep going."

It was also rare that I didn't make an appearance at Papa Jack's each day during those first few months after Harry passed away. A daily dose of love and hugs from my Papa Jack's family was one of the best antidotes for my broken heart.

At one point, I decided to make a quick trip to Anchorage. I wanted to prove to myself that I could do it, and I thought it might kickstart a plan for moving forward.

I flew in reverse of the night that Harry died. My first stop was Seattle, where I was able to visit with my friend Jennifer at the Marriott. In Juneau, I stopped by Max's firm after arrival and visited with my hospital client later in the day.

Coincidentally, Max was my seat partner on the flight to Anchorage the next morning. At one point, he asked me what my plans were. Still not sure, I said that I simply wanted to do something meaningful and significant. He suggested that my work in Nome had already qualified. I suspected he was trying to caution me on how I defined "significant," meaning that we can make mighty contributions without our name being cast in neon lights for all the world to see.

I was still thinking about Max's point an hour or so later when I opened the door to the condo in Anchorage. With a heavy sigh, I noted the Christmas tree in the corner—still fully decorated while Santa, Rudolph, and Yukon Cornelius sat quietly by. It was almost May.

Standing there feeling sad and forlorn, all I could think was, *It's time to take the Christmas tree down.* Later that evening, I lit the tree, turned on Christmas music, started the fireplace and cracked open a bottle of champagne. I sat in the dark with the lights of the tree and flames of the fire casting a gentle glow on all the wonderful Christmas memories I'd had with Harry. I crawled into our bed well after midnight and cried myself to sleep. The next morning, I took down the tree.

Something shifted in me during the trip to Alaska. By the time I returned to Georgia a few days later, a different type of low-grade sadness had settled in my soul. During our years in Alaska, Harry and I created beautiful memories. We had just spent nine months together there. It was also where I was when tragedy struck. Being back had aroused even deeper feelings of sadness, longing, and despair.

I started to cry. Nonstop. No sobs; just tears. Anytime. Anywhere. The accompanying feelings of sorrow were like none I had ever experienced. I didn't know it was even possible to feel such a bottomless, dark pit of despair. I called it the abyss.

Friends were noticing, and they were worried. I had to admit, I was worried as well. Few people knew that I had suffered severe depression before I met Harry. I was on high alert for its return.

But now, even though I was so tearful and, in such pain, at least I knew why. I thought it was normal, given the circumstances. So, I kept moving forward—one little baby step at a time. I started exploring online support groups. I tried to read books, but most were filled with prescribed stages of grief that included sadness, anger, and fear. Many of the online support groups had chat streams full of helplessness and victimhood. My heart broke for every person who was hurting, but I could not relate to their comments or the words in the books. I didn't want my experience to be only sadness, anger, fear and helplessness. I didn't believe it had to be that way.

One night while in bed, after tossing another self-"no"-help book onto the floor, I pulled up the covers and lay there thinking. The books weren't helping. There was only so much champagne one person could drink. And the therapist I had been using was a bit too clinical. That's when it hit me: *I need someone more spiritual.*

I threw back the covers and headed for my computer. It didn't take me long to find him. Already feeling a sense of relief, I fired off an email.

I met Bedford in 1996. I had been attending group therapy with my first husband, and once I learned that I was extremely codependent, depressed and struggling with a host of related challenges, including my marriage and career, I wanted to tackle it all head-on.

I wanted out. Not out of life, but out of the quicksand. I felt I was destined for so much more. For happiness and joy. I needed someone to point me in the right direction, and I didn't want to take forever to get there, wherever "there" happened to be. One day, in a private session with the counselor, I expressed my frustration with the slow progress of weekly, one-hour sessions. I was ready to learn and work on myself. I wanted something faster, stronger, better.

A few weeks later, driving a rental—a midnight-blue Mustang convertible—and acting on the recommendation of the counselor,

I set out from Savannah, bound for the hills of Tennessee. It was the longest road trip I had ever taken by myself.

It was a trip that changed my life.

The retreat was led by a badass but soft-spoken, long-haired, pony-tailed, corduroy-wearing hippie in sandals, who taught me and nine other people about our inner child and family of origin, and introduced us to the concept of God as the ideal father figure.

I cried during my first-ever meditation. Slept on a basic cot in a dormitory-type bedroom. Had my first massage. Learned with amazement how universal our individual stories are. And I started to feel a sense of peace that I had longed for, but never truly experienced.

I also experienced the first feeling that God, the Universe, Spirit, or whatever you choose to call it, had a remarkable plan for me. I just didn't know exactly what it was.

I left that transformative week, knowing I had learned from a gifted master. And that life would never be the same.

And . . . that I wanted a Mustang convertible!

In many ways, that trip was the catalyst for making changes that would eventually lead me to Harry. I put everything into myself. Into my marriage. Into my job. I opened up spiritually, and in the months following the retreat, I began to see, hear and feel the messages the universe sends us if we are open to them.

Less than two years later, I got divorced. I received a promotion at work, and started to feel I was worthy of a wonderful life and a fairytale relationship. I was playing tennis several times a week, spending quality time with friends, and especially enjoyed driving the beautiful coastal roads of Savannah in my very own Mustang convertible. GT. Midnight blue. Black top.

Many years had passed since that retreat, but as I made my way to my computer that night in 2014, I knew that if anyone could help me, Bedford could.

Bedford, who hadn't heard a peep from me in nearly 20 years, replied within the hour—even though it was late in the evening. I'm certain he didn't remember me, but I'd written what I'd like to believe was a compelling email with a suggested game plan. It concluded with, *Would you be able to help me get moving in the right direction?*

Bedford's response was exactly what I needed to hear. Although he couldn't accommodate me in his schedule for a month, he presented me with several options and concluded with, *Let me know what your intuition and inner healer are telling you, and we will go from there. You are held in thought and prayer. Take good care, Bedford.*

Though I had requested a series of extended one-on-one sessions, he had suggested I do two days with him, and two days in a small group. I bristled at the thought of a group setting, having a hard enough time in small groups of loved ones. But then I remembered how magical the first retreat had been. I told myself, *You reached out to Bedford for a reason. You either trust him or you don't.*

I read his email again. Then as he suggested, I called on my intuition. Moments later, I wrote back to him. *Your suggestion for July 8–11 in Nashville sounds perfect.*

I went to sleep that night, feeling a great sense of relief. I felt empowered by Bedford's recommendation for me to trust my intuition and inner healer. Even though we had not yet spoken, I had no doubt that he was going to understand my desire to do grief differently. I was so thankful that I had listened to my little voice, but it was early June, and July 8th seemed so far away. I was still crying so much that I'd started thinking, *Surely I will run out of water at some point!*

Though I never ran out of water, it helped that I now had three things to look forward to: a road trip to Savannah and Florida, my time with Bedford, and a visit from Paolo. I just needed to make it through the next couple of weeks. And then, as he had done in the days before the memorial service, my colleague and friend Kendall reached out with the perfect words at the perfect time.

I was working upstairs, in my makeshift office, when Kendall texted, suggesting that we talk soon. Still crying spontaneously, I let him know that I was game, but that it might be a one-sided conversation.

"I can take the tears if you can," he responded.

After I answered the phone the following evening, Kendall quickly got to the point. "What's on your mind right now, Cynthia?"

No surprise that I was crying. But I managed to say what was on my heart and mind, even though I honestly didn't know it was until I heard it come out of my mouth.

"Harry was larger than life," I whimpered. "He filled up a room completely. He filled up my heart. He had such a magnetic personality. And even though it feels like I've turned into a satellite dish for messages from heaven, I'm so confused. I just can't believe that someone so big in stature and spirit just . . . *ended*. And so, I find myself continually asking: *Where is he? Where did he GO?*"

After a brief pause, Kendall asked if he could share some of his beliefs. I tearfully gave him the green light. His next words were music to my ears.

"Cynthia, I believe that our loved ones are closer than we could possibly imagine."

Instantly, I felt a hundred-ton weight lift from my heart. But it wasn't just what he said, it was how he said it. With such certainty, conviction and confidence. At the time I didn't challenge his credentials to speak with such authority, because he had told me what I most wanted and needed to hear. He had given me permission to believe what I already felt to be true.

We spent nearly two hours on the phone that night. He went further into details about his faith. He spoke of his losses—a father, uncle and brother, all of whom had sudden cardiac events. His young son had died unexpectedly just a few years before. Kendall knew a lot about loss, and I could tell that his deep faith was more than a weapon in his arsenal against grief. It was also foundational to a life of peace.

I told Kendall about the cardinal visits. About the feelings that completely overwhelmed me. I told him about two vivid dreams I'd had after my father passed away, and how I was convinced it was him letting me know he was okay and extra busy in heaven.

I went to sleep that night with a tremendous amount of gratitude for Kendall's decision to reach out to me, and a peace in my heart that I had not felt in a very long time. When I woke up the next morning, I had stopped crying. A month later, I headed to the hills of Tennessee.

In our first chat, I explained to Bedford how broken I felt. I told him that friends were worried that I was depressed. Some had suggested I consider meds. He asked me what I thought about that.

I looked up at the ceiling with tears streaming down my face and feelings of frustration and despair. I admitted, "I had no idea that this kind of sorrow existed. It is so dark, and so deep, I call it 'the abyss.' And yet, even though I am in so much pain . . . I have never felt more alive!"

Bedford, now with short hair and wearing khakis and loafers, sat back in his chair. He stretched his arms toward the ceiling. "Cynthia, I am so glad to hear you say that. You're not depressed! You're *grieving*!"

As emotional as I was, I remember thinking, *Okay, Bedford, you get bonus points for that one.* And then I smiled.

He followed up with his thoughts on how poorly we grieve as a society. Though it is one of the ways in which we can grow exponentially in our wisdom, we typically feel we should put it into a box, shove it to the back of a dark closet, and get on with our lives. "But it just doesn't work if we do it that way. You know that already, don't you?"

I nodded and confessed that I didn't want to cover up anything. That although I had so much pain, even in the darkness I had encountered so much light. So much love. Amazing, beautiful things were happening. Then I shared some of the "Harry Ever

After" experiences, including the cardinal. Bedford smiled knowingly and spoke with conviction.

"Cynthia, you *do* know that Harry is here with us, don't you? He's right here! How awesome is that?!"

It was still early in the game for me. Even though I felt the same way, I had only allowed myself to consider "he will always be with me" in a figurative way. I could tell Bedford was speaking in the literal sense. As I had with Kendall, I appreciated Bedford's certainty and confidence.

I spent four incredible days of healing in Tennessee. Bedford had been right about the small group session. It was just what I needed, and a perfect complement to the one-on-one sessions with him. When I left on Friday afternoon, I had a newfound confidence that I could face the days ahead, and the world had eight more people in love with a red-feathered backyard bird and a larger-than-life guy named Harry.

I was also glad to have taken inspired action when I reached out to Bedford. It was the second time in my life that I made that beautiful drive back through the Tennessee mountains. And it was the second time that I was certain, after having been on the receiving end of Bedford's wisdom, that my life would never be the same. Just as I had the first time, I believed that God or the Universe had a remarkable plan for me. But this time, unlike twenty years before, I had a better idea of what that plan might be.

Chapter 7

The truth is, I had always had a general sense of what that plan was, because I had seen it every day for the first eight years of my school life.

Make you the world a bit better or more beautiful because you have lived in it.
— Edward W. Bok

The message was engraved on a simple wooden sign and placed in a strategic location on the Hancock Day School campus. It was hard to miss. If the school's founder, Emmie Ruth P. Hancock, had intended to brainwash us, it worked. At least it did for me.

I already thought the world was a beautiful place. My days before starting first grade were filled with sunshine and flowers. Once school started and I saw the daily mantra, the thought that I could actually help make the world even more beautiful filled me with wonderment and a constant butterflies-in-my-stomach excitement.

Though I was too young to understand exactly how my contribution would unfold, I wasn't too young to have a sense that my life had purpose. For the first few years of grade school, I accepted that this purpose was to learn, to explore and to grow.

In fifth grade, I fell in love with music. The love affair started with the hauntingly beautiful melody of "Over the Sea to Skye," which struck a literal and figurative chord with me. It continued with learning to play the clarinet, and teaching myself to play the Genie organ. Though I never sang in any formal settings, I was constantly singing with my friends. Instead of playing with dolls, we performed in front of make-believe audiences. We caroled every Christmas. I sang while I cut the grass, in the car, and for hours on end in my bedroom.

I also loved to read, devouring any books around the house that my parents or older siblings had read, no matter the topic or length. I couldn't wait for my grandparents to visit from Florida, as they came bearing mounds of magazines. I particularly enjoyed reading the essays and jokes in *Reader's Digest* and marveled over the stories and amazing photographs in *National Geographic*.

There was no greater day during the summer than when the pale green bookmobile sounded its horn behind our house. Tanya and I would gather our grocery bags of just-read books and rush outside, eager to step into the icy-cold library on wheels, to once again fill our brown sacks with adventure, romance and mystery.

By the time I hit seventh grade, the results of my early years of reading became clear as I completed homework assignments and book reports. The feedback on my writing was very positive, and I reveled in the attention I received. I secretly fancied life as a writer, composing stories by a roaring fire with snow falling softly out-side—an interesting vision for a young girl growing up in sweltering Savannah, Georgia.

I was also beginning to receive attention in athletics. With all endeavors, schoolwork, music and sports, I threw myself into learning and practicing with gusto. I was blessed with an unusual work ethic and ability to focus. I absolutely loved to practice, losing myself in learning and finding myself in mastery.

In the eighth grade, as I headed down the stretch of spring to the summer of 1979, I was creating. I was performing. I was growing. And I was looking forward to the continued development of my talents and gifts during the exciting four years of high school ahead of me. But trouble was brewing, and two significant events occurred within the next few years that changed everything.

The first occurred that spring when I learned, while watching the evening news, that my school, Hancock Academy, was closing. The campus had been sold to another school in town. Suddenly the exciting four years of high school with my classmates and teammates had been horribly disrupted. Just like that, a close-knit family of friends was thrust into uncertainty, having to scramble with decisions about new schools. My parents decided I would attend Memorial Day School, one of Hancock's staunch rivals, primarily known for its boys' sports teams. As an upcoming freshman in high school, I thought my life was over. But I would soon learn a lesson that would surface often, especially in the days following Harry's death. We can find gifts of light in even the darkest times. One of those gifts of light that spring was finding out one of Hancock's newest and best teachers was also heading to Memorial.

Carol Duberstein had walked into my eighth-grade English class just after arriving in Savannah from New York in the summer of 1978. She was loud, boisterous, direct, and had an edge unlike any teacher I'd had in my previous seven years of school. I could tell she was going to push us. I was mesmerized, and a little afraid.

But each time the homework and book reports came back to me, I'd find large, red As on them. Sometimes with a plus. Occasionally I'd receive comments like, *Subjunctive mood. This is an advanced topic, but you should know it. Come see me.*

So, I would "go see her," as instructed. From inside a plume of cigarette smoke, coffee and chalk, she would explain the concept in her New York accent and with a very direct, matter-of-fact manner. I knew early on that her intention was not to criticize me, but to make me better.

We were an unlikely combination, as I was shy and lacked confidence. But with each stroke of her red pen, my confidence grew.

I bloomed under the praise she lavished on me, and accepted the challenges she relentlessly sent my way. She was a passionate educator who took great pride and joy in seeing her students learn, grow and excel. Ultimately, we were a perfect match.

With "The Duber" heading to Memorial, life seemed less dismal. But she wasn't the only bright spot for me.

Many of the concerns I expressed to my parents about attending Memorial melted away as my new school added programs, built a gym, and started a school newspaper. The girls' athletic teams improved, and even enjoyed great success in softball and track. But the people were the best surprise of all: a wise and inspirational headmaster, compassionate office staff, excellent teachers and classmates that were bright and fun to be around, and surprisingly accepting of the new kid on the block.

And though I could not have fathomed it at the time, some of the connections that I made at Memorial, and which were dormant for over 30 years, became lifelines for me in the years following Harry's death.

The sale of Hancock devastated me and thrust me into a period of profound heartbreak for the first time in my life. It also gave me another first: experiencing the opportunities and gifts that can spring forth from the darkness of grief.

By the time I finished high school, I had won just about any athletic or academic award possible. I had formed connections that would turn into genuine friendships 30 years later. But perhaps most importantly of all, I had learned that my choice to embrace the unexpected circumstances had a direct impact on how I experienced them. As a result, my high school yearbooks are filled with comments from classmates about how much I smiled, and for three of my four years in high school, the smiles were as genuine as could be.

But by the time I graduated with that list of honors a mile long, the smiles on the outside were just camouflage for the tears on the inside. I was heading into my college years and what should have been a remarkably exciting time of my life, with a low-grade depression and the feeling that my life was over. Again.

The start of my senior year arrived, bringing the usual back-to-school giddiness from reuniting with friends, learning new subjects, and attending football games. It also brought the softball season, which had been moved from spring to fall.

By the time mid-November arrived, we had another region championship in softball under our belt, and I'd made the all-state team. We were starting our third week of basketball practice, which had been going really well. Until it wasn't.

One minute I was flying down the court, and the next, after a sharp cut to the inside, I was lying in a crying heap on the gym floor with a pain so intense that I nearly passed out. The doctor assumed it was the same minor injury I had suffered at the end of softball season. He gave me a flimsy brace, and said I could return to the court after some time off.

I knew he was wrong. Long before it was acceptable to challenge a doctor, I did. In one visit, I explained that the bottom part of my leg didn't feel fully attached to the top part. In another, I suggested it wasn't the same injury because of the pain, and the need to drain my knee during every visit. The doctor was defensive. It never occurred to me to ask my parents to change doctors. My home life was less than ideal, and there were financial challenges. All I could think about was not creating another doctor bill.

Eventually, I just gave up. And that was when everything changed. I had already stopped singing as much, a likely precursor to full-blown fear of singing in front of others that developed when I was an adult. Talking on the CB, another favorite hobby of mine, was no longer "the thing," and the Genie organ had been sold.

My dad, my absolute hero, was drinking. A lot. I didn't have the capacity at the time to understand the tremendous pressure he felt, or the pain he carried in his heart. All I knew was that I was scared, confused and heartbroken.

Years later, I self-diagnosed the injury after seeing a football player injured on TV. Ten years later, a doctor confirmed a completely ruptured anterior cruciate ligament (ACL)—one of the main ligaments in the knee. Back then, ACL ruptures ended athletic careers at worst, and, at best, were repaired with average success after major reconstruction surgery, a week in the hospital and months of rehab.

Nineteen years after the injury, I had reconstructive surgery. By then the surgery was performed on an outpatient basis and required nine months of rehab. I had been walking around on eggshells for nearly two decades, wondering when the next of countless blow-outs was going to happen. But after a lot of inner work, I had finally decided that I was worth it.

But as a senior in high school, I had nowhere near the level of confidence or awareness that I would later gain. All I knew was the flimsy brace didn't work and my basketball days were over. One of my primary outlets of escape and the means through which I received a lot of positive attention was gone.

It was the second traumatic event to occur in my relatively young life. Both times came when my future was looking exceptionally bright, and I was going full steam ahead. Perhaps that made them seem all the more devastating. But I would soon find out, just as I did when Hancock was sold, that tragedy can bring opportunity. Years later, I would look back and see clearly that the Universe was trying to point me in the right direction, and that it wouldn't be the last time it used The Duber to do it.

"I want you to join the literary team." Hearing a decision instead of a request, I grimaced. Though I had excelled academically, my preference for extracurricular activities had always been athletics. Joining the literary team was a disappointing consolation activity. But the region competition was coming up, and the team needed an essay writer.

So, I loaded up with *US News and World Reports*, climbed into the school van, and studied up on current events during the two-hour ride to the meet. I walked into the competition, drew my topic from a basket, went into a closet-sized room, and cranked out an essay in the allotted time.

Later that afternoon, I climbed back into the van, thankful that I had just read about Reagan's proposed Star Wars program. I returned to Savannah as the region champ in essay writing and, a few weeks later, I placed second in the state competition—same process, different topic.

I should have been elated. It was the first time my writing had been put up against something other than The Duber's red pen. It made the vision of fireside writing that much more believable. But I had lost my sparkle.

Spring of my senior year arrived. I had not applied to any colleges or universities, even though I probably could have attended most any of my choice. The thought of going off to school seemed selfish, and I didn't relish the idea of leaving my mom and Tanya to deal with my father by themselves. I halfheartedly applied to a couple of out-of-state schools, but was too late to be considered. At the last minute, I used a couple of private scholarships and entered Armstrong State College, one of the two four-year schools in town.

My interests had always been in creative pursuits. I even considered athletics to be creative—doing things with a flair and appreciating the beauty of a perfect play. And I had developed a love of talking, whether it was on the CB or delivering a speech. Expressing myself through writing, speaking, and performing in sports was very important to me. So, when it came time to choose a major in college, naturally I selected computer science.

In the mid-1980s, with the introduction of the personal computer, it was a promising field. I'm not sure that I even considered a career that would make my heart sing. I don't remember being counseled on anything other than deciding on a major that would help me land a secure, well-paying job. In my depressed state of mind, that paired well with my idea that it was time to grow up and do adult things, like make money and abandon my dreams. It never occurred to me that I could do both.

But the writing wasn't giving up that easily.

I received accolades from professors and an invitation to join the newspaper staff. And then, in my final required English class, I wrote a paper on the rise and fall of the American Dream in *The Great Gatsby*. Informing me that it was one of the best papers he had read in his seven years at Armstrong, the professor told me there was no need for me to appear for the final exam. "You've earned your A," he said.

The wonderful feedback was a most welcomed surprise. Unlike after the high school essay writing competitions, I was elated. I floated out of the professor's office on a cloud. I sent the paper to The Duber, who also blessed it with an A+++. It was the high point of my college experience and remains, to this day, one of my all-time best moments in life.

Yet, it never occurred to me that I should take a look at how the experience made my heart sing. It took three years and a Calculus II class for me to admit I had made a mistake with a computer science major. I finally determined that it wasn't a good fit for someone with my creative yearning and longing for self-expression. I couldn't imagine spending my working days in a room writing code. So, I did what any naturally creative person would do.

I changed my major to accounting. To the very career I swore off in high school.

At the time, I had a part-time job as a receptionist at a small CPA firm. I had quickly promoted myself into tasks far beyond typing and answering the phone. I knew I would have a job upon graduation, and the owners had become like parents to me.

The Charles Du Bos quote I selected as my senior quote, early in the last year of high school, before the ACL injury was:

The important thing is this: to be able at any moment to sacrifice what we are for what we can become.

Clearly, the same young woman who selected that quote was not the same one choosing accounting as her career. I had become uncomfortable enough to change my major, but not brave enough to follow my heart. So, the college student was now off to the races, heading in the wrong direction on the path of least resistance.

I mostly buried my desires and focused on being a success at what I had chosen. I graduated at the top of my college class and got promoted at work. Eventually, I became uncomfortable enough to change jobs, thinking that working in accounting for a large healthcare organization would provide opportunities to blossom beyond "bean counter." And it did in some ways. I was able to participate on quality improvement teams, conduct trainings and make presentations. But eventually, I began to use work to escape from relationship issues, the walking-on-eggshells anxiety from the ACL injury and, most ironically, from the discomfort of a career that did not fit.

After I met Harry and started my own CPA and consulting firm, I found great satisfaction in the teaching and advising part of my job. However, most of my projects were still fundamentally accounting in nature.

The universe had been patient with me. At every opportunity, it had provided me with clues and evidence that my life was not meant for sliding numbers into boxes or counting beans of any kind. Harry's death had certainly gotten my attention. But the Universe wanted to be sure that I was getting the message, so it sent an angel from my past to do the job.

She was one of the first to contact me when Harry passed away.

When I shared one of my first stories on social media in the early days after Harry died, the grades started coming in again. Only this time they didn't come in swooping cursive red ink. They were in words typed in an online comment.

After I wrote the first post about the cardinal, she surfaced again with her virtual red pen in hand. *Your creative talents have grown and manifest beautifully. I wish I could just hug you.*

When the red bird showed up for the fourth time, she was right there with him. *There she is, the creative writer in you. I hope you're keeping a hard copy journal of your musings.*

As I continued to write, she continued to comment. *When I see a posting from you, I read with gusto and my mind's eye pictures it all. And then I remember Cynthia in eighth grade, afraid to speak out in class, and recall your developing into Cynthia the valedictorian five years later. I still expect more great words from you, dearie.*

The Duber had always expected great words from me. Actually, she had always expected great everything from me. She pushed me and challenged me. When I did well, she rewarded me with praise and more challenge. When I fell short, she let me know without hesitation. In the years after high school, our contact had been sporadic at best, but the connection was still strong. Now she was back, her timing impeccable.

I was receiving reinforcement from The Duber. The cardinal had taken on a near cult following with my online friends, and it was spilling over into other writing.

Cherishing the attention and comments that were never in short supply, I felt very humbled by it all. One of the comments that influenced me the most was, *Thank you for expressing what we feel but cannot express ourselves.* It came from one of Harry's classmates whose husband had passed a few years before. It was then that my posting took on another layer of meaning. It began to feel like a responsibility—a calling.

I was fueled by my visit to see Bedford, and felt very strongly that the divine meaning in Harry's death was my rebirth. I couldn't shake the feeling that I was being divinely inspired to write about my experiences. It felt like my purpose was burgeoning. I thought, *Perhaps this is my way of making the world more beautiful.*

I felt compelled to see The Duber in person. To tell her what was in my heart, and to get her honest and unfiltered feedback. I knew

I could trust her to be straight with me, but it wasn't just about the writing. Carol Duberstein had been in my life since I was 12 years old. She knew my history. She understood my loss. I wanted to get feedback on my writing, but I mostly wanted to just be with this woman who had played such an important role in my life.

In late July, I decided to do my own version of a walkabout and head south in the "Cop Car," a silver 2004 Mercury Grand Marquis with darkly tinted windows. It came into our life just days before we got married, when Harry's employer changed its fleet. Harry complained about it endlessly with its "mouse fur interior and pleather seats." So I was surprised when he called me one day and said we could buy it for just a few thousand dollars. When I said, "You hate that car," he laughed.

"I do, but it's practically free!"

I think he secretly liked it, so we bought the Cop Car and mused that it was our "disposable" car. Since we were in Alaska so much, it was just fine for getting around when we were in town, but it was the last car either of us would have chosen. When my friend Geri saw the Cop Car in her driveway early in the trip, she asked with disgust, "What is *that*?!"

"It's the Cop Car!" I said, with a hint of adoration. Since Harry's death, it had morphed from a "make do" car into my trusty steed. After making it to South Florida without incident, I was glad that I had not put it out to pasture just yet.

I took great comfort in being with my mentor and friend. Carol Duberstein had loved me like a daughter and, like my mother, thought there was nothing I couldn't do. I had not seen her since 2003. During that visit, I was sitting on the floor of her home office as she dug out relics like our old school newspapers and copies of papers I had written. Suddenly she stopped, looked at me, and asked a provocative question.

"What happened to you?"

I was caught off-guard. Twenty years after graduating from high school, my teacher was implying that I had fallen far short of my potential. I knew the expectations were high for me. Even my high school nickname, "Hollywood," suggested fame and fortune. But she was right: I *had* fallen short. I was busted. I don't recall how I responded, but I do remember sharing that I'd just met a very intriguing man named Harry.

Eleven years later, it seemed as if the question had been answered, now in the context of what had occurred since I had last seen her. I felt like I was back in high school . . . I could see her with one of my papers on her desk, red pen in hand.

More than ever in my life, I need the A, I thought.

I could see her stroke the letter on the paper in bright, cardinal red as she shared her observations. I felt a lifetime of care and concern as she gently reminded me I had been part of something that many people only dream about . . . a love so strong and beautiful that it survived even death, as evidenced by the plethora of "signs" and the army of support and comfort that had surrounded me. When I talked about my game plan and asked her the question—did she think that I could turn my career in the direction of writing, teaching and speaking—the look on her face conveyed disbelief that I'd asked.

"Of course you should. If not now, then when?"

Just like that, she had added the coveted plus sign, leaving me with such a feeling of gratitude. Not just because I got a good grade on my paper of life, but because, as had been the case each time we were together, I learned more about this amazing woman who had been an ever-present influence. I had always considered her hard-charging, tough, tenacious, resilient, adventurous, and brilliant. But I had just seen a side of her that, though there all along, had not been visible through my lens. Of course, she valued excellence. And years before she had made an honest observation that I had fallen short of my potential. But after we finished our conversation that night, I realized that she was far more tender-hearted than I ever knew.

For she had just told me, without actually saying it, that the absolute best measure of success in life is not career achievement or living up to our potential.

It is simply to love and be loved.

I couldn't have received more beneficial feedback from The Duber if I had special-ordered it. She then suggested that we do a writing retreat to work on my first book, and combine it with some type of fun and adventurous trip. I agreed that was a stellar idea, and left my friend and mentor, feeling quite loved, encouraged and supported. A few days later, after visits with other dear ones, I pointed the car north.

I was deep in thought as I cruised up I-95. It had been an emotional trip. I had also reconnected with a Memorial teammate while in Orlando. I hadn't seen Sherry in 30 years, but she had been following my posts. In the corner of a Starbucks, with tears in her eyes, she thanked me for sharing my journey and pleaded with me to never stop doing so. Her outpouring of emotion was surprising and humbling. Once again, it seemed my writing about the cardinal experiences and other divine happenings was deeply impacting people.

My phone rang. I smiled when I saw the caller ID.

"Aaahhh . . . Buongiorno . . . ah?"

After I returned the greeting, he asked, "Where are you, my sister?"

"On my way to Savannah for a quick stop, then a visit with my mom on the way back to Braselton."

"And then what are your plans, Cynthia?"

"I think it's time to head back to Alaska. Start figuring out my next steps."

"Good! You know, if you ever need help in knowing what to do, just ask Harry. My brother will tell you."

"Oh, I know he will!" I replied. Harry had never been shy about sharing his perspective. Since he had seemed fairly present after slipping off to heaven, it seemed highly likely that, should I actually ask for his help, he would respond: *Whatever the Punkin wants! My feet have wings!*

Despite the lift from Paolo's call, I flung myself onto my hotel bed that evening, feeling completely alone. While I knew what my heart was calling me to do, I was once again that college student from long ago, not understanding that following my heart was an option.

I began to cry. The more I considered my options and longed for something I thought was out of my reach, the harder I cried. And then, taking Paolo's advice, I made an emotional plea, speaking with a trembling voice into the empty room.

"Okay, H. If you are really there, I need your help with a game plan, please."

Shortly afterward, I fell into a deep sleep. When I woke the next morning, I felt refreshed and eager to hit the road, and I had no thoughts of my tearful plea the night before.

Chapter 8

My mother lived on the outskirts of Brooklet, a small town near Statesboro, Georgia, about an hour's drive west from Savannah. That morning, I picked her up and drove into Statesboro to enjoy a tasty breakfast at IHOP, one of her favorites. It was the second time I had visited with her since Harry passed away, and again, our visit brought me great comfort.

As anyone who has journeyed through grief knows, the experience is quite unique for each person. Even though we may hear, "I know exactly how you feel," no one can truly know. But I knew my mother could relate to my situation. When my father was barely older than Harry, he was diagnosed with colon cancer and told he had six months to live. After a swift change in doctors, resection surgery and some chemo, he seemed to be out of the woods. Eight years later, we learned the cancer had returned. Death came quickly, two weeks later.

Years before his death, my father went through many difficult, dark years of alcohol abuse. He never missed a beat working or providing for the family, but he tortured himself with daily drinking and late meals that left him violently sick in the middle of nearly every night. Even so, my mother loved him dearly. Later in life, as the pressures in his life decreased, so too did his alcohol consumption. In between bouts of cancer, he stopped drinking entirely. He was semi-retired, and he and my mother were inseparable. He was her best friend, confidant and hero; it was a delight to watch them enjoying life together. So, my mother had lost her Prince Charming fairly young and quite suddenly as well.

After breakfast, I dropped her at home. Then I fishtailed out of her driveway as I always did, honked the horn, and waved out of the window. I could see her standing at the front door, waving back. I honked again when I turned right at the end of her road. Even though I couldn't see her, I knew she was still there, watching until she could no longer see the dirt-road dust kicking up behind my car.

There was no cell phone service at my mother's house, so a few minutes later, when my tires returned to pavement, my cell phone exploded with notifications. Several people had tried to reach me while I was in radio silence. One of them was Max, the auditor from Alaska. I had not talked to him since the plane ride from Juneau to Anchorage five months earlier. Max never contacted me to chat, so I wondered what was up.

After we exchanged greetings, I listened intently as he explained the purpose of his call. I took a deep breath and responded, "You know the concern I would have."

He acknowledged that and explained he was simply reaching out as a courtesy to his client. He suggested that, if I were interested in the opportunity, I contact the client directly.

Almost immediately after I hung up with Max, my phone rang with the daily call from Italy.

"Aaahhh . . . Buongiorno . . . ah?"

Paolo immediately sensed there was something on my mind, so I told him about the call from Max.

"Do it, Cynthia! Harry was so proud of you, and he'd love it. You should do it!"

When Paolo uttered Harry's name, I remembered my tearful plea the night before. When I got off the phone, I cried all the way to Macon. For two hours. Hard.

I had asked Harry for help the night before, and it felt like he had responded swiftly.

I know that your world shattered and that your heart broke into a million pieces sitting behind that desk in Juneau. I know that you have languished, punishing yourself for being there and not with me that night. And I know you feel like you ran away by not returning after my death. So, we are going to fix that, Punkin.

Go back to Alaska, a place we loved and where we shared so many special times. Where we chased rainbows, made snow angels, and drank more coffee than I could imagine. Reconnect with all of your colleagues and share with them the mob names I gave them. The Farmhand. Fingers. Stubby. The Handyman. Donnie G. Kenny G. And just plain old G. And take the Grief Monster to school by making great things happen from behind that desk in Juneau.

Why? Because we need to mend that broken heart of yours. Besides, you've been a little heavy-handed with the vodka, sister.

So, there I was, in the Cop Car, hurtling along I-16 at eighty miles an hour, at the tail end of two and a half weeks and 1,700 miles, with tears streaming down my face and an indescribable feeling of fullness in my heart. I felt cherished. I felt loved. I felt like a tiny speck compared to the enormity of the Divine, yet also as if I were part of the expansive and limitless Universe.

In the few months since Harry passed away, I'd had my share of divine moments, but none like the one I did on that day in the westbound lane of I-16. I felt the presence of something more magnificent than words, and I thought I should find out what it had in mind. So, once Macon and my tears were in the rearview mirror, I placed a call to Alaska.

Just over a week later, I landed in Juneau.

After a few welcoming hugs, I walked back into the office and sat down behind the very desk where I received the call from Death seven months earlier.

I noted the same books on the shelves. The same pictures on the walls. It was the same client with some of the same challenges. Everything seemed the same, yet I knew that wasn't the case.

I wasn't the same.

Not even close.

I had felt a sorrow that I didn't know possible, and lost an innocence I would never get back. I had cried more tears than I could imagine, and wondered repeatedly, *Where is he? Where did he go?*

Believing that Harry was still with me was one of my weapons of survival. I certainly had reason to believe that he was. After all, I'd had a seven-month soiree with a big red bird in the backyard, and other synchronicities including the recent highway experience that had left me feeling spiritually stalked in the best possible way. And yet, I refused to fully believe that it all could be real.

Now I was back in Alaska, and I had a job to do. I was about to meet with the one thing that *had* changed while I was away—the CEO. It was time to refocus. And have a cup of coffee. I had just enough time to swing by the break room before heading to his office.

I had been slightly apprehensive about my return to Juneau, despite the divine red carpet that had been rolled out for me. I just wasn't sure I was in the right place or doing the right thing. But as I walked into the break room, I felt a sense of comfort and ease. I took in the soothing aroma of Folgers, and noted that I had the room to myself, something that rarely happened. The break room doubled as the copier room, so there was typically a fair amount of traffic.

I opened and closed a couple of cabinet doors before finding the stash of mugs. I surveyed the inventory, looking for my mug from before—a colorful golf-themed mug, but all I could see were boring vendor mugs.

I kept searching, hoping that I would find one of interest, when a cup in the back caught my eye. It had a solid red line on the inside rim. Curious, I pushed the other mugs aside.

The cardinal was tucked into that dark corner of the breakroom cabinet, perched on a branch, just like he was on that frosty February morning when I saw him for the first time.

My heart beating wildly, I picked up the cup and admired it before filling it to the rim. It was old and chipped. I could feel the hot coffee through its thin porcelain. Though far from what Harry would have deemed a "proper mug," I thought it was perfect.

How's your coffee? I heard him ask with a mischievous twinkle in his voice. *Let's go, Punkin. We have a meeting!*

I went into the CEO's office and settled in. The CEO thanked me for responding so quickly to his request for help, and reiterated that it seemed "meant to be." He was referring to the fact that during our phone call a week before, I had explained that I was planning to return to Alaska and that I had availability. I had left out the part about my tearful plea to Harry from my hotel room. I glanced at the cardinal cup and imagined I heard, *See! I told you so! Hee! Hee!*

After the meeting, I headed back to my office. Or should I say, "we" headed back. Harry was in rare form. *You were a killer! The Legend of Golden Hair continues! Go Cynthee!*

I shut the door, put the cardinal cup on the desk, plopped down wearily, and thought, *Am I going completely crazy?* Then it all rushed in, and I felt myself back in that terrible moment, seeing the notebook page where I scribbled the name of the doctor and *Harry* during that horrific call.

Sorrow rose from deep inside. I had been afraid this would happen. But I had done so well up to this point. I pleaded with myself, *Not now!*

I looked outside and focused on the beautiful blue sky, the Gastineau Channel, the mountains, and the wispy clouds. I tilted my head back to keep the tears from falling. I took a deep breath and dabbed my eyes. I looked down at that cup—that beautiful, chipped porcelain cup, and I heard the assurance that I needed to hear.

I'm right here, Punkin. I'm right here.

Suddenly, a blanket of calm and comfort wrapped around me. Harry wasn't gone; this time I was sure of it. He was more alive than ever, and he was finding creative ways to let me know that even though his body didn't survive that night, his spirit and our connection did. I heard my voice from the night of Harry's service: *Harry and I spent a lot of time apart, but we were always together.*

I was still thinking about that at the end of the day when I slung my backpack over my shoulder and turned out the lights. This time, as I closed the door and left that office in Juneau, I thought, *The more things change, the more they stay the same.*

It took me over a week to share a post about the cardinal cup. While I wrote it down almost immediately and sent the story to my lifelong friend Denise, I held back on a more public share. I had begun to second-guess myself. But two significant events that seemed quite connected to the Divine had occurred in rapid succession: the call from Alaska the day after my plea for help from Harry, and the cardinal cup.

The mug had pushed me over the edge of uncertainty. In Alaska, eagles and ravens dominate the artwork, jewelry, clothing and coffee mugs. One would be hard-pressed to find a red bird on anything.

Not once did I believe that the "Ghost of Harry Past" had slipped into the breakroom ahead of me and planted that cup. But I did believe that a series of events had happened in perfect timing to land my hand on that mug at that moment.

I believed I was meant to find it. To connect the dots. To share the story. And so, I did.

Once again, the comments were filled with gratitude, love and encouragement. My friend Denise chimed in, *Been waiting for you to post this one, C! A very special, heartfelt piece. Written by both you and Harry.*

Denise was more right than she knew. It felt as if Harry and I had written the post together, but it also felt as if we were co-writing the next chapters of my life. That belief had become instrumental in my healing.

Another form of healing was taking place through my client work. It hadn't taken me long to find my rhythm; that had happened almost immediately. I arrived in time to help with some fairly large challenges and prepare for the annual financial audit. I was also assisting with the recruitment process for a CFO, providing training and mentoring for the accounting staff, and assisting with an upgrade to the electronic health record and financial systems. Focusing on something other than my own circumstances during the day brought welcomed relief.

The beauty of Alaska also had a healing power of its own. I only had to glance out of my window or take a short drive to feel the deep connection to earth and sky that had been part of my love affair with the beautiful state from the beginning. Bald eagles escorted me to the office, gentle rainfalls washed away my tears, brilliant sunrises brought the promise of new and brighter days, and crimson sunsets tucked me in at night.

Additionally, there was unspoken support from my client and other professionals in Juneau. They were all now part of my story. My healing. My return had not only provided me with an amazing opportunity to close the loop on the work with them, but also to receive comfort and compassion from them. Through their comradery, support and cooperation, it felt as if they were saying, *We are sorry that you suffered an incredible loss while with us. Thank you for coming back.*

It had never been hard to "come back" to Alaska. Having felt out of place professionally for most of my life, providing financial management services to small and remote community hospitals in Alaska seemed a much better fit than the small CPA firm where I started my accounting career, or the billion-dollar health system I left to start my own business. Though my engagements still carried a heavy focus on accounting, the added complexities of healthcare delivery in the Last Frontier intrigued and challenged me.

My engagements also increasingly included teaching and training. I was providing counsel to CEOs, conducting Board of Directors' training, and mentoring accounting staff. I loved the adventure of being in Alaska. Sometimes that simply meant braving the weather. One time that meant being whisked away to a board meeting in a sled pulled by a four-wheeler after landing on a snowy runway less than fifty miles from Russia's Chukchi Peninsula.

So, in the close-knit community hospitals of remote Alaska, where often the patients are friends, coworkers and family of hospital staff, I had found a professional home. It was one that required the depth of professional expertise I offered, but it also offered me something in return. An avenue through which I could more closely align with my true talents and gifts while making a difference for others. No matter the client or location, I found talented, committed, and enthusiastic people. And they had taught me a thing or two.

Through them, I saw that life in Alaska was much more about being and doing than about acquiring. They demonstrated "Work Hard/Play Hard" more consistently than I'd ever seen. There was no clamoring to find balance; it simply existed, ebbing and flowing around hunting seasons, flight schedules and the weather.

In the years before Harry and I made Alaska our home, and for a while afterward, I had no balance at all. I often worked sixteen-hour days for stretches that could last weeks. Sometimes that was because my clients needed intensive care and there was a lot to do in a short period, but it was also due to my old patterns. I was prone to overworking to camouflage uncomfortable feelings and emotions. Sometimes those sprang from missing my adorable husband. Sometimes they were a residue of feeling like I was not living up to my potential. Even though Alaska had helped me to be in better alignment than I ever had been, I still had miles to go.

When I returned to Juneau after Harry's death, I made a deal with myself that I would not bury myself in work, as I had earlier in my career. So, I took lunchtime drives or snuck to the Mendenhall Glacier after work and before the sun went down. If I stayed in town for the weekend, I worked some during the day and explored and took pictures in the afternoon. I was also writing almost every day, and I continued to share my writing and photos on social media. Maintaining connections had become one of my strategies for combatting the grief.

I also dove into a book that Tanya sent me—*The Right to Write* by Julia Cameron. Before knowing it was one of her more well-known quotes, I had underlined and highlighted a sentence that jumped off the page at me: *We should write because writing brings clarity and passion to the act of living.* I already knew that writing was bringing clarity to my own life. It was also bringing healing.

One night, as I drove to the hotel in the light mist that I had grown accustomed to in the rainforest of Juneau, I was thinking about the quote. I pulled the hood of my insulated jacket over my head and swung my feet onto the wet pavement. I was thankful for my waterproof jacket and boots, both gifts from Harry. *He's still protecting me*, I thought.

He was also still encouraging me to write. At least it felt that way.

Chapter 9

Friends marveled at the incredible "coincidences" showing up in my life. Comments flew onto my Facebook page, complimenting and thanking me for the photos I posted. Random coffee mugs, slid across the counter to me at Anchorage's Snow City Cafe, sparked deeply philosophical posts. Or comical ones.

It felt like I had turned into a human satellite dish, attracting and receiving signals to pay attention to the world around me. To engage with life and people in a way I never had before.

I was noticing changes in my professional world as well. I no longer needed to "discipline" myself about long hours. When warranted, I dug in, but late nights became the exception rather than the norm. I no longer needed their promise of escape. I was more interested in the bigger picture, in human connection, in telling a story—even if it were financial in nature.

Something magical was happening, though at the time, I did not fully grasp what it was. Now with perfect hindsight, I can see that my declaration of wanting a different life had summoned the Universe to provide me with even more miracles and magic.

I headed into November and the two-month stretch of the holidays. But this year, they actually felt like "the last days"—a period during which Harry and I had spent our last times together the previous year. It included big days. Thanksgiving. Harry's birthday. Christmas. New Year's. And the first anniversary of his death in January.

I knew it could be a brutal time, but I had planned ahead. Although I had lost my most cherished love during the year, I had plenty of loved ones still on earth, and they were lining up in big ways to shepherd me through the first "last days." Paula and Broughton were coming to Anchorage for Thanksgiving. I was doing a virtual birthday party for Harry on Facebook, before heading to Italy for Christmas. And on January 21, I would have a gathering to commemorate the one-year anniversary of Harry's death, before heading back to Alaska. Clearly, I had decided to use celebration as my weapon of choice in my face-off with grief.

For sure, I had some apprehension about the upcoming calendar, but I also had a sense of joyful anticipation. I had been telling myself for months that if I could just make it through the first year, everything would be fine. I was also looking forward to continuing my reconnections with friends.

What the $#@%?!?! Just how many vodkas did I have tonight?! I thought incredulously as I squinted into the darkness—not believing what I was seeing.

It was late November, and I had just returned from dinner with "Donnie G," another one of our Anchorage friends. It was the first time we had seen each other since Harry passed away. Donnie suggested we go to the tucked-away Italian place where he'd had dinner with Harry just weeks before his death.

Donnie wanted to talk about Harry. A lot. I was perfectly okay with that. While I'd had ten months to talk about Harry's passing, I knew Donnie had not.

But the evening had left me emotionally spent. When I got back to the condo, I turned on the fireplace and, instead of sinking into the usual chair, I settled onto the sofa.

I had been typing a post when I stopped to reflect, looking up from my phone and into the fire. Incredulous, I closed and opened my eyes. Then I squinted as I wondered just how many vodkas I'd had.

In the ten months after Harry had passed away, I had experienced more amazing moments than I thought possible. But never had I seen Harry staring back at me from the flames of a fire.

Feeling a wee bit crazy, I wondered if the grief had finally caught up with me.

I couldn't stop staring at it. It was actually only half of Harry's face, similar to his Facebook profile photo which shows one half of his face in the shadows. I was astounded that I had never noticed Fire Face before. But then again, I almost never sat on the sofa.

That night, I turned down the regular heat and slept on the sofa. The thermostat-controlled fireplace clicked on and off, keeping me warm on the outside and, for the first time, on the inside. I woke up several times to see that face staring back at me. It brought me an unspeakable comfort, but I also felt a little pathetic. I had already sprayed his cologne onto a pillow. This was going a bit far. But I quickly decided that I just didn't care. *Whatever it takes*, I thought as I drifted back to sleep.

Over the next couple of days, the condo was transformed. I now had company! As my new companion kept watch over my Thanksgiving prep, I began to look forward to the *click* that announced the fireplace turning on.

"There you are!" I'd say when the face appeared again. Instead of sitting in the kitchen cubby when I stopped for breaks, I sat on the sofa.

On Thanksgiving night, Paula sat on the sofa as well. Earlier in the evening and keeping with Brandt family tradition, we walked a block to Simon & Seafort's, one of Anchorage's most popular restaurants, for dinner. We had returned to the condo for after-dinner champagne and tree decorating when Paula sat down. She started talking about

Harry, saying it felt like he had been with us all day. She added, "The only thing that would have made today more perfect is if Harry had been here with us in the flesh!"

"Harry may be closer than you think . . . Take a look at the fire."

She stared intently into the flames. Her mouth dropped open as she looked at me wide-eyed and exclaimed, "Oh my God! Cynthia!"

In an instant, any worries that I may be crazy were wiped away.

The following week, I mentioned this to Bedford, who asked if I had ever listened to Beth Nielsen Chapman's album *Sand and Water*. He shared that the artist had suffered the loss of her husband and that the album was a channeling of her experience. And then told me about a song on that album that he wanted me to listen to right after our call.

I dutifully downloaded the song and, while sitting at my desk with Fire Face looking on, I listened to "Say Goodnight" for the very first time.

I will never forget the feeling I had, listening to the words as tears streamed down my face—especially the words Bedford told me to be on the lookout for: *In the spark that lies beneath the coals.*

I played the song over and over again. Each time it played, I heard Harry singing to me. I decided to make a music video as a birthday present for him. From start to finish, the video was filled with photos of what was and lyrical assurances of what would be, transforming doubt and uncertainty into hope and unwavering faith. Bedford told me he wept when he saw it. For a while, I cried every time I played it.

In my attempt to give Harry a present, I gave myself one—a fact I am quite positive he loved. A beautiful "Love-a-bye" with words of comfort, gently encouraging me to continue on, being *everything I want to be* while he was *right by my side.*

From the first night I heard it to this day, I cannot listen to the beautiful song without thinking, *If Harry had ever written a song for me from heaven, this would have been it.*

A few weeks later, I landed in Bologna, Italy. Earlier in the fall, when Paolo asked about my plans for the holidays, I teased, "Maybe I will come to see my brother."

After a brief pause, he said, "My sister. You could give me no greater gift than to come to Italy and spend Christmas with me and my family."

So, there I was, walking to the car, arm in arm with my Italian brother, his family by our sides. After an hour's drive to Paolo's, I had barely set my things down in the kitchen when he asked, "Did you see it?"

The "it" was a large framed photo that sat high on the kitchen wall between two oversized windows, right behind Paolo's chair. I had seen a smaller version of the photo because I had taken it, when Harry and I were in Italy for our honeymoon. It was a photo of Harry, with a joyful Sebastiano sitting on his lap.

Sebastiano passed away unexpectedly just over a year later, so I knew it had required a herculean effort for Paolo to place that photo on his kitchen wall. I was suddenly ashamed, feeling we had not done enough for him back then. He had suffered a loss I had no capacity to appreciate at the time. My eyes welled up and my heart ached.

For the next 10 nights, while our two angels looked on from the wall above, Paolo and I sat at the kitchen table until the wee hours, drinking wine and toasting champagne after everyone else had gone to bed. During the day, we visited with friends or drove to nearby towns so that I could see the sights. We each got to know Harry even better through one another and shared more about the losses that had broken our hearts. On the first night, I apologized that we had not done enough when Sebastiano passed away.

"No. No. My sister. You and Harry let me come stay with you in Braselton when I needed to. My brother Harry . . . he called me every single day for a year. That is what I needed more than anything."

I did not know about the daily calls, but now on the receiving end of my own, I could fully appreciate how meaningful they must have been to Paolo. I went to bed loving and missing Harry more than ever.

It was so hard to leave Italy. Though the trip had been draining emotionally, it had also been incredibly healing. And how could anyone not want to stay in Italy just a little longer? Especially with such a beautiful and loving family, who welcomed me wholeheartedly.

The day after my return, I was back on the porch in Braselton having Pellegrino, eggs and coffee. It had been dark and rainy, but the sky had started to brighten, allowing me to make out his raincoat of red in the crabapple tree. My phone rang as I rose to retrieve my glasses. It was my daily call from Italy. Paolo was checking on me after the long journey home. His call was perfectly timed with the arrival of the cardinal.

I smiled as I thought that my being away for a few months in Alaska and Italy hadn't seemed to impact the divine timing of my red-feathered friend. I refilled my coffee and watched other birds come and go while the sky struggled to brighten. Like so many times during the prior year, I knew that, up above the darkest of clouds, the sun was shining. A fiery sunrise had found me on an early-morning flight out of Bologna the day before and the window shade glowed amber on the flight from Rome to Atlanta.

That bright sun had set on this side of the world when the doors of the international baggage claim slid open the prior evening. My sister Tanya had told me that my favorite driver Jim would be waiting.

Jim and I had a most interesting conversation on the drive home, as I juggled phone calls and text messages. There's something insulating about talking from the backseat of a car to a virtual stranger. It's like "what's said in the limo, stays in the limo." Because of that, Jim knew how significant the holidays were for me. I'd met him weeks earlier after arriving in Atlanta on the first leg of the holiday journey. On the drive home that day, I had told him about Harry's passing and the upcoming trip to Italy. When he picked me up after Christmas, he asked me how the trip had been.

"Spending Christmas with Paolo and his family was as close to being with Harry as it possibly could have been." I added that it had involved some degree of emotional turmoil, of course.

"So, Cynthia. Do you keep a journal?" he asked.

When I didn't respond right away, Jim gave me an apologetic glance in the rearview mirror. "I'm sorry, that was too personal."

I set his mind at ease and confessed that I had been writing my way through my grief. I said that I had received some positive feedback and messages that my stories were helping others.

"Well, I've not read any of your writing, but if you write at all like you speak, you should write for a living."

Suddenly, I found myself sharing details of the last year with Jim. The signs. The messages. The awareness. The coincidences.

"You know, Jim, I feel that if I start writing, I'm simply not going to stop."

"What's wrong with that?" came the booming voice of the Universe disguised as that of my new friend.

After we pulled into the driveway, Jim helped me inside with my bags. I extended my hand, thanked him for the safe drive home and wished him a Happy New Year.

Moments later, I headed down the street to Paula and Broughton's. I had missed my friends, and it was time for a New Year's toast. Just after sitting down and taking a sip of champagne, I received a text message. It was from Jim, thanking me for my business, wishing me a Happy New Year, and encouraging me to get busy writing.

But there was more.

Don't screw the world out of a good read.

The Universe had spoken. Again.

Chapter 10

Prodding from the Universe seemed to work. During that day on the porch after my return from Italy, I wrote from morning to night. Story ideas, an outline of a new way of life, dreams, and posts. Even though the first anniversary of Harry's death loomed large, just over two weeks away, I felt excited—as if something amazing were just around the corner.

For months, I had been telling myself if I could just get through the first year, I would be fine. After all, I had returned to Alaska, climbed back on the work horse and ridden well. I had battled grief the entire time, but there had been no meltdown. No catastrophe. No curling up in a fetal position. In fact, the opposite seemed to be occurring. My heart was opening. I was seeing beauty all around me. Amazing synchronistic events were happening. Divine moments abounded. But dark feelings came on January 12 when I realized it was the anniversary of the last time I had seen Harry. It certainly took the luster out of the "around the corner" excitement the new year had brought.

I knew that one of the corners beyond the anniversary was a return to Alaska. Before the holidays, I had helped my client in Juneau recruit a CFO, and they had asked me to provide assistance with transition and an upgrade to their financial system. On top of the client work, I also had some soul-searching work to do on the next steps for me.

I wasn't sure how long I would be gone, and because I was feeling nervous about the one-year marker coming up, I thought it would help to get moving.

So, I hit the road in the Cop Car. A trip to Savannah would give me an opportunity to see family and friends before heading north once again. And it would give me some time to sort out what, if anything, I wanted to do about the one-year anniversary.

By the time I returned to Braselton a few days later, I'd reunited with four people that I'd not seen in over 30 years, and I'd hatched a plan for the one-year anniversary.

I had decided to invite a dozen people to the house for a happy hour of champagne and dessert. Though a part of me just wanted to pass the day and night quietly, I reminded myself that one of the best antidotes for my grief over the past year had been to celebrate. A two-hour party would allow us to honor Harry, and afterwards I would have plenty of time alone for quiet contemplation.

While I knew it was risky to host a dozen people on the anniversary, I told myself, *I can do anything for two hours.*

A few mornings after that decision, I was on my way upstairs to prepare for an afternoon conference call when I had a change of heart. It was beautiful outside, and I wanted to enjoy a few stolen moments on the porch.

I stepped onto the porch, fired up the laptop, and started typing. I could feel the emotion swell as I took myself back through the night that Harry died and the year since. How hard it had been, but also how beautiful it had been. How amazing it was to experience all the signs. Signs that happened repeatedly, and that led me to believe that Harry's spirit had lived on.

I bowed my head and closed my eyes, trying to still the emotion. A few seconds later, I glanced up, mainly to keep the tears from spilling out. But my tears gave way to sobs that racked my entire body. With my head in my hands, the tears continued to flow. Because at the very moment when I was writing about all the signs I had received, the cardinal had appeared once again.

When I looked up, I'd seen him perched on a limb high in the tree. He looked unusually majestic. Very large. Very red. Confident and triumphant. Very Harry.

At that moment, if I ever had a doubt that we were still connected, it ended right then and there. There had been too many coincidences, over the course of that entire year, to leave any doubt. I felt completely overwhelmed, as if I were being allowed a peek through a window that opened to something beautiful beyond belief or description. I felt humbled. And honored. I realized that the cardinal had appeared to assure me that Harry was still with me, and that I was being called to share my experiences. About the grief. About the love. About the connection. About the pain. About the beauty. About the celebration. About it all.

Seeing the cardinal had given me a boost of confidence about hosting the happy hour. It also gave me an idea. When the guests arrived, they were greeted with a smile, a hug and a bubbling flute with a cardinal and their first name etched onto the glass.

The flutes were an absolute hit, and so was everything else that night. With the cast of characters I had invited, a case of champagne, dessert and a huge platter of chicken salad croissants sent by a friend who couldn't attend, the reception turned into a full-on party that lasted until after midnight. I found out that I could do anything for two hours—and then some.

At one point during the night, I had the distinct feeling that the storm had passed. I pictured myself drifting on a life raft. Spent, exhausted, but alive.

Yes, I had survived, even though I'd said to someone in the early days after Harry passed that I felt "broken." But little by little, I was putting the pieces back together again with the help of so many. Along with the tears, sorrow and anguish, there had been learning, growth, love, laughter and living.

If Harry had been able to speak, I'm quite positive he would have said, "I can tell that you're feeling better, Punkin. You're starting to get your sparkle back!" Though there may have been a sparkle here or there, the journey was far from over. I was certain there would be worse times in the next year, as reality set in with a vengeance. But we had made it through a year riddled with holes that Harry left in hearts and lives all over the world. Although there were holes, I suspected we were somewhat thankful for them. After all, as a friend had said a few months into the year, "The only thing worse than losing Harry would be never having known him at all."

Yes . . . it was a horrifically beautiful year. But we had done our best to fill the gaping holes with laughter and love. My heart was mending a little more each day. As the night ended, I thanked everyone for being part of the village that had been with me on the journey to get my sparkle back.

The next afternoon, I headed upstairs to my office to do some administrative work. An engagement letter for the consulting work at the hospital in Juneau was at the top of the list. I had just put the finishing touches on it when my phone rang. When I saw the caller ID, I picked up the phone thinking, *Wonder what it is this time?*

It didn't take Max long to get to the point.

"I've got one word for you."

"Yes?"

"Sitka."

He had just met with the new interim CEO for one of his clients, the community hospital in Sitka. The CEO was Harvard-educated and a longtime Sitkan businessman who had been living on the East Coast. He had been called home to help in a pinch and he had no CFO.

"Max," I whined, worried he was about to tell me that the hospital wanted me for CFO services. I had all but decided to focus on a career change, but I knew it would be hard for me to say "no" to someone in need.

"I just suggested that he may benefit from having a phone conversation with you." The CEO had not headed a hospital before and Max thought it would help for him to get some input on critical success factors for his financial management function.

As the call continued, I learned more about the hospital and its tenuous situation. I disclosed to Max that the former CEO had contacted me a couple of months previously about providing some assistance. Now I knew why he had stopped calling. He had resigned and left town rather suddenly.

When I hung up with Max, I finished the engagement letter for the Juneau hospital. And then I called Sitka. I found the hospital CEO to be very professional, enthusiastic and even keel. During the call, we talked about the possibility of a short engagement to help them re-organize after the departure of his predecessor and the CFO. I offered to "stop by" on my next trip to Juneau. Less than a week later, after a 30-minute flight from Juneau, I touched down in Sitka for the first time.

Prior to that, my only knowledge of the quaint Alaskan town had been what I gleaned from a Sandra Bullock movie called *The Proposal*. During the two days of my initial visit, I didn't pick up many more specifics. The schedule had been fast and furious. However, that didn't stop me from feeling that there was "something about Sitka." It also didn't stop me from stepping outside on the second afternoon, after a particularly good meeting, to get some fresh air before my next appointment—a hospital tour.

It was a Chamber of Commerce day: blue sky, wispy clouds, fresh crisp air. Rumor had it that it was the first day the sun had shone in well over a week; not too surprising, since Sitka sits inside the Tongass National Forest, a rainforest that covers most of south-east Alaska.

Taking in the fresh air, I was thinking how thrilled Harry would have been. *The Punkin's in Sitka!* would have been the first of a string of messages he would have sent all day—funny messages, encouraging words, and probably a picture or two, his way of letting me know he was right there with me. That was exactly how I felt 30 minutes later, during the hospital tour, when I looked up as we approached the radiology department.

After the tour, I drafted an engagement letter for a short-term project to assist the hospital with establishing a best-practice financial management function. I met with the interim CEO briefly and told him how excited I was to work with him and his team.

And then, on my way out of the building, I stopped in front of the radiology department window. I looked around and noted that the only witness to the moment was a skeleton hanging in the corner just inside the glass. Not worried too much about his opinion, I shifted my gaze to the window. I stood there for just a moment and then I took a photo before leaving the building.

When I got into the car, I sat for a few minutes more, thinking of the millions of things that had to happen for that picture to be on my phone. I had been right the day before—there was something about Sitka. And now there was even more.

It was the second time in six months that I had been welcomed to a client hospital in Alaska by a cardinal. Both seemed to be waiting for me. To let me know I was in the right place. And that Harry was somehow right there with me.

Later, I would learn that it was a photo of a photo of a painting created by a six-year-old boy who lived in Washington State, the grandson of one of the radiology employees. It had been placed in that window just before my arrival.

The next day, when my 6:00 a.m. flight soared off into the dark Alaskan morning, I felt a stirring of excitement. Yes, there was something about Sitka, but there was also something about its community hospital. What it had been through. What it was still going through. I felt a connection to the people I had met, and I knew I could help them.

No doubt I longed to move away from an accounting-based career. On the surface, offering an engagement to the community hospital did not seem to honor that longing. But a part of me knew, even without the cardinal's welcome, that my landing in Sitka wasn't just about accounting.

I returned to Sitka about a week later. With a trip already planned to South Florida in mid-February, I wanted to make some headway on the new project before I headed down to the Lower 48. So, I flew in one evening in early February. When I woke up the next morning, my heart was light and I felt the most peace since Harry died.

It was so unexpected that I spent a fair amount of time that morning trying to determine what had brought it on. It could have been any number of things.

I had made it through the perfect storm of Harry's birthday, the holidays, and the one-year anniversary, when I wasn't sure I could. The holidays had been as perfect as they could have been. I was starting a new engagement, with a new client, in a new location.

It was also the one-year anniversary of the cardinal flying into my life, and he had just reappeared the previous week.

And then there was Sitka. I had woken up to a magnificent sunrise and a beautiful view of the Crescent Harbor. The wind, the sun and the cool temperature invigorated me. I felt lucky that somehow, despite the pain and sorrow, I was really healing, little by little.

That morning, not only did I enjoy the breaking of day from my room, I went chasing it. I found a great spot and threw open the car door. I took the first few pictures, thinking how beautiful it was, and wondering why I didn't get up early every morning. I darted across a busy street and to the foot of the John O'Connell Bridge, eager for the morning sun to wake me completely, and to feel the wind hurtling across the Sitka Sound.

It was wild and raw, and left me nearly breathless and giddy. I laughed out loud when I got back into the car, hair askew and chilled to the bone.

And yet, as I drove to the hospital, I was warm inside. I thought about the contrast to the night before, when the jet glided in under a moon so bright that the snow-capped mountains glowed iridescent pearls and the water glistened with liquid diamonds.

So, it seemed there was a calm the prior night before the good storm of sunshine, wind and laughter the next morning. A bit of guilt tried to ride in on the wings of a seagull, but I was so exhilarated, I was having none of that. Like someone parched from crossing the driest of deserts, I grabbed the canteen of joy and held on tight. A moment like this had been a long time coming, and I drank without apology.

It seemed fitting that on the morning exactly one year after the cardinal first appeared, I may have found my wings. Certainly, I was not quite off the ground, nor had I filed a flight plan, but I knew I was going nowhere without the wings—so progress was being made.

I enjoyed a few lovely days in Sitka, energized by that beautiful morning and the excitement of the new project. It felt good to focus on helping others once again, and I knew in my heart that I could make a difference for my new client.

I was also learning that I was well-equipped to make a difference for myself. On my trip to South Florida, I took an "e-break." I put the BlackBerry down for stretches at a time, limited my social media postings, and even backed off from taking many pictures. I needed to unplug from the electronics and just be.

When I couldn't sleep, I sat on the balcony, wrapped up tight in a blanket with eyes closed, listening to the pounding of the surf. On occasion, I would peek into the darkness and find the stars winking back at me. I'd smile, remembering how much I loved the sea, especially at night.

By day, I took in the sun, walked the beach, laughed with Brian and Paolo, and even "luxuriated" in Harry Brandt speak. I knew I was journeying into another phase of healing.

But I also knew the grief was certain to rush back in, just like the pounding Florida surf. It did as soon as I returned to Georgia, where I was making a brief stop before returning to Alaska.

With a vengeance, the Sea of Grief crashed on the shore in a stormy rage. For days I was tossed about, unable to find my balance or direction. I was physically sick. It all seemed so much worse because I thought I had my sea legs back.

But stormy seas leave treasures for us to find—seashells and sand dollars and starfish—there for our delight, should we choose to walk along the shore with our eyes and our hearts open to what we may find.

And so, I took that walk after the storm. With the sea gently lapping at the shore and a cool and comforting breeze drying my salty tears, I could indeed see the starfish of laughter and love, and cardinals and hugs, that had washed up on the shore over the past year. But unlike the early days of 2014, I knew that when the storm returned, I wouldn't be swept out to sea. Instead, I would walk along the shore . . . occasionally caught by a wave and sometimes with sand in my shoes. But I would keep walking, and when the storm was done, I knew I would find:

The sun on my face.

The wind in my hair.

And starfish in the sand.

I wrote about my starfish in the sand experience as I winged my way back to Alaska a few days later. It was perhaps one of the more dramatic and emotional posts I had written to date, and I hesitated to share it. But the little voice inside insisted.

When I landed in Ketchikan on my way up through southeast Alaska, I could see that the post had resonated with many people.

The feedback was stunning. The mother of one of my childhood friends wrote that my post was perfectly timed, as it was her deceased husband's birthday. He had been the love of her life, and she said my words helped her refocus on the treasures to be found in the pain and sadness. Another friend insisted that this passage be the centerpiece for a book about grief.

As usual, I was appreciative of the encouragement from my friends, but I couldn't help notice that something had changed. I was no longer a young widow trying to navigate the stormy seas. I was an experienced captain who had made it through many storms of grief, and I was being called upon to help others do the same.

It felt daunting to me. But I had just been reminded that my willingness to share my vulnerability had helped someone dear to me experience a bit of brightness in an otherwise bleak day.

The divine message had been delivered and timed perfectly with my return to Sitka and the new accounting engagement. The Universe was reminding me that the accounting engagement was okay for the time being, but I wasn't to forget the real reason I was on this earth. Or the real reason that I was in Sitka.

Over the next four months, the reasons for both unfolded in an exponential way.

I spent my days at the hospital, where the client engagement took a heavy turn toward teaching and training. And not just with the accounting department: with the senior leadership, the managers, and even the Board of Directors. Everyone I encountered was eager to learn. It was exciting for me to be in the teaching and process improvement mode—the parts of my professional life that I had loved the most. Unfettered by day-to-day activities of the organization, I could make tremendous headway over a relatively short period.

As the days got longer, I found myself gravitating to the outdoors when the client work was done. Or spending quiet time at the client-provided apartment, reading, writing or listening to music.

I had fallen in love with my Sitka home away from home, and named it "the Loft." It was a short walk from Crescent Harbor and the lively downtown area. A French door opened into the homey, cottage-style interior with hardwood floors, vaulted ceiling and lots of windows. When I stepped inside, it felt like every bit of the Loft wrapped me in a hug that said, "Welcome to Sitka, Cynthia!"

The inside beauty of the Loft was no match for the outside beauty of Sitka, which had treasures most any time of the day. I had already experienced the Sitka sunrise, but I wasn't quite prepared for its evening enchantment.

Since Harry passed away, I had been enduring a daily battle with "sunset sadness." No matter how I felt during the day, my mood sank as soon as the sun did. But then I discovered the Sitka sunsets. Before long, I started setting my "sunset" alarm, and took breaks to see them from the parking lot at McDonald's, the Ace Hardware or the grocery store. While I couldn't completely escape the daily deluge of emotion, the sorrow and sadness slowly gave way to a sense of serenity.

It was perhaps Sitka's serenity that also had an impact on an entirely different evening struggle that had begun after Harry's death. For a year, when I lay down, my entire body vibrated and buzzed. The first night it happened in Braselton, I thought Harry had left the Tempur-Pedic bed massage feature on, or that the HVAC units were causing vibration to the frame of the house. But 60 days later, when I rested my head on the pillow at the Seattle Airport Marriott on my maiden voyage back to Alaska, I realized it wasn't the bed or the house or the hotel. It was me.

But one miraculous night, after a couple of months visiting Sitka, I laid down to find the vibration completely gone.

So, Sitka, a charming seaside town in southeast Alaska, was having quite an impact on this girl from southeast Georgia.

Just months before, after getting the call from Max, I had simply booked a ticket without looking at a map. While onsite during my first visit, my phone alerted me about a ferocious storm warning for Baranof Island. Innocently, I had asked Ida, the long-time controller of the hospital, "Where exactly are we in relation to Baranof Island?"

Ida had smiled sweetly but the rest of her face gave it away. While she was quickly deciding how to reply diplomatically, I had interjected, "We are *on* Baranof Island, aren't we?"

Ida burst out laughing. I grinned sheepishly. Immediate rapport was established.

It was easy to build rapport on the beautiful island, bordered on the east by majestic mountains and on the west by the Pacific Ocean. A town with a spunky personality and something akin to Southern hospitality oozing from its pores, Sitka had been the capital of Alaska back in the day. With a quasi-cosmopolitan vibe, the tiny town of 9,000 boasted activities day and night. I was excited to be there.

That spring, I settled into a rhythm in Sitka that seemed to mirror Mother Nature. As the temperatures rose, the flowers bloomed, and the wildlife came out of hibernation, I too began to thaw from what had seemed to be the perpetual winter of Harry's death.

My camera filled with photos of the beautiful sights, and I cranked out Facebook posts almost daily. When I wasn't walking through the miracles of Mother Nature, I hit the community gym. Sometimes, I swung in late. "You know we close in 20 minutes, right?"

Undaunted, I would reply, as I signed in, "Twenty minutes is all I need!"

Just before climbing the stairs to the second floor where the machines and workout areas were, I would pause briefly to read the message, a Zig Ziglar quote, that had been painted on the face of the steps:

There is no elevator to success. You have to take the stairs.

Yes, I wanted to lose weight and get into shape. But I also knew the physical exercise was good for what ailed my heart as well. I also knew there was no shortcut to the grief process. No elevators. It was a step-by-step journey for sure.

My journey that spring included trips back and forth between Sitka and Anchorage. The whole one-way trip was three hours. After departing Sitka, we would fly to Juneau, sit on the ground for passenger and cargo swaps, and then head on to Anchorage.

Most of the time, I stayed on the plane during the stop in Juneau. I still felt the heaviness of being there when I got the call from Henry. But one day in March, I got off the plane during the pit-stop. I bought a cup of coffee, and then sat at the counter facing the runway.

I remembered Max on the phone, asking if I could see the trees on the other side of the runway. I couldn't see a thing, and Harry was gone. It was hard for me to imagine seeing mountains, or blue sky or the sun, ever again.

On that morning, just over a year later, I was struck by how different things looked out the airport window. The sky was gray that day, but I could see the trees, the mountains, and small ribbons of blue sky. From that day forward, passing through Juneau didn't have the same horrific hold on me. If God had instructed Alaska to help heal my broken heart, she was indeed following her divine orders.

It seemed as if the hospital and I were in a dance of mutual healing. Admittedly, I had suffered from bouts of workaholism several times during my adult life. In fact, one of the reasons I decided against an early return to Alaska in the weeks following Harry's death was that I knew I would work myself into oblivion.

When I returned to Juneau, I did a fairly good job of maintaining boundaries around the workday. When I got to Sitka, it seemed even easier.

No doubt I was tempted. There was no shortage of things to do, and the hospital, like me, was recovering from trauma.

On one occasion, I was scheduled to make a tricky presentation to the hospital board. I put in some extra time for preparation, and the presentation was very well received. I basked in the feedback and then, a few short minutes later, felt despondent as I walked to the car. There was no text from Harry telling me I had been a rockstar. No sitting at the table with him or providing a play-by-play of the evening via phone. No celebration. I was still feeling the sadness the following day, and so I took a walk, hoping that Sitka would come through once again.

That next evening, on perhaps the most beautiful walk ever, I saw whales for the first time. I was lucky enough to photograph them in action, with both of them breached and blowing water from their spouts. A few minutes later, a bald eagle soared past. And another bird, an Alaska Airlines 737, made its turn on the runway that juts out into the Sitka Sound. It gathered steam before bursting into the evening blue yonder, twisting and turning, up, up and away.

At the halfway point of my walk, I sat down on what had become "my" bench to relax and contemplate.

I noted a silvery sliver of moon cast on a perfectly blue background. I fancied how cozy it would be to curl up in its gentle curve. In other places, cotton candy had been brushed across the canvas of sky, leaving broad streaks. A short time later, they turned into bands of spun gold as the fiery sun dipped behind the snow-crested cone of Mt. Edgecumbe, Sitka's inactive volcano.

Despite the earlier sadness, everything that had happened over the last year and the seemingly long road yet ahead, I felt the enchantment and the splendor. It all seemed just for me.

I thought about a message I had found in the months after Harry died. He had sent it to a friend who had lost his parents and was still missing them. He had written, *You don't get over losing a loved one. You get through it.*

Now the wisdom of Harry's words was helping me get through his death. I was facing it as I could, filling the abyss inside of me with the beauty of life. Beautiful people, beautiful places, beautiful experiences—none of which could ever take the place of or erase a single beautiful memory of Harry.

I thought about the previous night, when I felt sad that there wasn't a playfully expectant text waiting after my big presentation. I reminded myself that he already knew how the presentation went, and that sooner or later, he would let me know that he had.

And then, sitting on my bench, I realized . . . he just did.

That evening, the message had come riding in on the backs of two whales. It flew past me on the wings of a bald eagle, and lit up the evening sky with ribbons of colors, like balloons at a party.

I smiled as I realized how perfectly festive the evening had been. It was one beautiful thing after another—reminding me of those Christmas mornings when Harry would continue to thrust package after package at me.

"Here! Open it. Open it!"

When he saw my look of horror at the odd assortment of patch-work paper, shipping tape and exposed corners, he would simply say, "I wrapped it myself."

But that night in Sitka, the gifts were wrapped perfectly. As I slipped under the covers in the Loft, I imagined curling up in the curve of the moon and being tucked in by the twinkle of a very special star that always seemed to be shining down on me.

That enchanted evening had been a turning point for me. I dove into the next couple of months with renewed enthusiasm. Though the Sitka project had evolved beyond the short-term engagement we had visioned, I continued to strike a good balance with professional work and personal healing. My spirits rose, and my weight dropped.

As spring began its turn toward summer, I began my preparations to depart Sitka for a few weeks. During our daily calls, Paolo and I had arrived at the perfect solution for how I would spend my upcoming 50th birthday, and what would have been my and Harry's 10th-year wedding anniversary.

It was time to return to Italy.

Chapter 11

I don't know who was more excited about my trip—me or my
clients. Until Sitka, I had kept a pretty solid line of demarcation
between my personal and professional lives. But little by little, I had
opened up. The people I had worked most closely with, the senior
leadership group and the accounting team, knew the significance of
the trip, and were very supportive in giving me a nice send-off.

The nightly 20 minutes at the gym, eating lean, and going
without alcohol had paid off. I had dropped another few pounds,
and was feeling energetic and strong. Aches and pains that
cropped up near the end of the first year after Harry's death
magically disappeared. Free from the "big women's" clothes shop
in Anchorage, I had been shopping at JC Penney when back in
town, and had a small selection of clothes ready for my trip. I also
grabbed a new hairstyle from the JCP salon before I hopped on the
plane to Georgia in mid-June.

I had planned my two-week trip to arrive in Italy on or around
the 20th. This would give me about ten days before my birthday, and
a few days afterwards. I had picked those dates for another reason:
June 20th was the anniversary of the accident that led to Sebastiano's
death. July 1 was not only my birthday and my and Harry's anniversary, it was also the anniversary of Sebastiano's funeral. Paolo
and his family had given so much to me. I hoped that my presence

during what was usually a dark time might brighten those days for the family, and give a little something back to them.

In the days before I touched down at the Atlanta airport, I had become a little nervous about going. I knew Paolo felt a brotherly obligation to care for me, but I didn't want him to feel pressured to make the bittersweet occasion perfect. And I was staying for two weeks this time instead of ten days. The four-day difference seemed huge. What if the family grew tired of me?

I couldn't shake the feeling that I was doing something wrong. Somewhere deep inside, I believed that if I had fun, there would be hell to pay. That "someone would end up crying," as my mother used to always say. And so much had changed in the six months since I had been there at Christmas. I was happier. I was healthier. I was turning 50, and I wanted to live life as fully as I could. This trip was about new beginnings, whereas the Christmas visit had been about grieving and surviving. I was heading into completely uncharted territory.

So, I asked my guardian angel for a sign that this was the right thing for me to do. "Cough it up, H," I demanded one evening shortly after my touchdown in Atlanta, and then promptly forgot my request.

Finally, the evening before my departure arrived. For a send-off, I had invited six of my best Braselton friends to join me for Friday night fish at Papa Jack's.

Never would I have imagined spending my 50th birthday and our 10th wedding anniversary with anyone but Harry. Under the circumstances, it could not have been more perfect than to dine with six of my closest friends at Papa Jack's before heading off to Italy. But by the time I headed home with Paula and Broughton, I was once again second-guessing the trip. Until we pulled into the driveway.

I could hear him the moment the car door opened. I thanked Paula and Broughton for the ride, and suggested I might return to their house later for a going-away champagne.

Once inside, I made a beeline for the porch. I could hear him from inside the house. I stepped onto the deck and in one motion, pulled out my phone while I glanced into the yard. I couldn't see him, but his song was urgent and loud. Not being able to photograph him, I did the next best thing and hit "record" on my phone. I glanced up to look for him again, knowing he had to be close.

I spotted him in the middle of the crabapple tree, singing at the top of his lungs. I dashed inside to grab my Canon Rebel with the long lens. He continued to sing, but just before I stepped back onto the deck, he flew away.

"Come back here!" I demanded as I went down the stairs into the backyard. I couldn't see him, but I could still hear him singing as loudly as he had been before. I listened intently and realized that he was somewhere in the front yard. After scurrying back inside, I darted down the foyer and rushed out of the front door. As I did, I checked to ensure the camera was locked and loaded.

Following the piercing sound, I turned left off the front porch. The song came in shrill bursts of four or five before a brief period of silence, and then another burst. I was standing between my house and the neighbors' during one of the lulls.

"Where are you?" I said in just the tone that Harry and I used to ask each other the same question—a question that really meant, "Why aren't you near me? Come closer!"

Another outburst from the cardinal gave away his position. I spied him, in all of his red-feathered splendor, sitting at the peak of the roof, beautifully brilliant against a perfectly clear and early-evening blue sky. The golden setting sun was shining directly on him.

"There you are!" I exclaimed, again using the same tone I would have with Harry.

Like a hunter with his prize game in sight, I slowly fixed the camera on my prey and began to shoot, although I suspected that he would fly away immediately when he heard the camera in action. But he continued to sing.

Eventually, he flew off to the backyard. I went back through the house in pursuit, but put my camera on the porch table before I stepped onto the deck. I must have known that I wouldn't need a camera for what came next.

This time there was no singing. No camera. It was once again like the first morning. If a dog barked, I didn't hear it. If a car drove down the lane behind the house, I didn't hear it. For about 10 seconds, what I heard came from inside my heart and soul as the cardinal sat in the tree, looking in my direction, perfectly still, and not singing a single note.

With his excited greeting earlier, it was as if he were singing to me, *The Punkin's going to It-lee! The Punkin's going to It-lee! You gotta get sacked up! Five a.m. will come early tomorrow. Hurry, Babycakes! The Mad Italian awaits you!*

And then with his quiet stare from the tree afterward, it felt as if he were telling me to relax. To trust that my path was indeed sure and true. Where I'd been, where I was, where I was heading. I knew in that instant that every decision made up to that point was leading me in the right direction. I was truly on a magical journey—one with a nasty detour, but still magical all the same.

I was thankful that my red-feathered friend had been there to see me off. By the next morning, the feelings of uncertainty had vanished, and I was smiling on the way to the airport.

It seemed that H had come up with an answer—the cardinal approved my Italy trip. I set out the next morning on my journey with renewed confidence that it was the perfect thing to do.

And perfect it was. It started the minute I heard Paolo call out to me at the Verona airport as I scanned the small crowd. It ended two weeks later as the sun rose over the rolling, green Italian countryside, eavesdropping on our early-morning conversation about my plans for the future as we made our way back to the airport. In between, I experienced one of the most transformative experiences of my life.

It was my fourth trip to the beautiful country to visit Paolo and his family. The first trip had been a honeymoon that Harry and I took nine months after we got married. We spent a glorious week as guests of Paolo, and, as had been the case so many times over the years, the three of us had a marvelously fun time. We visited Paolo's factory, hosted friends at his house, dined with the family at his parents' castle and almost daily at a neighborhood restaurant.

On that trip, I was mesmerized with the beauty of the northern Italian countryside, its slower pace of life and Marietto, our handsome and stylish guide who piloted us through the channels of Venice, with stops at Harry's Bar for the best grilled cheese sandwiches and coldest vodka I'd ever had. On an afternoon that I'll never forget, I took a coffee with Harry and Paolo on the veranda of a restaurant on Lake Garda in the picturesque town of Sirmione—the town referenced in Harry's Match.com profile.

We returned a few years later, on my birthday and our anniversary, just hours before Sebastiano's funeral. The service took place in the beautiful, centuries-old small church that sits on the corner across the street from Paolo's house. Before the service, we stood outside as friends, dressed in black, rode up on bicycles and arrived on foot. Family members sat in the tiny church while friends and colleagues attended the service from outside. Dear Paolo, with so much on his mind and heart, sent someone to find us, asking that we sit inside with him and his family.

My third visit was the first Christmas without Harry. Even though there was plenty to be sad about, one of the things I had loved the most about that visit was once again hearing the church bells from my third-floor attic bedroom.

On the morning after arriving on my fourth visit, I woke to those beautiful church bells ringing and a canopy of blue in the skylight, as I thought, *Every day should start this way.*

That same evening, the skylight framed vivid lightning, dancing to the rhythm of pounding thunder and pattering rain. As I fell asleep to my personal light show lullaby, I thought, *Every day should end this way.*

For fourteen days and nights, that pattern continued. Of course, not every night brought flashes of lightning, nor did every day paint the skylight blue. But each morning and each evening, along with the hours in between, my heart and soul were imprinted with the picture of a life I so desperately wanted to live.

Often up before anyone else, I took on the morning routine of tending to Ben and Tilley, an adorable golden retriever and a white Yorkshire terrier. I had never been a dog person, but Ben cast a spell on me and I fell deeply in love. He had to be touching me. Leaning against me. Resting his head on my bare foot as I sat outside taking a coffee, while enjoying the beautiful garden and the sunshine and the church bells and the birds singing to me in Italian.

It was on one of those mornings, as I sat there while my hair dried in the early-morning sun, that I realized the ever-spinning merry-go-round of my life had stopped.

For thirty years I had been working hard, bolting from one personal crisis to another, and not treating myself very well. Even during my years with Harry, I battled depression and experienced long stretches of full-blown workaholism. Never believing that I could slow down, I had nearly run myself into the ground. But Harry and I were working a plan for a slower lifestyle that would provide an opportunity for us to be together much more. Knowing that we were embarking on that journey made his untimely departure that much harder to bear.

But something had started in Sitka, and once I got to Italy, without work to occupy my time or thoughts, I was finally able to be still.

Those mornings in the garden were precious to me, as were the family times at the kitchen table, with the portrait of Harry and Sebastiano watching over every meal from their place high on the wall.

Paolo's sons Jacopo and Lorenzo took turns fixing me the perfect coffee before they left for their days. On some mornings that first week, I went to work with Paolo. Sometimes I stayed home, but always we would have lunch together. In the evening, after dinner, I would climb the stairs to my attic room and fall asleep under the bolts of lightning, twinkling stars or moonbeams shining down on me from beyond the skylight.

As the first week ended, Paolo suggested that I try something different the following week.

"Cynthia, you should get out and see some sights!"

It was incredibly hot during that second week, with temperatures consistently in the 90's. And yet, the heat did not bother me. The sun cream I purchased was my secret weapon. It also didn't hurt that I had lost a lot of weight, had been exercising, and unlike during my Christmas visit, Paolo and I were mostly abstaining from wine and champagne.

On my first day trip, after boarding the train and taking a seat, I felt a sense of excitement. I was on a train in the north of Italy, heading to Bologna. Just me and my backpack. I didn't speak the language—well, except for ciao, grazie, espresso, prosciutto and Pellegrino. What other words could I possibly need?

I had a spunky new hairdo that was more perfect for the trip than I anticipated. After letting it dry naturally in the Italian morning sun, I returned to my room to style it when I discovered it needed no styling at all. Soft and swirly, it seemed perfect for my dangling earrings. The high temperatures called for a white sports skirt and a lightweight multi-colored spaghetti strap top. I had makeup and a pair of comfy, strappy sandals in my backpack, in case I wanted to freshen up and slip out of my walking shoes on the train ride home and be ready for whatever the Mad Italian had in store for dinner.

We had only been rolling for a few minutes when I took a selfie to memorialize the beginning of the journey. I had felt a bit of sadness edging out the excitement, but I was not prepared for what I saw looking back at me. Or rather . . . who.

The photo intrigued me for many reasons, one of which was that it was completely unfiltered. Literally and figuratively. If I'd had sleeves on that day, I would have been wearing my heart on both of them. That photo seemed to capture the very essence of my life's experience since Harry's passing and how I felt at that very moment. The dance of life and death. How the darkness and light coexisted— both equally important to the journey and the lessons learned.

I had put my elbow on the ledge of the window and was resting my head against my fingertips, deep in thought. My eyes hinted of tears. The shadowy left side of my face revealed sadness and pain. The lighter right side showed a slight smile. It was a photo that seemed to say, *Life is so beautiful. Even when it's not. And this birthday adventure, that I already know to be life-changing, has come at such an incredible price.*

I glanced at the photo a few more times on the way to Bologna. Each time I looked at it, I became more protective of the young woman looking back at me. I didn't see a soon-to-be 50-year-old woman; I saw a vulnerable young lady who needed love, protection and permission to have fun that the 50-year-old version of me was finally prepared to provide. In that moment, I decided I would do just that.

For several days that week, I wandered the streets of Bologna, Verona and Florence. On the morning I went to Verona, just before Paolo dropped me at the station, he said, "You know, Cynthia. Venice is just a short train ride from Verona." I had laughed, not wanting to attempt anything more complicated than a straight shot to Verona and back.

And yet, as I had breakfast while watching another Italian day come alive, I thought, *Well . . . why not Verona for breakfast, and Venice for lunch?!*

So, on the day before I turned 50, I enjoyed a leisurely breakfast in the town of *Romeo and Juliet*, followed by lunch at a café on the Grand Canal in Venice, as the beautiful songs of gondoliers filled the afternoon air. Before, after, and in between, I was more than content to sit back and watch the Italian countryside go by.

After dinner that night, Paolo advised me that we were going to have a family meeting in the kitchen the next morning. With everyone gathered, the family presented me with a variety of gifts that included a special birthday card from Sitka. I was deeply touched that my relatively new client had made such an effort to ensure that I received their birthday message half a world away.

Paolo announced that the family had also decided that I was getting Ben the dog for my birthday. They had made arrangements for him to travel home with me. Of course, they were kidding, but I wasn't the only one who had noticed something magical was happening—even with the animals.

At lunch, Paolo told me that there was a surprise birthday party for me that evening.

"If it's a surprise, why are you telling me?" I teased.

"Aahhh, Cynthia. We are not very good at keeping secrets. You were bound to find out!"

And so, he then filled me in on the plan. After lunch, he would take me back to the house so I could collect whatever I needed for the rest of the day, and then he would drop me at his parents' home for the afternoon. After work, he and the family would join us, and we would have dinner and the birthday party.

I suppose that I shouldn't have been surprised, with the number of amazing things that had happened in my life since Harry passed away, that my 50th birthday celebration would take place in an Italian castle. Despite my not knowing Italian and his parents not speaking English, we had a lovely time together that afternoon—just the three of us.

I drank grappa and ate salami with Paolo's father, and had my first "chat" with Paolo's mother after I sent her a Google translated message via WhatsApp as she sat quietly across from me. I'll never forget the look of surprise as she picked up her phone and saw the message I had sent: *It is so lovely to be here with you in your beautiful home.* I even took a little nap that afternoon in one of the dark, cool rooms off the grand entrance. It's hard to describe the feeling of love and protection emanating from Paolo's parents.

The festive evening started in the downstairs kitchen with a champagne toast by Paolo's father. Then we dined at the beautifully set table that was laced with confederate jasmine—my favorite, handpicked from the garden by Paolo's mother just before dinner.

Afterward, we went upstairs, where there were more presents to open, and then we enjoyed a piano concert performed by "Maestro," the boyfriend of Paolo's sister Roberta. At one point, I heard Roberta make a comment to Maestro with the word "Americano" in it. Shortly thereafter, the familiar tune of Johnny Mercer's "Moon River" filled the castle. Tears came to my eyes as I looked at Paolo. "Do you know this song?" When he looked puzzled, I explained, "It's Moon River! You crossed Moon River with Harry when he took you to our house in Savannah!"

"You're kidding!" he said, and then excitedly translated the coincidence in Italian.

Eventually, the perfect evening came to an end. Back at Paolo's house, I climbed the three flights of stairs to my attic bedroom, carrying a gratitude-filled heart. I had expected to feel terribly sad. But I simply wasn't. I had promised that young woman that it was okay to have fun. And what better time to make good on that promise than on her birthday? Besides, the day had been too perfect and festive for sadness. I was also hoping, as the skylight winked goodnight, that my birthday celebration had given Paolo's family a better July 1 than they had had in quite a while.

The next day, I was on the train again. Destination: Florence!

This trip required me to ride to Bologna, change trains, and head to Florence. I was undaunted by the itinerary. After all, 48 hours before, I had spontaneously decided to add a Venice round-trip to the day. What was a little train change in Bologna?

It had grown even hotter as the week progressed, and it was a steamy 96 degrees when I got to Florence. I'm not sure if Paolo was a bit nervous because I was farther away from home than the other two ventures, but he had checked in on me a couple of times during the train ride.

Eventually, the phone had grown quiet, and I became fully absorbed in my day. As had happened every morning, my eyes welled with tears as the realization sank in that I was in the beautiful country of Italy. And as was the case every day, I was simply content to wander aimlessly, taking in the sights, the sounds, the smells. It was impossible to not feel open-hearted and spiritually awake. The heat and sweat only added to the feeling of being completely alive.

For the first time in my life, my skin was turning brown. Even as a lifeguard during my late teens, my very fair skin had only ever burned from the sun. But for nearly two weeks, the Italian sun had been painting my body a subtle bronze during my mornings in the garden and my days walking the streets of northern Italy. In many ways, it had also been infusing my heart and soul with heat—a sort of simmering desire for a life that included much more "living" than I had done up until then.

After I had been walking for a while, I ducked into a café to have an aqua con gas and to charge my phone. A short while later, I left the dark cool café and stepped into the sweltering, busy Florence street.

This time, perhaps because I had allowed myself to cool off completely, the heat seemed particularly oppressive. Moments later, when I came upon the entrance to an inviting garden, I slipped inside.

It was incredibly beautiful and soothing. Lush landscaping, tall trees and a perfectly placed bench provided me with a few moments to cool off before I continued deeper into the garden. As I came upon what looked like a driveway and a couple of cars, I thought, *That's odd.* I looked around a bit more before the startling realization: *I think I'm in someone's backyard!*

Seconds later, I was certain I was. Giggling, I continued on the loop of the walkway, heading back to my starting point. As I walked up to what would now be my exit, my smile quickly disappeared as I thought, *Uh oh!*

During the few minutes I had been inside, someone had closed the door through which I had entered. It was not only closed, but locked as well. Even with a tug or two, it wasn't budging. Nor did it look like it ever had! *Medieval,* I thought as I stood there and stared.

I didn't panic. I saw the humor in what had happened. I knew I had two choices: I could call Paolo and get him to airlift me out, or I could attempt to solve the problem myself. I opted for the second option as I retraced my steps. Certainly, whoever had closed the door couldn't be far away.

Shortly thereafter, I encountered a woman gardener. She didn't speak English and my limited Italian vocabulary, mostly composed of food words, wasn't going to be much help. I knew that I could call Paolo to translate, but I wanted that to be the last resort. So, I simply smiled, pointed back toward the medieval door, and then put my hands together in what I hoped would mean something akin to "I am no threat to you. I come in peace."

It did the trick. She laughed and escorted me back to where it all started. And then *I* laughed as she walked up to the door, reached through some foliage on the right, and pushed a button that magically opened the seemingly impenetrable door.

And just like that, I was free! The gardener returned my heartfelt "Grazie!" with a smile and a wave. And I was on my way again.

As I continued to wander the streets of Florence, other possible outcomes of my garden experience began to haunt me. The heat was getting to me, and I was feeling separation anxiety as the time for my departure was now less than 48 hours away. And I had not had lunch.

So, I decided to call it a day, and began the trek back to the train station. I had not been walking very long when I happened upon a cab driver who was unloading fashion mannequins from his car. They were quite lovely and quite naked. I greeted him and confirmed he spoke English.

"When you finish with these lovely ladies, are you available for a lift back to the train station?"

Minutes later, I was enjoying another experience of the bustle of Florence, watching storefronts and people come and go from the comfort of a refreshingly cool cab.

At the station, I double-checked my departure times and headed to a nearby restaurant. I had plenty of time for lunch and to reflect upon the day in the welcoming café with red and white checkered floors that reminded me of Papa Jack's.

On one hand, I was quite sad to be leaving. On the other, I was ready to get started with my new life. I had always felt in the deepest part of me that life was supposed to be enjoyed. I believed in true love and fulfillment. In my younger years, I wanted to be as happy going to work in the morning as I was to head home in the evening. As I got older, I didn't want my work and life to be separate. I wanted to live a mission, something that was as much a part of me as my beating heart. And I didn't buy into the idea that any of that was fantasy. After all, I had already experienced true love.

I was deep in thought about all of this as I made my way back to the train station after lunch. As I watched the countryside blur past me on the ride from Florence to Bologna, I continued to contemplate a mission-centered life. One in which I could tell people "yes" instead of the "no" that so often came with CFO consulting work. As I got closer to Bologna, I studied the train schedule again. I had a very quick connection, with no room for error.

As soon as we stopped in Bologna and I was standing on the platform, I had a momentary lapse in my sense of direction. I was tired from the heat and the garden experience. Knowing I had little time, I trusted my instincts and headed for the connection.

But when I walked up and glanced at the routing for the train, I didn't see Paolo's town as a stop on the route. *I must have been mistaken*, I thought. I hesitated, just long enough for the train doors to close. My heart sank, because now it would be hours before I would be home.

Suddenly, out of nowhere, several people rushed up and began banging on the doors and trying to pry them open. Amazingly, the doors opened. I took a quick step forward, but then hesitated again. A quizzical look from a woman standing next to me seemed to say, *Well? What are you waiting for?*

I still didn't know if it was the right train or not. Suddenly, as a lifetime of hesitation flashed before my eyes, I didn't care. Not one little bit. Just as the doors started to close again, and with a feeling of reckless abandon, I leapt. As I vaulted blissfully into the unknown, I had one thought:

Just jump on the damn train!

I plopped down into my seat, barely able to contain the emotion I was feeling. If I had felt free when the medieval door swung open hours before, I wasn't sure at all what this new feeling was. It was freedom on steroids. In that moment, the young woman on the train departing to Bologna and the 50-year-old woman departing from Bologna became one. It seemed impossible that I would ever let anyone or anything hold me back, ever again.

From the moment in Paolo's garden when I realized the merry-go-round had stopped, to the moment I "jumped on the damn train," I had glimpses of the life I wanted to live and the person I wanted to be—the person I already was. In two short weeks, I had become as completely and unashamedly the most authentic I had ever been. I tanned for the first time. I had no fear, no frenzied excitement or tension. I temporarily adopted a dog, and it seemed totally natural for me to be riding trains through the north of Italy with no agenda and no real timeline.

For the first time in my life, I felt totally carefree. Totally me.

In the days and years since then, I have rarely shared my emotional experience of the trip. I didn't want anyone to tell me I had fallen under the spell of the Tuscan sun. Or that it was a vacation, and real life was nothing like that. Because I believe that it *was* real life. I, of all people, know that life isn't always smooth. But I'm convinced that the day-to-day life that we generally accept as "real life" isn't real at all. How could it be?

What part of our "real life" days provide an opportunity for the merry-go-round to slow down? For us to hear the whispers of our souls? To be in touch with what makes our heart sing? How could we possibly hear the whispers over the noise of what we've defined to be our real life?

The emotional life that I experienced in Italy was the life I didn't know I craved. Yes, I knew that I wanted something different. But during those two weeks, I felt limitless. And for the first time ever, I didn't believe that I needed permission from anyone to do anything.

I wrote very little while I was in Italy. I posted periodically on Facebook to share my location and the sights I knew my friends would appreciate. And I captured snippets of things here and there to help me remember. But the trip to Italy wasn't about writing at all.

It was the best kind of test drive possible. I got to see and experience, for two weeks, what living without limits might feel like. A newfound connection to my heart, my intuition, and to the world around me had started with my return to Alaska the previous fall. In the spring, the connections deepened in Sitka. And during two summer weeks in Italy, any remaining resistance to an open heart and who I was meant to be seemed to slip away—just as the Italian countryside had, through the windows of the daily trains.

No, the trip had not been about writing. It had been about preparing to write. To write authentically and from the heart, I would have to *be* authentic and to have an open heart. I would need to take risks—to jump on the damn train, not knowing for sure where it was going.

So, while my body was journeying from one Italian town to another, my heart and soul were on a journey that went far beyond the lines on any map.

As I prepared to fly home, I thought about a "quoto" I had made with one of my photos and Aberjhani's quote from his book, *The*

River of Winged Dreams. The photo was of sun, sky, plane and sea, and the quote was:

> *A bridge of silver wings stretches from the dead ashes of an unforgiving nightmare to the jeweled vision of a life started anew.*

Losing Harry and the aftermath had indeed been a most unforgiving nightmare. But daily since then, I had been on the receiving end of so much love and encouragement—perhaps more than any one person deserved.

That encouragement included assurances that eventually the tears would transform from sadness to joy, and that the sun would rise to days filled with hope and happiness, rather than dread and despair.

On the day of departure, I turned to see the molten glow of the new day peeking over the edge of the early-morning Italian countryside as we drove to the airport. I smiled, knowing that all the promises had been kept.

It's been said that "life begins at 50." While I don't disagree with that, given the incredible timing of my experience, I actually believe that life begins when we decide it does.

When we decide we are worth the fight. When we decide to cast aside expectations of others and become who we were meant to be. When we decide that living a meaningful and experience-rich life is not optional.

Sometimes it takes difficult decisions. Sometimes it takes jumping on the damn train.

That's when life really begins.

Chapter 12

The silvery wings of the jets that carried me to and from Italy were a bridge stretching between the nightmarish life without Harry and the promise of a new one. A new me. As I flew back across the Atlantic, I thought about the cardinal's appearance the night before my departure from Atlanta, and the message that seemed to come with it. A message from Harry that my path was sure and true. That everything was happening exactly as it should, and that I was indeed on a magical journey.

By the time I landed back in the States, I knew that my life would never be the same. That I would never be the same. I had left a ton of grief on the railroad tracks of northern Italy, and in its place flamed a burning desire to live passionately and to laugh without apology. To follow my heart, no matter where it might lead me.

Even so, I knew that I had a lot of work ahead of me. Literally and figuratively. I had to lead my Sitka client through its annual financial audit. I also had a lengthy list of personal to-dos that had been pending for far too long.

Perhaps most importantly, I knew that two weeks under the Tuscan sun wasn't enough to erase my many self-limiting beliefs and deeply ingrained patterns that could cause stumbling blocks to my growth.

But I was closer than I had ever been to creating the life I believed I was meant to live. For the first time, I could see such a life with me actually in it. I didn't dread the hard work ahead. I knew the results would be worth it.

And I had a plan.

To be reminded of that plan, all I had to do was reach up and touch the pendant that Paolo had given me for my birthday. It was a gold smiley face with tiny diamonds for eyes. It hung from a simple brown ribbon tied around my neck.

"Keep smiling, my sister," he said. And that, I decided, was exactly what I planned to do.

My strategy to "keep smiling" seemed to enhance my satellite dish abilities as the number of signs and synchronicities continued to mount. Not only was I smiling, but I was seeing smiley faces everywhere. It was happening so often that I suspected Harry had gotten bored with the cardinal and had hijacked Paolo's smiley face. Or that I was now getting unspoken encouragement from my Italian brother half a world away.

One night, after meeting friends for dinner in Homer, Alaska, I felt nudged to take a detour on my way to the hotel. It was 10:30 p.m. after an incredibly long day. Even so, I followed my intuition and headed for the Spit, a narrow finger of land that stretches four and a half miles into the Kachemak Bay. Dotted with bars, shops, restaurants and marinas, it's a popular spot for tourists and locals alike. As I drove, I reflected on the heaviness I was feeling after a festive night of friendship and music.

Despite the flame sparked in Italy and the trail of smiles I was leaving everywhere I went, I still was not living in alignment with my gifts. I experienced a pervasive guilt for even thinking that I deserved a life of happiness. If I chose myself, I felt as if I were abandoning others. I kept thinking that if I could just get the merry-go-round to stop like it did in Italy—if I could just have some quiet time, if I could just sleep in my own bed for a stretch—I could figure it all out.

But instead of carving out time for contemplation and rest, I loaded my schedule with travel, events and client commitments. I constantly entertained my friends on social media with playful posts and majestic photos of Alaska. Sometimes I wrote long, brave reflections about my journey that always ended with a "can do" attitude. And though the smiley faces were showing up constantly, I added my own smile a good bit as well. And in those moments, the smiles were totally genuine.

But as I headed toward the Spit that night, I wasn't exactly smiling. I was deep in thought and in tears. I knew I was emanating a glow and always wearing a smile. Something magical was indeed happening. I could see it in my pictures. I could see how people reacted to me. I was surprised by the person looking back at me in the mirror, in a good way. It seemed that I was getting a glimpse into the beauty and magic that this world offers and it showed.

At the same time, I felt out of place. Frustrated. I wanted to comfort and make a difference for people as my mission in life, not squeeze it in between debits and credits. I wanted to tell people "Yes!" instead of "No," or other words of caution that came with my line of work.

And I missed Harry so much that night. We wanted to, but never made the trip to Homer. So, the beautiful drive and fun-filled evening spawned an intense feeling of regret that we had not made the time to do it.

Mind you, I wasn't lonely. I wasn't feeling like *why me?* Actually, I wasn't sure exactly what I was feeling. It just didn't feel good.

When I reached the Spit, I found it to be hauntingly beautiful. With the night nearing eleven o'clock, the sky and the sea were beginning to take on the same silvery blue, making it tough to see where one ended and the other began. That's when I realized exactly what I was feeling: confusion. Where did I begin? Where did I end? What did I want? What didn't I want?

I was happy, and I was sad.

I longed to call somewhere "home," but felt at home anywhere I was.

I had a left-brain career, but found joy in right-brain activities.

I craved connection, but yearned for solitude.

I missed Harry, yet felt him so close.

And though I had felt completely broken, I also had never felt more alive.

I was crying because I knew I was on an incredibly beautiful journey filled with unbelievable experiences, glorious places, exciting adventures, new friendships, and old friendships that had grown deeper and richer. I was crying because that incredibly beautiful journey had come at such a horrific price. In that moment, I really needed a close friend. To hear an encouraging word. To feel a comforting hug. To see a reassuring smile.

The world went into slow motion as I drove past. I blinked and refocused, thinking surely the descending darkness and my tears were playing tricks on me. Still crying, I started to giggle when I realized that wasn't the case. It was real, and it was working, because now I was smiling. And then I started to laugh. I shook my head and exclaimed, "Really?!"

I made my way to the end of the Spit, and as I turned around and headed back, I realized that my spirits were now heading in the opposite direction as well.

It was right at 11:00 p.m. when I pulled into a small driveway just off the Spit, where I sat quietly, gazing up at a beautiful, carnival-like smiley face. It was about two feet in diameter, and painted the typical yellow. There was an iron loop with some wire on top that looked like a little tuft of hair. It sat atop a pyramid-shaped buoy about six feet in diameter at the bottom, with alternating ribbons of pastel colors. I'm guessing it was about eight feet tall, including the smile. Sitting off on the side of the road among dilapidated boats, floats and fishing gear, it appeared to have a found a permanent home in a junkyard of the sea.

As the silver-blue night turned to black, I wondered how many times it had "rescued" someone else from an ocean of sadness. How many times a captain sailing in a raging storm had gotten back on course seeing the slightly crooked smile, bobbing and swaying in a dark night, providing fresh hope of weathering the storm and making it to shore.

There's no doubt in my mind that I was supposed to be driving along the Spit at that very moment in time. I'm sure the buoy had been sitting there for years. It didn't just magically appear.

But something propelled me to make that drive late at night, in a strange town, after a very long day. I should have made a beeline for the hotel, but something told me I wasn't quite done with the night—or perhaps the night wasn't quite done with me. Perhaps the night had that reassuring smile I needed. And while it took a few more months for this captain to change course, that night, my path was no longer dark and unsure, but well-lit by the sunshine of that rusty and slightly lopsided smile.

After a few more months of intense client work and several cross-country trips, I had a reckoning with myself. I admitted just how hard things had been since returning from Italy, seeing the vision of what I wanted my life to be like, but feeling it was out of my reach.

My strategy had been to keep smiling. To keep moving. I had not yet learned that the changes I needed to make had to first come from the inside. I was still trying to force my way into happiness through external events. But I finally had to admit that I was also trying to outrun the sorrow.

I was so tired. Exhausted, actually. So, I did what Forrest Gump did when he'd had enough of running.

I. Just. Stopped.

I made a 60-day plan to incorporate as much quiet and rest into my schedule as possible, while also tackling the rather long list of personal to-dos and wrapping up onsite work in Sitka. I also made another decision: I would spend the holidays in Anchorage by myself. Friends and family seemed nervous about this. I suppose I was, too. But my little voice was pretty confident it was the perfect thing to do.

I knew from the previous year that decorating for Christmas was an antidote to the holiday blues, so immediately after Thanksgiving, I put up the tree and decorated the condo. For the last several years, putting up the tree was my absolute favorite thing to do.

One year, I was extremely busy on a client deadline and so, in an unusual divide-and-conquer move (simply because we did everything together), Harry offered, "Shall I go chop down a tree at Lowes?"

"Okay. But make it easy on yourself, Paul Bunyan. Artificial. Pre-lit. White lights."

"My feet have wings!" he exclaimed.

Later that afternoon, he insisted I take a coffee with him and then inspect the tree. He was proud to have gotten a good deal. "I stole a Christmas tree," he declared when he got back.

So, I acquiesced and ripped into the box. And then with a disappointed, "Oh no!" I looked up sadly.

"What's wrong, my Punkin?"

"Colored lights!" I lamented.

The look on Harry's face was priceless. It may be the one time that he seemed even remotely embarrassed. After all, he was always thinking ahead, always doing exactly what he said he was going to do.

And yet, there we sat with a Christmas tree of colored lights.

He leapt to his feet. "Fear not! I will immediately return it and fetch a tree of white lights for my princess!"

It was awfully tempting, but it had started snowing and blowing, and I couldn't ask him to do that.

So, I heard myself say in a reassuring tone, "You know, I'm thinking that colored lights may actually *be* the ticket. We need some contrast to the lighter hues in here." By the time the tree was up and branches arranged, we were howling with laughter.

Every year since then, I've held my breath just before plugging in the tree. And especially those first two years after Harry passed. I wanted nothing more than for every single one of those colored lights to work. On my home-alone Christmas that year, without fail, the tree burst into color as I heard Harry bellow, *Flame on!* Later, I sat at my desk, enjoying the beautiful mixture of the colorful inside Christmas lights and the outside city lights. I had indeed come to love the tree of many colors.

It will always remind me, long after it shines its last bit of color, that many times in life we get the tree of colors when we'd wanted and expected the one with white lights. And many times, though it may take a while before we realize it, the one with many colors is actually the perfect tree for us.

By the time New Year's Eve rolled around, I had very much enjoyed the holidays. I continued to work on my list, and had every holiday meal at Simon & Seafort's, where I quickly became a regular. I walked in the snow to see the play *A Christmas Carol* on Christmas Eve, and stopped off for a hot toddy on my walk home. All the while, one of Harry's high school friends, Donna, who had also popped out of a virtual birthday cake at his Facebook party the year before, kept me company via texts.

As the New Year approached, I created a pictorial New Year's wish with a holiday photo of me taken by Harry a few years back and a quote widely attributed to Albert Einstein. *Learn from yesterday. Live for today. Hope for tomorrow.* I re-read his words of wisdom on New Year's Eve. They rang even more true for me as I stood on the cusp of a new year, after gaining firmer footing the previous 60 days.

Life isn't meant to be about regret or fear. It is a gift we have been given, a blank canvas awaiting its masterpiece. We will make mistakes. We will have losses. There will be pain. But the beauty in it all is that every single minute of every single day, we have a chance to start over. To begin again.

We aren't meant to forget. We are meant to remember. And if we remember without regret or judgment, we create our best chance to learn. And therein lies the means by which we grow—we become stronger and wiser. We get a chance to live a better day, every day.

Thus, we learn to hope, and in turn, perhaps we hope to learn. At least I do.

Oh, how I learned over those first two years after Harry passed away, and every year since then. Eventually, simply remembering, without remorse and regret, came easier. The reward was a chance to live each day more fully, with more joy and a hint of sparkle. I learned to hope again.

I also learned that I'd need to dust off parts of me that had been shelved during my time with Harry in order to thrive during my time without him. To spend time in nature. To listen to music. To take more photographs. To reconnect to people from my past, and deepen connections with those in my present.

And to write.

I was more convinced than ever that the horrifically beautiful life I was living was to be captured and shared with those who needed assurance that the light shines in the darkness. That magic and miracles are happening around us, every day. That our loved ones are closer than we could possibly imagine. And that it's never too late or too impossible to follow our hearts.

In the end, the growing pains of 2015 were my Christmas tree of many colors that provided me with great wisdom and strength, as well as a hunger to situate my life in support of my dreams much sooner than later. My 60-day plan to end the year had been perfect, and I was planning to add another 60 days right behind it.

Even though I had much to celebrate, I didn't toast at midnight on New Year's Eve. Instead, I sat quietly by the fire with only the tree for company when the New Year arrived in Alaska. The sounds of new beginnings floated in through an open window. Car horns and an occasional "Happy New Year" sounding from the darkness lured me onto the balcony. I was surprised to hear church bells ringing and see the snow-covered mountains that stretched out before me decorated with colorful splashes of fireworks.

It was quiet except for the sounds of the city. I had not watched the ball drop in New York, nor was I playing music. I had made it through the holidays without incident, and so I wasn't about to let "Auld Lang Syne," a song capable of stirring up sorrowful emotions even during the best of times, derail me as I stepped across the threshold into the New Year.

After the short visit to the balcony, I turned off the tree and headed to bed. I felt peaceful and ready. While enjoying the sounds of the New Year in Anchorage, I thought about 2015 and all that came with it. With surprise, I realized that it had been one of the best years of my life. As my head hit the pillow, I was filled with joyful anticipation that 2016 would be even better.

Chapter 13

On the first night of the new year, I picked up a book I'd started reading nine months before, *The Power of One*, by Bryce Courtenay. It had been gifted to me by one of the many friends I inherited from Harry.

"It's one of the best books I've ever read," he said over fried chicken at Papa Jack's one afternoon. "I think you'll find a little bit of our boy in it. The first 50 fifty pages are a bit tough, but stick with it."

I did stick with it, and did indeed find some Harry in the main character, Peekay.

> As I sat on the rock high on my hill, and as the sun began to set over the bushveld, I grew up. Just like that . . . I knew . . . that I had permission from myself to love whomever I wished . . . I knew that when the bone-beaked birds returned I would be in control, master of loneliness and no longer its servant. You may ask how a six-year-old could think like this. I can only answer that one did.

Those words conjured up images of all the stories that surfaced after Harry's death as evidence that he was wise beyond his years, even when he was a small boy.

The further I got into the book, the more I saw traces of myself in Peekay as well. And then, in the wee hours of January 2, near the end of the book, I discovered the reason why I had taken so long to get there.

I was home again just as the moon was rising over the valley. The pain, the deep dull pain under my heart, had lifted. Sadness remained, but I was now proud that Doc had achieved what he wanted to do. And we would always be bound together, he was very much a part of me. He had found a small, frightened, and confused little boy and had given him confidence and music and learning and a love for Africa and taught him not to fear things. Now I didn't know where the boy began and Doc ended. I had been given all the gifts he had. Now that Doc was resting right, I knew we could never be separated from each other.

As I read those words, I felt the swell in my heart begin. I had to wipe my tears in order to finish reading. They were big, wet, sloppy tears. I clutched the book to my chest, rolled to my side, then burrowed into the bed and held on for dear life as sobs wracked my heart and soul.

It took a few days for me to realize that I had been sobbing out the best kind of tears. Tears of truth. Tears of relief. It was as if every single beautiful or horrific moment of the last two years was being acknowledged or released in the tears rolling down my face. I knew I had taken so long to read that book, because the words would surely have missed their mark if I'd read them one moment sooner.

Even before Harry died, he reveled in our connection. "We are psychically connected!" he would say, as if there could be nothing finer in life. He also reveled in my successes, and wanted nothing more than for me to be happy. To be my best self. He was driven to share his knowledge, and I was an insatiable student. The night of his service, I had confessed, "Being married to Harry wasn't just a relationship; it was an education."

And so, I had seen through the words of Bryce Courtney that Harry was my "Doc."

My gift of gifts.

As I read those beautiful, heart-piercing words, I could see that Peekay was the small boy who started out as Harry and grew into Cynthia—learning along the way about "The Power of One." And I knew it was all real: the connection, the magic, the love. I had been reading "our story." It was now up to me to write the rest of the story, chapter by chapter, using the gifts I had been given, and following the path that Harry so lovingly laid out for me, through cardinals, songs, smiles and friends.

And in those few magical moments, it felt as if he put his arms around me, held me tight and whispered, *Happy New Year, Punkin! Happy New Life!*

For the first time, I really, truly believed it. I *knew* without a doubt that I could and would keep going. I would live joyfully, knowing that my connection to Harry would always be there. Not keeping me from moving forward, but ensuring that I did. My tears turned to those of relief, because I really needed to believe that.

I had a lot to be thankful for and to celebrate. I was doing as well as I seemed to be. The smile on my face was real, as was the joy in my heart. It had been a beautiful holiday season. I had missed times with family and friends, but I'd needed the solitude. I knew I had a long way to go, but I had made tremendous progress, and one of the most significant healing moments I had ever experienced had just occurred. If the first hours of the year were any indication, 2016 was indeed going to be an incredible year.

I planned to start the year with the same peaceful approach to work and life that I had implemented in Anchorage during the holidays. To shift from professional accounting work to creative endeavors. But as I had on numerous occasions, I once again went in the opposite direction.

Not only did I take on more work with existing clients, I added a new one. I over-traveled and under-slept. It was self-sabotage at its best, and I became more and more anxious, angry, frustrated and exhausted. By the time I got back to Alaska in mid-February, after two back-to-back cross-country trips, I could barely function, and all of my hopes and dreams of a shiny new year had lost their luster.

During that frenzied time, I also publicly proclaimed that I was going to write a book. Fear and feelings of unworthiness, or having done something wrong, surfaced. *What if the cardinal sightings are just my grief response? I'll definitely have to change my career. Who wants a CFO or trusted advisor who believes her dead husband is sending messages from heaven through a bird in the backyard?*

On top of that, I was scheduled for a business conference in Las Vegas at the end of the month. I wasn't looking forward to it at all. Vegas had been such a special place for me and Harry. I didn't relish the thought of going back there without him.

And then I found out that Celine Dion was going to be performing in Vegas the very week I was going to be there.

Celine's music had played in the background of some of the most intense, emotional times of my life. I didn't listen to her very much after I met Harry because he introduced me to jazz and, since life was so very good, I didn't need her broken-heart ballads to sustain me. For a while after Harry died, I found it very difficult to listen to music of any kind. When I did listen, and tried to sing along, I felt very inhibited. I literally couldn't carry a note. The beautiful voice I seemed to have when I was younger had disappeared.

Once I braved music again, I found myself seeking out my old friend. Two of her albums were particularly comforting to me. I started most every day listening to *A New Day Has Come* and for my evening and weekend listening, I often tuned to *Loved Me Back to Life*.

When I learned about her husband's death earlier that year, I thought of Celine often. I knew a little something about losing a husband who was so much more than a husband . . . a business partner, a mentor, a colleague, a best friend, a confidant, a teacher, a coach, a cheerleader, a knight in shining armor . . . someone who thought you hung the moon, and because he did, sometimes you actually could. Someone who reveled in hearing your dreams, never asking "why?" but "why not?"

I had wondered when she might return to work, and how she would pay tribute to her great love. In one of her interviews about returning to Vegas following her husband's death, she shared a belief that they would always be together. I knew a little something about that as well.

I had not been planning to see any shows while there. SEAL Team Cynthia: Get in. Get out. No casualties. But when I saw that Celine was going to be in Vegas, I decided it was meant to be. And I decided to have a virtual "Date Night" with Harry. So, I bought the best ticket I could, and a new blouse for the occasion. I made dinner reservations at The Palm, where we had dined frequently. When Celine walked out onto the stage that Wednesday night, we would all be there: me, Harry and her husband René.

I knew I would cry during those special songs, "Because You Loved Me" and "My Heart Will Go On." Especially that one. But I suspected the tears would be bittersweet, triumphant tears. For me. For Celine. For all of us who have loved deeply and lost profoundly, and yet . . . we go on.

Excited about the turn of events, I did something I almost never did. I posted my plans on social media. Three people from my life before Harry let me know that they would be in Vegas at the same time. Then I learned that a colleague from the Nome project was attending the same conference.

So, a trip I was dreading turned into an incredible reunion to be spread out over several nights of my stay, with Date Night falling right in the middle of them. It felt like the Universe was my concierge—arranging things perfectly to give me exactly what I needed.

Even so, the pervasive feelings of dread returned just a few days before my departure to Vegas. I was still exhausted from the back-to-back cross-country trips down South and a demanding work schedule. I had convinced myself that Date Night was silly, and that I had overindulged in purchasing a ticket to Celine's show. I felt out of sorts, and certain of only two things: I was in crisis, and heading to Vegas for a business trip, the first one since Harry had passed away, didn't seem like a very good idea.

Chapter 14

The minute I stepped onto the plane in Anchorage, my mood shifted. My seat partner was wearing a shirt exactly like the one Harry was wearing the night he passed away. Like Harry, he told entertaining stories, was quick to laugh, and had a twinkle in his mischievous 95-year-old eyes. We toasted with coffee and champagne, and were so cozy that the flight attendants thought we were traveling together.

In the days leading up to the trip, I marveled at the number of friends I was going to see and kept thinking, *I wonder who will be next?* Only moments into the trip, it appeared Harry had answered, *Well . . . a guy named Walt. Sitting in my seat and wearing my shirt. A nice touch, don't you think?*

As my next flight took off into the Seattle night, my spirits lifted even further as the memories flooded in.

My inaugural trip to Vegas was twelve years earlier, in 2004. I was also dreading that trip, even though I was going with Harry. He had been making trips to Vegas since he was a youngster, accompanying his father there on business. Eventually, the trips turned into his own business trips and raucous romps in the desert with friends and colleagues.

"It's adult Disneyland!" he would tease. The more he insisted it would be fun, the more I resisted. I couldn't imagine there being anything I would enjoy in the smoke-filled casinos of seedy Las Vegas, except for his company. But in March 2004, I agreed to go.

When it was time for me to fly home four days later, I didn't want to leave.

Instantly, I found a lot to love about Vegas. And over the years, the list grew. Chopper rides and picnics in the Grand Canyon. Dancing fountains, pirate ships and erupting volcanoes. Elton John and *The Phantom of the Opera*. Lavish meals, free-flowing champagne, and an "always-on" vibe that felt surprisingly right.

I smiled as I thought about that first trip. Part of my dread had less to do with Vegas, and more to do with me. It wasn't just my first trip to Vegas; it was my first trip with Harry anywhere. He had traveled all over the world. I had not. Even though he was well aware of that, I didn't want it to show.

But I took to the travel like a duck to water. When Harry beamed at me during dinner, my last night there, and proclaimed, "Traveling with you is soooo fun!" I felt like I had won a gold medal. Giddy from the compliment or the Conundrum wine, I blurted out, "I don't want to leave!"

To which Harry smiled and replied, "Then stay!"

And so, I did.

The truth was that I didn't want to leave Harry. More than the shows, attractions and food, what I loved most of all about Vegas was seeing him in his element and enjoying the company of some of his closest friends and colleagues. It seemed that everywhere we turned, we ran into someone he knew. I never grew tired of seeing their faces light up, or of watching him mesmerize a table full of people with his stories, many of which seemed just a bit hard to believe.

It was clear that Harry was known far and wide, was respected as a man of high intellect and integrity, and that he knew how to have fun better than most. In Vegas, I found reason after reason to be prouder of him than ever, for the effortless way he made people smile, laugh and feel safe. When I told him so, he would smile slightly and simply respond, "Vegas. It is my town."

Eventually, it became my town, too. I even traveled there a few times by myself for business, or to see a show with friends. But it was never as much fun without Harry.

As the plane began its descent and I spied the Strip glowing in the darkness, I thought about my new friend Walt and how familiar and festive he had been. I hoped that it was a message for me that things would go better than I was expecting.

But by the next morning, the dread had returned, along with a physical discomfort from the first business attire I had worn in over a year. I was missing the more casual comfort of Alaska. And I was missing Harry.

The conference boasted an attendance roster of over 40,000 people. When I walked into my first session, I saw ten-top tables stretching as far as the eye could see. People buzzed around, grabbing coffee, finding seats, and chatting in the aisles. Everyone seemed so happy and excited to be there. At one time, I would have been, too. Despite a perpetual dissatisfaction with my career, I would have been activated by the energy in the room, eager to meet people and learn something new. But not that morning.

My life was so different now. My heart was so different. A wave of certainty hit: my current career would never satisfy my soul. I had known that for years, but that morning I felt it from my head to my toes. As I looked around the huge room, I thought, *I don't fit in.*

I should have been happy for that clarity. I didn't want to fit in. But I was shrouded in sadness. When we were asked to introduce ourselves to our table, a tsunami of anxiety hit. I heard the speaker outline the questions: Who was I? What did I do? Where did I live? Why was I here?

I didn't see it as a simple introduction. The questions were existential for me. I had been desperately searching for the answers for two years, and still didn't have them. I was exhausted from pretending to be someone I wasn't. I briefly fantasized about simply saying, "Hi. I don't know who I am; I'm a misfit in my career. Home is where Harry is and since he's dead, well, it's become complicated. And I have no clue as to why I'm here. But I *do* know that my name is Cynthia. It's a pleasure to meet you."

However, I didn't think my tablemates deserved a Monday morning meltdown, and I certainly wouldn't have wanted it to find its way back to my clients. So, I delivered my typical spiel while doing my best to hold back the tears.

After the painfully long session, I staggered out of the room and into the swarm of attendees in the conference center hallway. The sensory overload from the number of people and the volume of their voices was excruciating. All I could think of was that I so desperately wanted answers to those introduction questions. And I wanted Harry back.

With tears in my eyes and despair in my heart, I felt completely alone, certain that there wasn't a single person among the 40,000 that I could or would want to connect with, personally or professionally. My best friend who made my world beautiful just by being in it was gone, and I was sure that I would spend the rest of my life without ever experiencing that kind of connection with another human being.

As I navigated the crowd, I longed to return to my room and crawl under the covers. Or better yet, jump into a bottle of champagne and pull the cork in behind me. But I knew that wasn't the answer, so, I slipped into the ladies' room to freshen up. It was time for my first reunion.

I met Phillip and his paternal twin David during my freshman year of high school. Quintessential Southern gentlemen even at the age of 14, they had befriended me, a new student who'd transferred from rival Hancock Academy. We quickly found shared interests of laughter, sports, and their older brother Bryan, who flirted with and pursued me relentlessly from the start.

After crisscrossing each other in the friendly skies for years, Phillip and I had finally landed in the same spot at the same time. That afternoon, we headed out on another journey, covering 35 years in three and a half hours that went by in the blink of an eye.

David joined us by phone for a few minutes, and I smiled at one brother while I talked and laughed and joked on the phone with another. David agreed to give his parents a hug for me, and moments later he called back. Phillip answered and then simply handed the phone to me.

"The hug was delivered, and they send one back to you. But Phillip will have to deliver it because my arms won't stretch that far."

I burst out laughing. No one watching us or listening that afternoon would have guessed that it had been 35 years since we had seen each other, except perhaps the two devilish angels looking on. Two and a half years before Harry passed away, Bryan had passed away just before his 50th birthday. So, our visit was somber at times. But we also laughed a lot, imagining that the two of them had connected in heaven and conspired to bring us together that afternoon.

Over the previous two years, I'd had a lot of special moments with friends. But my reconnection with David and Phillip felt like reuniting with a family I didn't know I had lost. It wasn't about reliving high school memories. It was about experiencing the bond that formed in our early years, and continued through our separate but similar experiences of loss and laughter and love since then. It was about what life takes from us and what it gives back. That afternoon, it gave back plenty.

As I reluctantly unfurled from our goodbye hug and watched Phillip head down the escalator, it wasn't lost on me that within minutes of my desperate feelings of disconnection, the twins had shown up, bringing joy to my heart and light to my day. Tears welled up as I watched Phillip disappear. I knew that I didn't want us to break our promises to stay in touch.

While the visit had alleviated my feelings of disconnection, it didn't take long for darkness and despair to return. Throughout my trip to Vegas, the vicious cycle repeated. I'd wake up each morning and burrow under the covers, not wanting to face the conference with its sea of people. Sometimes I would stay there, blowing off the morning sessions, but I would rally for the afternoon client meetings and system demos.

In the evenings, I came alive for my personal reunions. No longer the impostor of the daytime events, I reveled in a sense of freedom and authenticity. Conversations were filled with laughter, toasts to Harry, celebrations of reconnecting, and chats about my journey and desire to change direction professionally. I hated when the evenings ended. Already missing my friends, I also dreaded what the mornings would bring.

The morning of Date Night was no different. I skipped the morning sessions and burrowed under the covers. I wanted to feel excited, but the more I tried, the worse I felt. While I was looking forward to the Celine Dion concert, I still felt silly about my virtual date with Harry. It suddenly seemed pathetic for me to have conceived of the idea. I was also very stressed, knowing that my client work in Alaska was piling up while I was at the conference. It was important for me to be at the afternoon demos that day. So, at the last possible minute, I headed to the conference. Before I left the room, I hung my new blouse in the bathroom and laid out shoes and jewelry for the evening. No matter how silly it seemed, I was going to do it. Date Night was on.

In the days leading up to the trip, I had gone shopping in Anchorage for a top to wear for the special night. I wanted something elegant that would go with my all-purpose little black skirt. When I saw it on the rack, I knew it was the one. The bottom layer was solid black with spaghetti straps. The top layer, with three-quarter sleeves, was black sheer accented with designs of ivy. A scoop neckline left plenty of room for my necklace. While I had not turned Harry's ashes into diamonds, I had a dusting of them embedded in a cobalt-blue glass pendent. I knew it would look perfect hanging from its black rope chain.

I stayed at the conference later than planned that day, so when I returned to my room, I was glad everything was handy. I quickly dressed, giggling as I slipped on the blouse. My angst from the morning was already fading away. "Try to contain yourself tonight, H," I teased as I gave one last glance in the mirror, fluffed my hair and walked out the door.

"I don't know . . . what do you think?" I asked.

"You might as well go big!" she replied.

"Or I might as well go home!"

She laughed and said, "I like how you think!"

After enjoying dinner at The Palm, I had arrived at the Coliseum. As the bartender poured my prosecco into a large plastic cup, I smiled. One of Harry's favorite sayings was, "Go big or go home."

And then it started . . .

Stop stealing my stuff! You're always stealing my stuff.

I only steal the good stuff.

Get your own stuff.

When the bartender gave me a cup of ice to keep the beverage cool, I laughed and thought, *Giving me ice to keep prosecco cold is like giving the Brandts a wine stopper.*

I heard that.

Did not.

Did too.

But it's true.

Indeed, it is.

Are you going to talk all during the show?

I might . . .

Really?

Whatever the Punkin wants!

I made my way to my seat and took part in the pre-show festivities of photographs and meeting my seat partners. When I heard a woman behind me speaking in French, I turned around and said, "Bonsoir! Comment allez-vous?"

She got so excited and asked me, in English, if I spoke French.

"Un peu," I said, and Harry revved up again.

I knew you were going to get busted one day! Run into someone who really knows French! And then he laughed his famous-among-friends French laugh, *Hon hon hon!*

Pretending to ignore him, I chatted with the couple sitting on my right. After the woman commented on my outfit, I explained that it was a special night and why. She said, "You know, Celine just lost her husband."

"Yes, I know. So, I'm here to pay tribute with her . . . to a very special kind of love. I think she and I have that in common. Hi, I'm Cynthia."

She reached across her husband and extended a hand. "My name is Angel."

I shook her hand and smiled back.

"Of course it is."

The show had barely started when I got my first dose of full-body chills. The message was written in big, white letters, on a huge black screen hanging above the stage.

In her own words, Celine acknowledged that her career had been her husband's "masterpiece" and that she knew she had to continue.

As I sat there in the Coliseum and read those words by Celine Dion, I felt as if they were my words, too. In so many ways I felt like I had been Harry's masterpiece, and that I must become the best I could be, to honor that. So, her words went straight to my heart. I don't even remember what song she led with. Perhaps she talked to us first. It's all still a blur. What I do know is that I cried for the first fifteen minutes of the show.

Eventually the tears stopped, and I sat mesmerized, watching and listening to the woman who had been singing in the background of most of my adult life. I had seen Celine in Vegas years before, but on this night, her stage presence was different. Or perhaps it was I who was different. Likely it was both. She was as powerful as before, perhaps even more so. But this time, she was far more captivating. With a blend of vulnerability, resilience and triumph, she seemed to be singing the songs from the deepest part of who she was.

And she had added some humor, at one point showing some leg from a slit in her long gown. "That was for René," she joked as she glanced toward the balcony section. I laughed and looked down at the sleeve of my special purchase, thinking, *And THAT was for Harry!*

There was one more thing for Harry. And for me. I had been waiting for it all night. It's perhaps one of the most iconic songs of all time. And even though it's a perfect song for anyone who has lost a loved one, the song had taken on new meaning for me after Harry's death, and even more so after my visit to see Bedford months later.

During the last two days of my visit, I had participated in a small group session, as he'd recommended. Each attendee had an opportunity to work through a session of psychodrama. There was no assigned order; each person went when it felt right. Afterward, Bedford played a song while the group sat in contemplation and reflection.

I was the last one to go, on the last day. In one of my sessions with Bedford earlier in the week, he told me that a therapist in training was going to attend. "I think you might like him," he had said with a smile. No wonder. Matt was "very Harry." Tall, dark and Italian-handsome, his presence filled the room. When my session came on the afternoon of the last day, I chose Matt to be Harry. While I spoke, Bedford provided the script to Matt, masterfully transforming him into Harry. It was one of the most healing experiences I'd ever had, and there wasn't a dry eye in the room afterward. I was exhausted, physically and emotionally, from the intensity of it all. I sat back in my chair with my eyes closed, awaiting "my" song. Bedford had chosen well. More tears rolled down my face as Celine started to sing "My Heart Will Go On."

Halfway through the song, I felt a sensation of heat. Opening my eyes for a quick peek, I saw that I was the only one in the room bathed in sunlight streaming through a window high behind me. Certain that it was divine confirmation of all that had transpired that afternoon and in the months since Harry passed, I closed my eyes and listened to the rest of the song as I felt the warmth of universal love and Harry's spirit shining directly upon me. It was the first time I remembered thinking they could be one and the same.

So, I had no doubt that would be the last song of Celine's show. The grand finale.

As soon as she started singing "My Heart Will Go On," I shivered. It was much more powerful to hear the song in person, after all that I had experienced in the previous two years. Consumed by the music, her passion and the energy from the crowd, I couldn't imagine feeling a song more deeply.

Afterward, I joined the audience in a raucous round of applause. As we clapped, I felt a wave of sadness. It reminded me of how I felt at the end of every fireworks show I had ever seen, knowing that the grand finale had just exploded into the night, while wishing with all my heart that it had not.

As the applause died down, I realized my wish had been granted. The show wasn't quite over. As Celine began her concluding remarks, I could feel a buzz of excitement from the audience. *Would there be another song? What could it possibly be?*

As Celine's remarks gave way to the song's familiar introduction, I put my elbow on the left arm of my seat and rested my head in my hand. When Celine started singing "Over the Rainbow," I started crying softly.

The tears were unlike any I had cried before. The more she sang, the more they flowed, falling like raindrops onto my lap. Though there were 3,500 people in attendance, for a life-changing three minutes or so, it felt like it was just me, Celine, and our two angels, Harry and René. I had no idea where I was, but it didn't feel like the Coliseum any longer. It was so beautiful, so pure, so true. I felt an overwhelming sorrow and sadness. And yet, I also felt a love beyond description.

And I felt Harry's presence like never before.

When it was over, I stood up, gathered my things and glanced sheepishly at the couple sitting next to me. They were also gathering their things and so I chose to escape, simply stepping into the aisle. But moments later as we inched along with the crowd, I felt a hand on my back. I turned around to see the "Angel" from my row smiling at me. I smiled back as she took my hand and gave it a reassuring squeeze. She nodded and winked without saying a word.

I was already shaking. The interaction with Angel only made it worse. Or better. Something miraculous and magical had happened. I was sure that I would never understand it or be able to explain it. After exiting the Coliseum, I ducked into the ladies' room to center myself and to apply a fresh coat of war paint after all the tears. When I looked in the mirror, the woman looking back at me was not the same one from the mirror in the hotel room hours earlier.

A part of me wanted to return to that room immediately. I wanted to capture the experience in words, hoping that by doing so, I would be able to make sense of it. But another part of me knew that wasn't possible. Not yet, anyway. Besides, the night was young, and I didn't want it to end just yet.

The balmy, bustling night of the Vegas Strip seemed oddly comforting to me after the cosmic experience of the Coliseum. By the time I reached Lavo, a restaurant in the lobby of the Palazzo hotel, I was feeling a bit more grounded.

But over the next couple of hours, I had encounters and experiences that left me in a spiritual swirl and the echo of Harry's voice in my head: *It's Vegas, baby!*

For fifteen minutes, I had a hushed conversation in the hotel lobby with one of our favorite friends in Vegas, Johnny Love. After I told him about Harry's death, he immediately turned the conversation to all things he loved about Harry. And then, with a steady gaze he said, "Okay . . . so you know he's in a better place now, right?"

I nodded. "And I think the 'better place' is much closer than we may think."

As I walked away, I felt the same way I did watching Phillip disappear down the escalator the day before. I didn't want it to be over. And apparently, neither did Harry.

The night is young, Punkin! I heard him say. *Let's go find a nightcap!*

If I had heard it once, I had heard it a thousand times. Harry's adaptation of a famous line, delivered in a raspy Godfather-like voice every single time we had wine together.

"Vito . . . pour the wine."

After a short stroll, I sauntered into Canaletto's, which was next door to where Phillip and I had lunch. I perched at a high-top table in the bar area, thinking that a nice Italian coffee and some dessert would be the perfect nightcap. My smiling server appeared before I even had a chance to get settled.

His name was Vito.

An hour later, after Vito poured the wine, and I enjoyed dessert and an espresso afterward, I began my reluctant walk back to my room. As I passed the high-limits room, I felt a tug on my arm. *Come on, Punkin! Spin the big wheel!"*

That's not roulette, I replied dryly.

You know what I mean! The night is still young and I'm . . . feeeeeling . . . LUCKY!

I had already passed the entrance, but I reversed course, and settled at a machine in the near-empty room. A few minutes later, I hit a royal flush and my machine erupted with the *Ding! Ding! Ding!* and flashing lights of a $1,200 jackpot. As I gathered my pocketbook and secured the cash, I thought, *I guess he really was feeling lucky, wasn't he?*

I stepped lively out of the high limits room and noted that it was still not even midnight. I couldn't have had a more perfect night. Even so, the evening felt "unfinished." So, I stopped by the TUMI store and splurged on a $400 backpack. It was fun and felt very "Vegas" to buy something extravagant with our winnings, and to have a memento to commemorate the night. Now, many years later, it seems a small price to have paid for a constant companion and the perfect reminder of the magical, miraculous evening.

After slipping into bed, I sent a photo of the jackpot poker machine to Paolo with no explanation. Moments later, my phone rang, and I answered to him doing his best impersonation of Harry's French laugh. It was morning in Italy and, though at the office, he seemed content to talk at leisure about our fun times with Harry in Vegas. He was glad I stopped to see Johnny Love. We laughed about the jackpot, he applauded the purchase of my "memento," and the call ended much like it started. But this time it was both of us—trying our best to mimic Harry's French laugh.

After I hung up, I rolled over, spun the little wheel of my iPod and landed on what Harry and I called "the beautiful music." The real name of the album was *Beautiful Thoughts.* I had played it for the first time years before on a night in Vegas when I was having trouble sleeping. Its beautiful spa-type music instantly became our lullaby, but I had not played it since just before Harry's death.

When the music began to play, I knew that Date Night had finally come to an end. I snuggled under the covers and could hear his soothing voice, sounding as if all were right with the world.

Ah, the beautiful music plays once more. Thank you, my Punkin. What a fun night!

Chapter 15

Despite the magic of Date Night, the vicious cycle continued the next morning. Not only was it wreaking havoc on my Vegas visit, it had been a debilitating pattern for most of my adult life, repeating with such frequency and predictability that I had come to accept it as just the way it was.

It originated in my early years. My dad's rage always seemed worse when something really good happened for me. But it was best summed up by what my mother said when she saw us laughing and having fun: "Better stop that or someone's going to end up crying!"

I know now that both of my parents loved me and wanted only the best for me. Their actions and beliefs were coming from their own limiting thoughts and patterns, but those messages were like the worst kind of one-two punch ever. The resulting beliefs—to not be happier than my father, and that having fun and being happy would cause something bad to happen—were deeply embedded in me as a child. Those beliefs were still driving my thoughts and behaviors, forty years later.

And they were hard at work in Vegas while I slept after Date Night. By the next morning, they had totally eclipsed the sparkle of the previous evening. I woke in a paralyzing darkness of guilt, dread, anxiety, and the feeling that I had done something horribly wrong.

Once again, I had landed right back in the doghouse, and was positive that I was going to end up crying.

Feeling totally incapable of facing the day, I burrowed farther under the covers. I worried, and I fretted. I chastised myself for having fun. For missing my continuing education sessions. For wanting to be happy and fulfilled. For procrastinating about selling our real estate, turning off Harry's cell phone, and everything in between. For returning to my Alaska client after Harry's death. For believing in the magic I had experienced the night before. I even chastised myself for missing Harry. I punished myself about all of this and more, as I lay in a silent heap of hysteria.

All the while, another part of me was watching this unfold with quiet fascination. This higher part of me knew that everything about the night before had been real, and that everything up to that point had been perfect. I had been exposed to so many divine moments for a reason. My heart was the true compass, not the punishing voice. The version of Cynthia that surfaced each night in Vegas was the truer version of me than the daytime one ever would be. This higher part of me was the same one that came to my rescue the night Harry died, and so many times since then. Just when I was about to give in to the darkness and call off the entire day, it came to my rescue again by saying in a still, small voice, *Get out of bed.*

I threw back the covers and launched into action, ordering room service and showering. I dressed festively and reviewed my schedule while I ate. As I stepped into the palatial hallway of the Venetian and closed the door behind me, I felt like a Roman gladiator who had risen from the floor of the Coliseum to fight once more. Only there wasn't a raucous crowd cheering me on. There was just that small voice whispering to me, *There you are! Now, let's go make it a great day!*

To be honest, I was a little unnerved that I could go so quickly from being a heap of hysteria to a Roman gladiator. I wondered if I were manic-depressive on top of everything else. It would take many years and a lot of hard work before I realized that an immediate change of state was available to me at any time. I could be in complete control of how I felt and how I reacted to life's circumstances, including the worst of what the punishing voice could hurl my way. But that day, I was just glad to be vertical and on my way again.

I didn't have any trouble getting out of bed the next morning—my last full day in Vegas. With nothing between breakfast and a dinner reservation at Canaletto's, I had a stretch of open road to make good on a promise I had made to myself—to complete a summary for the first book before I left Vegas.

For hours after breakfast, I sat at the Grand Lux Café, writing down my thoughts and observations about the week, thinking it would be good to clear my mind and heart before working on the book summary. As I processed the week, allowing as much honesty into my observations as possible, I came to a significant realization.

Every one of my reunions reminded me that there had been a Cynthia before or apart from Harry, and that my need for connection and love could be met if only I would open my heart to it. I thought back to times in my life, before I met Harry, when I had been the one organizing the fun. Creating experiences for my nieces and nephews. Hosting family gatherings or being a calm guiding light among colleagues and staff.

No doubt I blossomed during my years with Harry. I'd learned so much from him, and the time in Vegas had demonstrated that. At times, I actually felt like Harry. But this trip was also a perfect opportunity to remember "me."

I opened a journal file created months earlier and found two sentences that said it all: *It is as if I have become the child we didn't have. The best part of each of us.* In that moment, I understood the perfection of the week, divinely designed to bring clarity of heart and soul.

Later that evening, I strolled into Canaletto for my "last supper." Beautiful music floated through the air as a violin and flute duet performed in the square. I sipped prosecco while I thought about the emotional morning and the quiet afternoon that followed at a sun-drenched table in the beautiful Venetian garden. The dark moments during the week seemed to have been outshone by the abundance of magical moments. I was feeling triumphant. In fact, I had decided that I was "winning."

As the evening continued, I found it more and more difficult to embrace the concept of my next-day departure. I was scheduled to return to Sitka, but I didn't feel ready. I hadn't come close to processing everything that had occurred during the trip, including what happened at the Celine Dion show. *Especially* what happened at the show. In Sitka, I would dive right into the mountain of work and bury the deep, raw emotion that needed to be expressed.

I was exhausted, and knew it would take every bit of energy I had left to get packed and make an early-morning flight. On top of that, I didn't have my book summary finished. Suddenly, it was like I was transported back 12 years as I thought, *I don't want to leave!*

I saw Harry's mischievous grin in response. *Then stay!*

And so I did. My new plan provided for a more leisurely departure. What actually happened is that I ate and drank generously on Saturday, stayed up quite late, and barely woke up in time for another reunion made possible by my change in schedule.

Sunday night came and went, and I still didn't have my book summary done. I wasn't packed. I still didn't want to go straight back to Sitka. I was stalling, and my consumption of food and beverage had continued to increase.

I changed my Monday flight to Tuesday, and I booked a backup flight for Wednesday. Afterward, I headed out to dinner and found the perfect spot to enjoy a lovely meal and finish the book summary. But shortly after sitting down, I felt a wave of sadness. It was time to face whatever was causing my reluctance to leave.

I knew a couple of reasons. First and foremost, Vegas reminded me of Harry, and my time at the Venetian reminded me of my beautiful times in Italy. I had created my own little neighborhood at the Venetian. I had reconnected with dear friends and made new ones.

The feelings of being alone and disconnected had vanished. What had emerged was a Cynthia who had last been seen jumping on the damn train in Italy nine months before. I knew she was one more thing that would get buried under the mountain of work awaiting me in Alaska.

And then there was Celine. It's not like I met her or got a selfie, but I thought about her "getting back to work" without her husband, her mentor—a man who had been with her for most of her life. I wondered how she was doing, especially after the show when the curtain went down.

I finished my dinner and pushed my plate aside. I fired up the laptop, determined to finish the book summary. I was close. But once again, I found myself resisting. I had grown tired and emotional, but I decided to "lean for the tape," as Harry and I used to say. A short while later, I stared at the laptop screen, stunned. Unbelievably, it was done. I re-read the last paragraph. Instead of feeling accomplishment as I had expected, I felt a rock in the pit of my stomach. I quickly snapped the laptop shut, overcome with a feeling that I had just done something horribly wrong.

I cried myself to sleep that night, and I woke the next morning fairly convinced that I would not be getting on a plane that day. That is, until I had a phone call with my friend Juli. She had noticed that I was still posting on social media from Vegas, long after I should have been back in Sitka. She texted, asking if I had time for a chat.

A short time later, we exchanged pleasantries before she asked, "So what's going on?" I knew I was busted. The false bravado behind which I answered the call crumbled, and my voice started shaking as I told her *exactly* what was going on.

"You need to get out of that hotel. Today."

It was the first time she had ever spoken to me so directly. Or so firmly. Juli and I were only acquaintances when Harry passed away. But we developed an instant bond over a three-hour coffee break several weeks after his death. When she learned that I was still in Braselton, she sent word to me through Paula that she would like to visit with me. And on a beautiful March afternoon, while the cardinal frolicked in the backyard, this woman who I hardly knew comforted and advised me on things that she had found helpful when she was widowed in her twenties.

I listened intently and was thankful for her willingness to share. Eventually, she confided that her first husband had been one of two American officers killed in the North Korea Axe Murder Incident of 1976. Occurring in the Joint Security Area of the Korean Demilitarized Zone, it was an incident that almost led to war.

I was horrified and in awe of this woman who had chosen to share such a horrific event in her life, in an attempt to smooth the path for me. I was also incredibly grateful. I knew she had walked the path. I trusted her. She had a wisdom, a gentle demeanor and an approach to probing my thoughts and intentions that didn't feel intrusive or judgmental. And it didn't hurt that her voice was soft, smooth and full of comfort.

But that morning, almost exactly two years after we had that first coffee, I knew she meant business, and that she was right. Before we got off the phone, she insisted that I tell her, step by step, what I was going to do to ensure that I would be on a plane that evening.

It worked. I was on a plane to Seattle that night, but my final destination was Anchorage. Not Sitka.

For years, I joked with Juli that, had she not intervened, I may still be shuffling around the Venetian, in my slippers and bathrobe, hair askew and dragging a bottle of champagne behind me. Back then, it wasn't a laughing matter. I was a complete mess, and the strategy of going to Anchorage was to provide me with an opportunity to get myself together before interacting with my clients in person—I had three of them in Sitka.

I knew that I needed to process the events of Vegas more completely. I had made a good start in the final days there, but was nowhere near finished. I hadn't let myself think at all about the Celine show, or the feeling of having done something horribly wrong by finishing the book summary.

The night I returned to Anchorage, I sat down to write about the Celine concert. I went deeper and deeper into the night until Celine finally returned to the stage for that one last song. My fingers picked up speed and flew across the keyboard as I recorded what I was seeing in my mind's eye and feeling in my heart and soul . . .

As the music began, I turned off my camera. I put down my phone. And I closed my eyes. And for an amazing three minutes or so, I felt like Celine was singing to me and me alone. The tears that came were different than any tears I have cried. They were painfully cleansing, as if they had been stagnant at the bottom of my soul for two years—now drawn way up high. And there were lemon drops and chimney tops and bluebirds . . . lots of bluebirds.

As Celine sang to me, I didn't just see Harry smiling, I could FEEL him smiling and sending me a wealth of reassurance.

"Punkin, the sky is so blue and the dark clouds really are far behind me. And troubles? Well, they have melted away like those tasty lemon drops. Remember how the birds always began singing when they heard your voice? Well, bluebirds are everywhere, always singing of our love. So, please don't cry, my sweet baby! Remember what you said at my memorial service. 'Harry and I spent a lot of time apart. But we were always together.' Nothing has, could or ever will change that.

"So, chase your dreams, my princess, because they really do come true. And when the time comes, just look for me above the chimney tops . . . That's where you'll find me.

"Until then, remember I am close. Just like Celine said— even though René is not with her physically, he is even more present. It's true! We are sitting up here in the balcony having a great time. Even though I don't speak it, you know that I can laugh in French, so we are getting along just fine."

And for a few magical moments I was with Harry again, "Somewhere Over the Rainbow."

By the time I finished typing, I was shaking and sobbing uncontrol-
lably. I jumped up from the computer and paced around the condo,
almost as if I were trying to escape the sobs. But they stayed with me
and only grew deeper. Quite different from the cleansing ones I had
experienced that night in the Coliseum, these were painful. My lungs
hurt. My face hurt. My head hurt. My heart and soul hurt.

Eventually, I walked back to the computer, saved the file without looking at it, and turned off the computer. I continued to cry
throughout the night and when morning came, I was horribly sick.
I couldn't get out of bed for days.

Even when I started feeling better, I could barely get out of bed.

I knew I was in trouble. I contacted Bedford and scheduled multiple hour-long sessions for every day that week, and put some on
standby for the following week. We talked through it all, and little
by little I felt better, but I was still spending a lot of time in bed. And
then one afternoon, I had an experience very similar to that morning
in the Venetian when I threw back the covers and leapt out of bed.
But this time, it wasn't because of my still, small voice. It was a message from David, one of the twins I had reconnected with in Vegas.

David had sent me a beautiful message just as the Celine show
was starting a few weeks before. He had messaged me occasionally
since then. I answered one or two of them, but didn't really engage.
He kept sending them.

Then one afternoon, I decided to respond and learn a little more
about this person who was so kindly continuing to check on me.

I knew that David had sustained a traumatic brain injury from
a car accident many years before. He had endured more surgeries
than one human being ever should, had long-term health effects
from the accident, a host of other muscular-skeletal diseases, and
had recently been diagnosed with PPMS—primary progressive
multiple sclerosis—the kind for which there is no treatment. Even
though facing paralysis and possible blindness one day, he had an

optimistic outlook, a kind heart and a refreshing sense of humor. The accident had ended his promising journey to a career as a physical therapist. So, he had become a certified dog trainer, taught himself photography, loved working with kids and all things related to God.

After reading his message that afternoon in which he shared more details, I felt embarrassed and ashamed. *What problems do I have, compared to this man?* I thought.

Not only did his message motivate me to get out of bed and stay out, it also was the first of what became a daily string of communication between us. He was a very good writer, and I enjoyed reading his messages. When we were younger, David was the incorrigible twin with a nonstop smile, a revolving door of girlfriends, and just enough goofiness to make him adorable. When we reconnected, I had expected his sense of humor. I had not expected his emotional depth, wisdom or faith. I could never have anticipated that half a lifetime later, it would be the still-humorous but now wise man who held out his hand and pulled me out of the abyss.

I confided in him about the darkness I was experiencing. Surprisingly, he already knew, confessing that he was overwhelmed by the sadness he saw in a selfie I'd posted on Date Night, even though everyone else saw "festive and fun." From that first online chat and for several weeks, he raised my spirits almost every day. I sent him books about Alaska. When I finally landed in Sitka at the end of March, he was there virtually and kept me company while we chased a beautiful sunset. In between, he shared more about his faith in God, the pain of losing his brother Bryan, and his admiration for the love that Harry and I had shared.

One day, after I made it back to Sitka, I was talking to David on the phone as I walked along Crescent Harbor. I had just told him how sorry I was for everything he had gone through.

"Cynthia, don't be sorry for me. That accident actually saved my life." He explained that even though it nearly killed him, it put him on a path to his own spiritual awakening and being more clear about what was really important in life.

My daily interactions with David and my sessions with Bedford pierced the darkness that enveloped me after Vegas. David was a living, breathing example of someone who had also decided to not let a tragedy do him in. It was a good time for me to be reminded of the same pledge I had made to myself the night that Harry passed away. Through Bedford's wise counsel, I was able to see more meaning in the events of Vegas, what they triggered, and the blessings in them.

No doubt I could see the incredible beauty of what was happening while I was in Vegas and days later at the keyboard. In those moments of crying in my seat at the show and at the keyboard in Anchorage, I felt a love bigger and deeper than I thought possible. It felt like a total and complete connection to the Universe, and showed me that the ordinary, ho-hum of everyday life was actually quite extraordinary. In that moment, I felt even more love than when Harry was alive. It was overwhelming. Incredible. Beautiful. I felt unworthy of it, and a bit afraid of it.

I was in a place I had never been before, experiencing the bliss people expect when they die and go to heaven. Only I wasn't dead. Somehow, I had just experienced heaven on earth.

I also had no doubt in my mind, heart and soul that, as my fingers were flying over the keyboard, I was recording a conversation that had actually occurred on the night of the show, and continued when I was back in Anchorage. It felt as if Harry were in heaven, and that I had been able to "visit" him there.

Despite the power of the cardinal from the back porch in February 2014 and all the other divine moments since then, this dialog was the closest I had come to truly experiencing Harry after his passing. He seemed joyous, full of life, playful and funny, just as he had been on earth. I felt our amazing connection and his love for me. With his enthusiastic spirit shining through, it felt like he was saying, *Punkin, go do your thing. I'll be right here when you get home!*

How could I be sorrowful about Harry being happy and joyful wherever he was?

I couldn't. Through my sessions with Bedford, I realized it was necessary to accept the gift of this chat with Harry so that I could put my grief in perspective. This was my only chance to see even more truth hiding beneath it.

My life with Harry had made all the unsatisfactory things in my life seem okay. Manageable. I didn't have to look at the unhappiness with my career choice, or the pervasive feeling that I was in the doghouse. After losing him all over again after Vegas and the second wave of grief that came with it, I was no longer distracted from what needed to be addressed in my own life.

From this perspective, I could see even more clearly the pattern of opening and closing, of going from lightness to darkness that was playing out daily in Vegas. It had occurred after my birthday trip to Italy and had been recurring in longer cycles for as long as I could remember.

In Vegas, the darkness into which I awoke each morning was actually grief. But it wasn't wholly the grief of losing Harry. It was also grief for losing me, the most authentic part of me, that had appeared the night before, but had already retreated by the time the sun came up—hiding under an ill-fitting career and my own self-limiting beliefs.

I had identified the feelings of pain and sorrow as being from grieving Harry, when they were actually about not honoring the most authentic part of myself. The part of me that refused to believe that the happiness, the laughter and the feelings of joy were all illusions. That the divine—which had filled me with a beautiful, white light of truth—was coincidence to be shrugged away.

Even so, the feelings of losing Harry were still pretty acute while in Vegas, and only grew more intense after returning to Anchorage. Later I would realize that the feeling of doom that hit me right after completing the book summary came from a knowing that something very painful but very necessary had happened while I was there.

It had taken two years and a trip to Vegas to admit that Harry was gone. And . . .

It had taken two years and a trip to Vegas to realize that I was still here.

It would take me many more years and trips into the darkness of the abyss to realize that the profound grief of losing Harry had morphed into the profound grief of losing myself, over and over again.

Ultimately, that grief was the most debilitating of all.

Chapter 16

The lessons from Vegas were painful, but they were worth it. I was beginning to see that if we fill ourselves with what makes our heart sing, it's easier to let go of what doesn't. During that spring in Sitka, for the first time, I not only heard the sweet melody of surrender to my heart's desire, but I began to truly respond to it.

After returning from Vegas, I notified my clients that I would be working remotely, and would be less available for a couple of months. It was a bold move for me. I couldn't remember a time when I'd voluntarily put my needs ahead of my clients'. But I wanted and needed to get back to Georgia. My mother's health had begun to decline, and I had a long list of personal affairs at the house in Braselton that had been on hold since Harry passed away. I thought the time and distance would also provide an excellent opportunity for me to plan a career transition.

Within days of sharing my intention with the hospital's accounting staff, Ida, the controller, announced her retirement. She had worked at the hospital for 30 years and she led the accounting department. The hospital was heading toward year-end and its annual audit, so her departure was going to leave a gaping hole at a critical time.

Because I felt an insatiable desire to help others, especially in their time of need, I offered to cut my remote work short. This would provide transition time with Ida, and ensure that all year-end activities went off without a hitch. I would ride back into Sitka on my white horse, weeks earlier than planned, to save the day. Fueled by adrenaline, and despite giving up some of the time I'd set aside, I headed to Georgia. In a prior lifetime, I would have just canceled my trip. It was a step in the right direction.

I was looking forward to being back in Georgia. Besides spending time with my mother and handling many personal affairs, I was going to see Phillip again. This time, he was bringing David with him. During our reconnection in Vegas, we were pleasantly surprised to discover that they both lived just over an hour from the house in Braselton.

When I saw them pull into the driveway, I bounded down the garage stairs to meet them out back. Even though it had been over thirty years since I had seen them together, I was struck by how different the twins were in appearance, also seeming to reflect differences in their personalities.

Phillip was a solid refrigerator of a man, standing at 6'4." David had feigned being afraid of him, saying that he was "freakishly strong." His short-cropped auburn hair, seeming unchanged from high school, topped a lightly freckled face that often reflected a serious nature. But when he smiled from under a thin mustache, the serious countenance disappeared and hazel eyes twinkled with mischief.

In the weeks of getting to know David after Vegas, I learned that his body was wracked with disease and pain. He was slow to exit the car, but after he unfurled his 6'7" frame from the passenger seat that day, it was hard for me to imagine him being afraid of Phillip or anyone else. He, too, was solidly built, though a bit more gangly. In high school, his hair was curly and black. Now, mostly covered by a baseball hat, it appeared to be close-shaved and tinged with gray, as was his mustache and goatee. When I saw his smile for the first time in thirty-five years, I noticed how it matched his smiling hazel eyes.

After hugs, we visited for a short time at the house before heading to lunch at where else but Papa Jack's. As usual, the crew took great care of us all while teasing me about bringing my bodyguards. It was nonstop sweet tea, fried chicken, hugs and fun. At one point, I found myself with my head on the table, laughing hysterically. Another time, I glanced over to see Phillip laughing so hard he was crying.

It occurred to me later that no one observing the raucous table would have guessed that it had been 35 years since the three of us had had any real contact. And that left me wondering—what was the connection, and when did it really start? Why did it feel like something clicked into place in Vegas just months before?

I don't profess to understand the mysteries of life. But I know that the time we spent together as freshmen in high school created a bond that lasted for 35 years. I suspect that my relationship with their brother Bryan was also a part of the bond. Bryan was two years older than us, and my first serious boyfriend. He had pursued me for years before I finally said yes, midway through my senior year in high school. We dated for a couple of years after I graduated high school and were in touch periodically for twenty years after we broke up.

Because of our bond, Phillip reached out to me when Bryan passed away in 2011. That day, Harry and I sat in the kitchen in Anchorage for over an hour while I talked about Bryan and the rest of the family.

The next day, I headed back to Nome. After Harry dropped me off at the airport, I wandered into the Hudson News store with Bryan and his family still heavy on my heart. Almost immediately, a bright yellow book caught my attention. I picked up *The Happiness Project*, read the back cover and put it back, thinking, *I have enough happiness right now!*

After continuing to scan the shelves, my gaze once again landed on the yellow book. Reluctantly, I picked it up. A couple of pages in, I stopped and stared at the nearly blank page with a quote by Robert Louis Stevenson:

There is no duty we so much underrate as the duty of being happy.

I may as well have had another book in my hands—my 1981 high school yearbook. Because the only other place I had ever seen that quote was in that book. In my mind's eye, I could see Bryan looking back at me from the page and the wise words of Robert Louis Stevenson directly below his senior portrait. Bryan's selection of those words for his senior quote had caught the attention of my sophomore self. But they really hit home with me as I stood in that Alaska bookstore, over 30 years later. If happiness had eluded Bryan, in that moment, I was certain that it no longer did.

I didn't know then how many more times over the years ahead I would find myself in the middle of similar experiences. That day, I simply felt my eyes fill with tears, my body course with chills, and my heart beat wildly fast as I became completely certain that I had been divinely guided to pick up that book. To receive Bryan's message.

When I flipped one page backward in the book, I knew I was also supposed to deliver it to his intended recipients. I found another one-liner on a blank page that I had entirely missed the first time through:

For My Family

I bought the yellow book that day. And while I never read it, it was my constant companion for a couple of years—on my nightstand in Nome for almost a year before making its way to my nightstand in Anchorage. After Harry passed away—and despite realizing that unlike that day in the airport, I was now very short on happiness—I put it on a shelf, behind the closed door of a closet. I had never mustered the courage to share the story with the family. It seemed too soon right after Bryan passed. Then as the years went by, it seemed that too much time had passed.

But when Phillip and I reconnected in Vegas, he mentioned how touching my cardinal stories were. David quickly became a big fan of them as well. I knew it was time, so I shared the story—first with their mother, and then with each of them. Their reactions confirmed what I knew in my heart by then: that we all want to believe that our loved ones are still with us.

And so, it was as if we were all guided back to each other. I was able to connect them to the Bryan that they loved and, in many ways, they connected me to Harry with their large physical presence, wicked sense of humor, gentlemanly ways and big hearts. As I would come to realize over the years afterward, the feeling I had in the store in Anchorage was the absolute certainty of being connected to the divine.

So, I was not at all surprised when we were back at the house after lunch at Papa Jack's to hear Phillip say, "Your cardinal is in the tree."

David and I were sitting side by side on one of the red leather sofas in the great room looking at photos. Phillip was in an armchair across the room from us. I was facing the windows to the porch and backyard and glanced up, expecting to see the cardinal in his usual place—among the leylands or in the crabapple tree. When I didn't see him, I returned to looking at photos with David.

A few minutes later, Phillip said, "He's still there."

And then a few more minutes later . . .

"Does he always sing that much?"

Finally, I couldn't contain my curiosity or excitement. I had been back for several weeks and hadn't seen a single cardinal during that time.

That day, the cardinal was sitting in an unusual place: in an evergreen tree at the end of the porch. Positioned perfectly for only Phillip to see him, and singing at the top of his little-bird lungs.

"Whatever you do, don't open that door, Phillip!" David warned and giggled nervously. "Harry's gonna come in here and peck our eyes out!"

I burst out laughing. "No . . . I don't think he's jealous that you're here, I think he's probably singing a message to Phillip, like . . . "What the hell are you doing in my chair?"

David's eyes grew wide. "That's Harry's chair?!"

"Well, it *was*," I said.

Phillip bounced out of the chair and we all laughed. Despite David's warning, I opened the door to the porch. For the first time, the cardinal did not fly away upon hearing it open. I was nearly halfway across the porch and able to get a beautiful photo of him, before he took flight. I returned to the great room, where we laughed and joked about the cardinal. It felt like the sun was shining a bit brighter and the birds were singing louder and more sweetly . . . not just outside on a beautiful June day, but inside my heart, as well.

I think on some level, I had thought maybe the magical days of the cardinal were over, because he hadn't appeared since I returned. I didn't plan to be an old gray-haired lady sitting on the back porch wearing black and waiting for my red-feathered friend to appear. I never once thought that Harry had "come back" as a cardinal. But I had come to believe that the cardinal was a sign from above, delivered in a "Very Harry" way—easily recognizable, and sent at precisely the right moments—when I needed a hug, a smile or an "Atta girl."

That day, it was all of that and more.

When David and Phillip walked into the house, it was as if a black-and-white picture turned to color as the house came to life before my eyes. Once again there were smiles and laughter and love—the best kind of decoration any house could have.

And then there was that special accent of color that arrived on the wings of a red bird perched just outside the porch.

An accent to affirm that even after my darkest days, the sun would shine again. The tears would turn to laughter. The sorrow, to joy.

An accent to greet David and Phillip. To say, *You are welcome here, and thank you so very much for loving my Punkin and making her laugh again.*

The cardinal continued to sing after David and Phillip left, though he stayed hidden while doing so. His song made me think about the hardest but perhaps most rewarding lessons I learned in the wake of losing Harry.

Yes, the cardinal sang a song sent from above. A song to remind me to love and to trust and to have faith. Hard-fought lessons that helped me know, at the bottom of my heart and the depth of my soul, that our best way through so many things in life—perhaps through all things in life—is not to hold on so tightly, but to let go completely.

To love.

To trust.

To have faith.

Kind of like the two-and-a-half-year game of "peek-a-boo" with my red-feathered friend. My ears could hear his beautiful song. My heart was open to the love he brought from above. And on days like that beautiful afternoon in June after David and Phillip departed, I had trust and faith that even though I could not see him . . . I knew that he was there.

A few days later, I didn't have to have faith to know he was there.

I had been for a two-mile walk in the heat of the day. There was a nice breeze blowing, so I sat down on the front porch steps and sipped my water, pleased with my midday efforts. After a few minutes, I decided to check the bird feeder before heading upstairs to my office and an afternoon of client work.

I walked around to the garage, grabbed the bag of Songbird Delight and headed into the back yard. I felt a little guilty when I noted the empty feeder and realized that it had probably been empty since before I returned from Alaska.

I filled it to the rim and headed back inside. I was on my way to my office when I stopped at the bottom of the stairs, near the front door, to make a call. I was leaning against the chest that sits just inside the front door when I heard a chirp, and caught something out of the corner of my eye.

This time he was in plain sight, on the front porch—on the first step, almost right where I had been sitting. It looked like he was eating a worm.

I had never witnessed a visit to the front porch. Thankfully I was quick enough to snap a couple of photos before he flew away. And then, in a bewildered daze, I walked two steps to the front door and glanced out to see if he had landed somewhere close by. I didn't see him, but what I did see sent chills down my spine.

It was the key to the front door, sitting on the top step. I must have put it there when I sat down to relax after the walk. It was like the cardinal was saying, *Oh Cynthee! Don't forget the key!* And then when looking at the pictures, I zoomed in to see that he had not been eating a worm after all. It was dark bird seeds—just like the seeds that now filled the feeder to the rim.

I could only conclude that he swooped in and grabbed them from the feeder immediately after I left the backyard, flew to the front porch, and put them down for me to see them. And with proper manners, he had gathered them up before he flew away. I fancied that he was alerting me about the key and expressing gratitude. *Thank you! These seeds are quite tasty! But what took you so long?!*

Well, maybe it was that and more.

I was on an unbelievable journey that had been paved with heartache and moments of beauty beyond belief. All along, I felt in my heart of hearts that there had to be something remarkable in store for me. That I still had things to do. That my story was not over. I had to think that, because it was the only way I could make sense of the pain.

Even so, as "remarkable" began to unveil itself, I doubted it. Even when the blessings rolled in. Even when the signs were coming out of the woodwork. Even when things just seemed to fall into place, I challenged that it could be possible. Because on some level, I wondered . . .

Why me? Why in the world me? Didn't I already have enough remarkable?

And then the cardinal showed up on the steps and I heard the whisper again.

Oh, but there's more, Cynthia. So much more. The key is on the first step. Yes indeed, the key to getting from where you are to where you are meant to be, is taking that first step.

It occurred to me that day that the first step wasn't some her-culean task to be accomplished. Rather, it could be nothing more than to stop asking "Why?" and to start asking "Why not?" To stop holding on so tightly and to let go completely.

It was wise counsel indeed, as I certainly had a long list of to-dos ahead of me. But the visits from the twins and the cardinal had infused me with energy, and prompted me to consider a different approach. Perhaps I could learn to swap my long list of to-dos for a letting go of sorts. To invite more of my intuition in. To be guided more by my heart than my head. And so I turned toward July, ready to celebrate my birthday and eager to see what my next trip around the sun would bring.

Shortly after my birthday, I got a taste of what that would be. The "letting go" started and didn't stop all year. But it wasn't exactly the letting go that I had in mind.

Ten days after my birthday, my mother died.

In less than 24 hours, she went from home, to the emergency room, to hospice and then to heaven. As I sat by her side the night before she passed, it was hard to imagine just a couple of days prior we were laughing as if there were no tomorrow, not knowing that tomorrows were actually in short supply.

Earlier that evening at the hospice house, I read that talking to or reading to the patient was recommended. I visited the nursing station and asked for a Bible. We never went to church as a family, and the only praying we did together was saying grace before dinner. But one of the things my mother saved from her younger days was a small book of prayer. Memories of her mother, visiting us from Canada and on her knees praying every night before bed, passed through my mind. Some-how it seemed important for me to read the Bible to Momma that night.

I sent a message to David who had become my "personal preacher," asking for recommendations. He responded almost immediately; *The book of John is known as the book of love. I'd start there.*

That night, as I read the Bible to my mother, I was oblivious to the nurses who came and went. Later they confessed how touching it was to walk in and hear me reading. When I wasn't reading, I talked to her, as I had done so many times on the phone, in the car, at the kitchen table. I told her about my dreams and plans, and promised her I was really going to be okay.

Then there was our chat about heaven. Excitement filled my voice as I described what I thought it would be like. "And even better than that!" I had said through my tears as she lay quietly.

I laughed about her seeing Daddy again and wondered out loud what his first words to her would be. I asked her to please tell Harry that I knew he had stayed close, and that I thought using the cardinals was quite clever of him.

I napped at 4:00 a.m. for an hour. When I woke, she was noticeably different. Closer. And yet, I wasn't ready to let her go.

"Let's take a coffee, H!" I had suggested as cheerfully as I could. I returned to the room with my cup and sat with her until other family members arrived.

Later that afternoon, while I rested in a hotel, and with two of her grandchildren and my sister Tanya by her side, angels whisked my mother off to that incredible destination I had described. She passed on the same day in July that Bryan had six years before.

To most, my mother was quiet and demure. But I always knew that underneath, she still was that adventurous soul who, with only a plane ticket and a promise he'd be there, boarded a flight in Newfoundland, Canada and headed to Savannah, Georgia. As promised, my father had been there to pick her up. I'm sure he was there once more, to take her hand, swing her into his arms, and waltz her on to the dance floor in the clouds.

I still miss everything about her.

I could write pages and pages about a woman who was so much more on the inside than she ever showed on the outside. Even during her final days, she kept smiling, laughing and joking, never showing concern or fear, or giving us any sign that something was wrong.

In the end, she died exactly how she lived.

I took a photo of her 60 days before she passed. It's one of the most precious photos I've ever taken. We were in the bride's dressing room as my soon-to-be niece prepared for her big day. I thought my mom looked so regal, and she seemed already in a frame sitting by the large mirror. When I started taking pictures, she put up a fuss and wouldn't smile. Finally, I said, "Hildie, you may as well smile, because I'm going to keep snapping away until you do. Love the camera, Momma!"

And then it happened.

A beautiful, knowing smile. A look of triumph in her eyes.

Now, when I see that picture, I imagine that she was actually saying, *I did it, Cynthee! I've had an amazingly beautiful, adventurous life. I am happy. And I'm ready. All is well.*

I'll always be thankful that my family entrusted me to be with my mother on her last night on earth. I continue to miss everything about her. But I know her legacy lives on. And I know she lives on. In heaven. In my heart. And everywhere in between.

While I was reading to my mother on her last night, I received a message from my dear friend Sandi, who was married to Pops, my first husband's father. Pops was in the hospital, and not doing well.

I had known and loved them both for over half my life. They became family through my first marriage, but remained family because of our friendship, love for one another, and the joy of spending time together, no matter how many years fell in between.

Sandi called me the day after she and Harry spoke on the phone for the first time. "I just have to tell you that I'm in love with your husband!"

"Join the club!" I laughed. "It's a big one!"

Sandi traveled to Braselton immediately after learning about Harry's death. I had promised her I would return the favor when the time came.

So, the morning after my mother's funeral, I headed south to Orlando, Florida. I spent the next week at Pop's bedside, mostly in the hospital and some at home. For extended periods of time, I sat with my hand in his as we talked and remembered and made promises. Other times, I just sat back, watching and listening, as two people who shared a precious love walked the tightrope of holding on and letting go. When I left Orlando that July, I felt certain I wouldn't see Pops again.

A few weeks later, I got the call, just before flying back to Sitka and right into year-end audit preparation for my client. Sandi understood my professional priorities and insisted that I return to Alaska as they were not going to have the memorial service right away. I was already later than expected returning to Sitka because of my mother's death and the trip to see Sandi and Pops. By the time I got back, Ida had retired. Even though I missed the transition time with her, the remaining accounting team rose to the occasion, and we completed the audit and regulatory filings without a hitch.

By Thanksgiving, I was ready to return to Braselton to be with family and friends. A few days before departure, I received heartbreaking news from Savannah. Glenda, a dear friend and former employee, was entering hospice care. And John, also a dear friend and one of my first mentors in the healthcare industry, had passed away.

I went straight to Savannah and spent a magical morning with Glenda. A few weeks later, I returned to Savannah to deliver the eulogy at John's memorial service and just before Christmas, I returned to Savannah for Glenda's funeral.

That's when I hit the wall. In less than six months, four people who meant the world to me had passed away. By "coincidence," I was with three of them shortly before they passed. I delivered eulogies for two of them. I had barely caught my breath from Harry's unexpected death, and the passing of another former employee and dear friend Betty, who had passed away six months after Harry.

I was reeling from the string of deaths. My husband. My mother. My first father-in-law. Two of my best friends and former employees. And my mentor who I had loved and admired for twenty-five years.

Through it all, I had continued to work at a frenetic pace while living like a gypsy—trying to figure out where home was, professionally and geographically. I had been flying by the seat of my pants, doing nothing perfectly, but everything the very best I could with everything I had.

I spent Christmas Day by myself, in bed, in a hotel in Savannah. I was probably a little depressed, but mostly just exhausted. Somehow, I got myself going by early evening and walked to the Chart House for dinner. It's the restaurant where Harry and I met in person, and was one of the few places open that night. Shortly after I sat down, David called to wish me a merry Christmas. I was thankful for his perfectly timed call. Afterward, I returned to the hotel and sat in the lobby, by the fire, until the wee hours of the morning, thinking and writing.

I knew I had a choice about how to view the events of my life. One of those choices was to think of them as horrific. But the truth was, in the midst of every single storm, I received refuge.

When I lost a mentor, two more appeared. When I doubted deep connections with others, David and Phillip appeared. When I missed the sense of family I had with Harry, John's family welcomed me. When I needed a hug, my phone rang. When I felt trapped in my career, outlets to express my gifts appeared.

When I lost people in my life, I got back plenty. As I sat there on Christmas night, I realized that the plenty came in beautiful packages of love and joy. All the right colors. All a perfect fit. And they didn't come just at Christmas; they came any time I was open to receive them, and courageous enough to peek inside. The gifts were actually about giving, not receiving. To create. To express. To comfort. Opportunities to do the things that my heart had been craving. They were a perfect fit, indeed.

With the relentless string of deaths behind me, I headed into the New Year with a renewed sense of purpose. The six months after my mother passed away had further convinced me that writing and speaking were foundational to my professional future. Therefore, it seemed a perfect time to reactivate my game plan. To take some quiet time, listen to the whispers from my soul, and finally follow my heart.

Chapter 17

When I returned to Alaska after the first of the year, the sheer magnitude of work to be done was daunting, even for me. Ida's position had not been filled, so I was covering it, and my list of projects was growing. While I was able to provide great value to my client, I was showing little evidence that I valued myself. My health began to show signs that I was out of alignment as I experienced episodes of shutdown in which I was not able to function—physically or mentally—for days. My list of personal to-dos continued to grow. I was fueled by the desire to help others, and I knew I was making a difference for my clients. But the more I accomplished for them, the more my own life seemed to be falling apart.

By the time May arrived, I was in crisis mode. I continued to serve my clients with a smile. I continued to write well-received posts on social media. To be in constant contact with close friends. But the amount of overwhelm and anxiety I was feeling on the inside was almost more than I could bear. And it didn't help that I now had a friend coming to visit me. My condo in Anchorage was in disarray, as I was in the middle of a "purge." There was no way that I could take completely off during my friend's visit, as I had a big budget presentation to make. I didn't feel prepared at all. In fact, just days before she was scheduled to depart Baltimore, I almost called it off.

I had met Mary Beth just months before Harry and I got married. She worked for my very first client at a hospital just outside of Washington, D.C. One evening, she invited me to dinner, and the rest was history. We quickly became friends, always striking the perfect balance between professional and personal. Ours was simply a friendship "meant to be."

The year before her Alaska visit, she had gone from one doctor telling her "There's nothing I can do" to a cowboy surgeon telling her, "I think I can get it." She had undergone a series of life-saving surgeries to remove a tangly growth that had wrapped around her spinal cord at the base of her neck. Just before the surgeries began, she commented on social media that Harry was one of the angels who would be holding her hand through it all.

They had formed quite a connection before he passed away. Super smart and with a great sense of humor, she was a good conversational match for Harry. She saw things very clearly and was not afraid to speak her mind. But she always did so in a way that was respectful and laced with care and concern.

In the end, I decided that there was no way that I was going to pull the plug on her trip. Mary Beth was lucky to be alive. She had been through hell. I wanted her to experience the majesty of Alaska. I thought to myself, *If any of my friends could come to Alaska and still enjoy it while I am embattled in a firestorm of intense work and personal chaos, it would be Mary Beth.*

I couldn't have been more right about that. With her perfect sense of adventure and ability to roll with what life throws her way, Mary Beth sidestepped boxes in the Anchorage condo and slept on the pull-out sofa in Sitka. When Edna, a friend of mine from Nome who had worked for my client there, texted that her cancer was now terminal, I asked Mary Beth, "How would you feel about a day trip to Nome?"

She had simply nodded and said, "Let's go!"

One night, as she sat in his chair in the kitchen, we talked about Harry, about loving him and losing him. I was once again reminded, as we both let the tears roll unashamedly down our faces, how many lives Harry had touched in a most profound way.

"We both needed this," Mary Beth said at one point. She was more right than she knew.

I had no idea, when I contemplated calling off the trip, just how much I needed Mary Beth's visit. Because she understood the industry, the demands of the work, and me, she was the perfect companion during those intense days. In the end, however, the perfection had little to do with work.

On the morning after my budget presentation, we took a 6:00 a.m. flight out of Sitka and arrived in Anchorage around 9:00 a.m., just in time for breakfast at Snow City Cafe, one of my favorite spots. It was packed as usual, but before long, Mary Beth and I were seated at a two-topper right in the thick of the morning action.

I was past sheer exhaustion. For six weeks, I had been averaging about four hours of sleep a night, and had facilitated several highly emotionally charged issues for my client on top of the budget work. I was stressed about Mary Beth's visit, even though she was rolling with the punches. And the conversations about Harry, while very welcome, had also been emotionally draining.

But when the server set my coffee cup down, all the exhaustion disappeared instantly. Not because of the coffee, but due to the mug in which it arrived. Mary Beth and I just stared at each other.

"Oh my God!" she squealed.

As I stared at the coffee cup in front of me, I could hear Harry's voice: *I'm on both sides so I can keep an eye on both of you!*

I looked over at my friend, noting that she was wearing cardinal colors of red and black to match the red birds on my coffee mug. No doubt Harry was with us, just as he had been during my years of grief. And while holding Mary Beth's hand during surgery, knowing that she would sit across from me a year later—showing me that miracles do happen, if only we believe.

During breakfast that morning, Mary Beth confessed part of her intention for the visit: to convince me to leave Alaska and my accounting career. She shared her opinion that my writing was comforting and inspiring to others, and that I needed to be closer to friends who could provide the support and love I needed.

But she also confessed that, after being there for a few days, she understood the allure. She could see the connection I had with my clients, and with the majesty of all that is Alaska. In the end, she concluded, "All I'm saying is that you should be writing full time. Period. Find a way to do it."

After breakfast, I walked her to the church around the corner, and then headed back to the condo to tidy up before we started our Anchorage adventure.

I was thinking a lot about what Mary Beth said when my phone rang. I smiled and fired off a text, *I'll call you right back.* I scurried to the condo, turned on the fireplace, and sank into a chair. When she answered, I said, "Hello Duber!"

She got right to the point. "Have you started on your book yet?" When I stuttered into an explanation about work, she cut me off. "What are you waiting for? Are you afraid of something?"

It was hard not to connect the dots. The birds on the coffee mug. Mary Beth's "Find a way to do it." And now The Duber. I began to reply when she cut me off again.

"I'm editing my daughter's book, and I want to be editing yours, as well. I'm not getting any younger, kiddo."

She suggested that we carve out some time together. To take a cruise or for me to visit with her for a week. We would lay out all of my writing from the years since Harry passed, and begin to piece it together. I knew better than to disagree. Besides, I really wanted to do that.

When Mary Beth returned, I told her about the call from The Duber. I let her know that I had promised her I would find a way. It was the second time that morning I had made such a promise.

Mary Beth smiled. "Good. Then it's settled."

Not long after Mary Beth departed for Baltimore, I made plans to return to Georgia and pick up with the plan that I had devised the year before. To take the first steps in being true to my word. One of the items on my to-do list was to make a decision about the house on Skidaway Island in Savannah.

My tenants were out of town, so I had arranged to meet my dear friend and expert handyman, Wise Old Al, at the house. Al and his wife Nanette had been the first friends that Harry and I made as a couple. Al had retired twice, once from the Marines and once from the City of Springfield, Ohio. Still sporting a Marine crew cut, he spoke in a raspy, Clint Eastwood voice and had a swagger to match. Though retired, he had a very active handyman service on the island. He had been a godsend to me in the years since Harry passed, looking after the house and even me at times, sometimes showing up in the white utility truck, sometimes on his Harley. We were going to make a list of what needed to be done to prepare the house for sale or for me to move back in.

As I talked to Al, I thought about the cardinal, and wondered if he were going to make an appearance. After all, I was sitting in almost the exact spot where Harry's chair used to be, I was talking to one of his best friends and, when I looked out of the window, I could see a bird feeder that Harry and I bought and placed very strategically during the first few days of sharing a home together. The conditions were ripe for the cardinal to swoop in. But he didn't. At least not that day.

I returned to the house the next day to meet Al again. We were both sitting in the same spots we had been the previous day and our conversation was winding down. It would soon be time to go. We had been so busy I hadn't given the cardinal another thought.

That's when I saw him. My face must have lit up as I reached for my phone.

"What is it?" Al asked.

As I took a picture and started the video, I whispered, "A cardinal."

Almost instantly, the bird fluttered out of sight. I walked to the door and spotted him between a flower pot and the deck railing. Al had followed me. The cardinal came back toward us, hopping across the deck. He glanced up before hopping into a flower pot two feet from where we were standing.

Al began to fill in the voice, "Hey there! What's up? Just came to check on you guys."

I added, "Got any coffee?"

Al replied, "Yeah, I got some coffee . . . "

The cardinal spit out some seeds, hopped down from the flower pot, and walked toward us, looking up at us as he approached.

"He sees us here, and is still coming this way," Al said incredulously.

"Unbelievable!" I whispered as I kept the camera on him.

"This is nuts!" Al exclaimed. The cardinal was now literally at our feet, the glass door the only thing between us.

Then he looked up, made eye contact, and flew away.

We turned and stared at each other, then returned to our seats, stunned. We talked about it briefly, but it was so unbelievable that words seemed inadequate. Coming close on the heels of the coffee cup with Mary Beth, it seemed to be an important message for me.

I left Al with instructions that we should proceed with getting the house ready for me to move back when the current tenants moved out. They had been planning to move to Charleston for some time, and I wanted to be ready when they actually did. I also asked him to get me a quote for adding a screened porch in the back. I had a lot of writing to do.

I returned to Braselton, feeling that I had made a little headway by deciding to return to Savannah, eventually. I had just walked in the door when I got the message that Edna, my friend in Nome, had passed away. Even though I was expecting it, the news hit me particularly hard that night. Over the course of the next couple of days, I thought a lot about how to change the trajectory of my life, and I cried about my friend.

Finally, one afternoon, as I was feebly attempting to complete some client work, a wave of anger and frustration washed over me. Despite the professional deadlines, I pushed back from my desk, grabbed a book, a journal and pen David had given me, and headed for the porch.

I was still writing when the sun came up the next morning. After that first night, I got some sleep each night, but I stayed on the porch all day and often wrote by candlelight until well into the evening. I didn't stop for four days.

I was certain friends thought I was inside, curled up in a fetal position, feeling depressed. But by retreating to the porch, I was actually moving forward.

It was one thing to think that I was unhappy, in the wrong career, and off-course in life. It was another thing to see it in black and white. The book I took with me, *Do What You Love and the Money Will Follow*, was ragged and held together with a couple of rubber bands. Its well-worn pages, with underlines and highlights in a variety of colors, showed how many times I had read it over the years. But it had never been about hoping the money would follow; it was about finding what I loved. During those four days on the porch, the book's wisdom and thought-provoking questions seemed new and fresh. Later I would realize that the words of the book had not changed at all. I had just become more ready to receive them.

The book became my teacher. I let it ask me questions, and I answered every one of them and more. I explored my values. I listed all the examples in my life so far when I had taken a risk. As I made the list of risks, I noticed a pattern: the risks that were motivated by faith or confidence turned out well nearly 100 percent of the time.

The risks that were motivated by fear or the feeling of "I should," did not. As I realized the significance of this finding, I could hear Harry assuring me that my sense of intuition, my little voice, would light the way. I could now see that clearly, in black and white, on the pages of my journal.

Ending the risk analysis with two examples, I wrote:

Having faith and walking away from professional situations that were unhealthy not only liberated me, it propelled me into new adventures, my own business, and ultimately nine magical months with Harry before he died. Operating from a state of fear and ignoring my intuition led to my leaving Harry in Braselton and not insisting on aggressive attention to the issue. That cost me the greatest love I've known. And it cost Harry his life.

It was a moment of reckoning for me. There could have been no better lesson for me to understand the power of intuition than this one. I didn't know it at the time, but saying "It was my fault," out loud, or writing it on the page with no one there to tell me it wasn't, eventually unlocked my ability to release more of the tremendous amount of guilt I had been carrying.

They were powerful lessons, and I felt motivated to design a game plan for how to move forward. I revisited the five values I had listed early on. At the top of the list was "honesty," which is basically the practice of telling the truth—in all situations. I knew that in order to practice honesty in my life, I had to know the truth.

The truth had been perfectly laid out on the prior pages. I had described what made me happy. What memories filled me with joy. What actions made me feel as if I counted in my own eyes. What traits or characteristics, when expressed, made me glad to be me. What kind of person I was at my best, and how I looked and acted during those times.

When I revisited the very short list of important goals I had never made time for, my eyes welled up as I focused on the two at the top of the list:

Writing a book or two
Learning piano

When I saw those two goals, I realized that they weren't just goals. I knew that my life would never feel complete unless these activities were an integral part of it—not just a goal to check off the list. And I also knew that the woman who yearned to write a book or two and learn to play the piano would never live an honest life sliding numbers into boxes. No matter how much money she made doing it, or how she rationalized it as helping others, or how much she loved her clients.

This was a turning point for me. I realized that it was critical for me to take the newfound awareness and high emotion and use it to devise a game plan, and to take action on that plan. I knew that I'd feel fear, but I was determined to press ahead. So, for guidance in developing a plan, I used another well-worn and perfectly titled book in my library, *Feel the Fear and Do It Anyway*. I also researched strategies used by those who lived in alignment with their mission and values.

By the time my porch session was over, I had devised a detailed game plan that included how I could gracefully serve my clients while also creating the personal space I needed for continued transformation. This meant that the hospital would have to hire a replacement for Ida, my current engagement would be extended with a firm end date, and more of my work would be completed remotely.

I also outlined in great detail what my ideal home would be, without regard to the real estate I currently owned or specific geographic location. I created a vision for physical vitality, financial freedom and spiritual growth.

Turning to the tactical, I made specific plans for incorporating rituals into each day that would support and nurture me. I also took a few moments to remind myself of the good things that happened during the four days on the porch.

The daily fresh air, sunshine and birdsong lifted my heart and soothed my soul. I ate very healthily, abstained from alcohol, and felt a profound sense of peace and calm. I agreed to carry no more grudges against myself, and I noticed that every bit of bodily pain I had been feeling had disappeared.

The cardinal, true to form, visited often during my time on the porch, singing from the crabapple tree or doing high-speed passes across the yard. Just after my epiphany about living an honest life, I wrote, *I have all that I need to do what needs to be done.*

Since physical vitality was at the top of my list, I returned to Savannah once more before heading back to Alaska. The sole purpose for my trip was to re-engage with the doctor who had treated me for about twenty years before I moved away. He had begun a concierge medicine practice, and the timing seemed perfectly aligned with my recently declared priority of health and vitality.

The visit started off in rare form as I realized that his long-time assistant's last name was Cardinal. But the best part of the visit was the doctor's enthusiasm and care. He was genuinely interested in partnering with me, and at the end of the visit, gave me a hug and said, "This is the beginning of the next phase of your life. And it's going to be great!" But we both agreed that it was going to be up to me.

As I prepared for departure to Alaska, I sat down with my journal and re-read the list of good things that had happened on the porch. The days on the porch had reminded me of who I was. What I wanted. Why I was here. I knew that I had challenging days ahead and that liberating myself to live an honest life would not be easy. I also had come to appreciate, perhaps for the first time, the importance of my career up to that point, and how it could serve me in the future. I had helped build a hospital that made Edna's last days more comfortable, and that had helped so many other patients and families receive care, sometimes end-of-life care, in a beautiful state-of-the-art facility.

But the woman I described in the pages of my journal needed to fulfill a higher purpose—to be expansive, creative and free-spirited. I had just developed a plan to move in that direction. My doctor provided a perfect reminder that it was up to me. So, I headed back to Alaska with a plan in hand, the energy and resolve to accomplish it, and the acknowledgment that if I were going to be a writer, then it was time for me to start acting like one.

Chapter 18

One of the first steps I took to become a writer was to register for a writer's bootcamp in October. While I had been writing for my entire life, I had not had any formal training, except for what I learned from my excellent teachers in school and college, or through occasional business writing seminars over the years of my professional life. I knew I didn't have to fly off to the opposite corner of the country for a conference to begin my training. There were hundreds, if not thousands, of ways for me to do that, right where I was.

But attending the conference wasn't just training for me. It was "acting as if." Pretending that I was already a professional writer. It was a significant step, with equally significant commitments of time and financial resources. Booking the conference was me saying out loud that what I wanted mattered, and that a conference to kickstart my writing career was as natural an event on my calendar as an accounting project.

No doubt the carrot of the conference was behind my drive during those first 60 days back in Anchorage. I focused and finished. I worked hard during the day and accomplished much for my clients. In the evening and under the watchful gaze of the midnight sun, I hit the streets of downtown Anchorage, chasing my goal of walking five miles a day.

I slept well and ate well—experimenting with how many ways I could prepare fresh Alaskan halibut, my favorite. When I had a taste for human interaction, I went to dinner with Donnie G, or sauntered next door to Simon & Seafort's or just up the block to the Crow's Nest on the 20th floor of The Hotel Captain Cook. In either of Anchorage's most popular restaurants, I was sure to find a familiar face behind the bar, or greeting me with a smile at my table. I was also driven by the inner work I'd done on the porch, which had a profound impact on how I viewed my work, myself and my future.

Even so, I knew from prior experience that it didn't take much for me to abandon personal plans when professional needs arose. So, I made sure to view the conference as a professional endeavor. This was a shift in mindset, and a first line of defense against a derailment.

I executed the game plan flawlessly for 60 days, and was confident that I had put the odds for success in my favor. But with another 60 days stretching out in front of me before that southbound flight, I woke up one day feeling a little off. A tiny chink in the armor of confidence and calm had appeared. And then, before I knew what happened, the tiny chink turned into a gaping hole. My confidence disappeared and progress came to a grinding halt. Again.

I've never known what to call it. Over the years I've referred to it in a number of ways: The Resistance. The Shutdown. The Cave. The Spin. It's an insidious feeling of sadness, rebellion, frustration and sorrow, all woven tightly together into an emotional and very heavy wet blanket. It results in a paralysis of sorts—a deep desire to withdraw from any stressors or pressures, and my inability (or perhaps more accurately, my unwillingness) to sit down at my desk and work.

Two return trips to Braselton, during those two months, may have triggered it, or at least contributed to it. For the first time in fourteen years, when I walked into the house on the second trip, it didn't smell like Harry. It didn't smell like home, and that made me sad.

The sadness deepened as I experienced feelings of not belonging—of knowing that Braselton was not my forever home. This was especially emotional for me because it was in Braselton that I had felt the most surrounded by love in the eight months after Harry passed away, and many times since then. I could not have asked for more support, encouragement and love. I had developed deeply personal friendships. My "family" had grown exponentially. It scared me to think of my life without Braselton and all that it represented.

But something happened to me during the four days on the porch and in the two months after my return to Anchorage. A transformation had begun—one so profound that the first and only place that had ever felt like home suddenly didn't. Ironically, I felt alone and isolated in Braselton. I realized that the cocoon of Alaska had provided me, not only with an opportunity to begin again, but also with an opportunity to distance myself, literally and figuratively, from the memories of what was, and the broken dreams of what would never be.

The trips to Braselton didn't seem to be the only triggers. I injured my Achilles tendon and stopped exercising. My journals included notations of surprise that I'd eaten junk food.

But perhaps the biggest trigger of all was an inordinate amount of stress that surfaced during the first week of September. Hurricane Irma was raging as a Category 5 hurricane in the US Virgin Islands. With a condo in St. Thomas and two houses in Georgia, I had three properties potentially in the path of the storm. I was quite concerned about my tenants and other friends in St. Thomas who were most assuredly in harm's way. And I was upset with myself that I had not yet sold the real estate.

I was watching the consequences of my inaction playing out in real time on the Weather Channel from Sitka. I had traveled there, despite my desire to serve my clients remotely. I thought it was the right thing to do, since my engagements would be winding down over the coming months.

Almost immediately upon arrival, I felt the gloom and doom of being back in the "Dungeon," the affectionate nickname we all called the financial offices which were located on the lower level of the hospital. This time, the feelings of darkness were magnified by the helplessness that I felt regarding the storm. Even though the properties escaped relatively unscathed, the relief was not enough to reverse the spiral. During that trip to Sitka, I missed some time in the office due to flu-like symptoms that I believe were a precursor to a full-blown episode of darkness that was waiting for me back in Anchorage.

The shutdowns had been going on with me for my entire adult life. Sometimes they would come after an extended period of intense work. Other times it would be after a noteworthy success or accomplishment.

For a long time after Harry passed away, I didn't seem to have any of them. For the first eight months, grief took center stage while I got my feet under me in Braselton. For a while, when I did have episodes, I attributed them to grief. But then I noticed that they didn't necessarily occur when I felt grief, or after intense periods of work. They were happening after I had done something significant for myself, or had taken a break from the accounting work. Or after I allowed myself to have a vision of a different life. Or after the trip to Italy, and the trip to Vegas.

This was one of the first times I could remember it taking place in advance of a planned event. The work I needed to do was neither difficult nor unpleasant. I loved my clients, and wanted to serve them at the highest level. But I found it almost impossible to sit down at my desk. And so, the list of things to do grew longer, the runway on which to do them grew shorter, and I grew more and more anxious.

Bound and determined to "get to the bottom of it" once and for all, I put my journal and favorite writing pen in the kitchen cubby along with a spare laptop. When I wasn't struggling to get work done at my desk, I was there researching and journaling. I explored articles on self-sabotage and procrastination. I stumbled across a paper on pathological avoidance disorder. I re-read the books *Feel the Fear and*

Do It Anyway and *Building Your Field of Dreams*. And I re-read the mini-book I had written while journaling my way through four days on the porch.

I read about being a "co-creator" with God and about forgiveness. I studied articles such as "Recognizing the Voice of Inspired Insight" and "A Workaholic's Guide to Beating Anxiety."

But I didn't just read the articles and books. Zigging from articles to help me diagnose myself and zagging to articles about crafting a life of fulfillment, I took notes on each one of them, and then studied the notes as if my life depended on it. It sounds dramatic, but I felt as if I were fighting for my life. As if I had some kind of invisible web around me that was preventing me from functioning at the time I most needed to.

There were many times in my life that I attributed it to having reached my maximum propensity to consume accounting work. But I knew the career dissatisfaction was likely only a symptom of the real issue. Whatever it was, I knew that if I didn't identify it and "fix" it, then it was only going to follow me into my writing life. Completing the client work and ending the engagement with Sitka as gracefully as possible was quite important to me. I desperately wanted to understand what was preventing me from doing the very thing I thought would set me free.

After studying a great deal of material, I took a moment to identify the exact emotion that surfaced when I thought about sitting down at the desk to work.

I recognized it immediately as sadness. A sadness that I would lose myself if I sat down to work. That I was abandoning myself by doing so, and that another day would lead to another week, another month, and eventually another year of not living in alignment with my values and gifts.

Then a stronger swirl of emotion emerged—frustration laced with powerlessness—as I saw myself continuing to do something that I really didn't want to do, but not having the voice to say, "No. I choose something else."

I thought again about how much resistance I had to the trip to Sitka. I didn't want to spend my days in the basement producing financials. I didn't want to read policies or decide on personnel issues. I didn't want to immerse myself totally in client work while my personal life was calling out so urgently for me.

In that moment of journaling, I realized that it was the exact scenario that had occurred when Harry passed away. My gut instinct had been to stop everything and give my personal life, my husband, my undivided attention. But I had not. I was at my desk working at a client site at the very time he had collapsed.

I wrote *GUILT* in large letters in my journal. As I sat there staring at the word, I took my pen and started drawing big circles around it. Over and over and over again, bearing down so hard that I nearly cut through the thick paper.

It all flooded in. I felt guilty for Harry's death. For working too much when I could have spent more time with him, and for now making a life without him. For sitting in his chair.

The guilt was pervasive and stretched into the far corners of my life—even beyond life with Harry. I felt guilty for billing my clients. For my ability to smile in the darkness. For enjoying some degree of financial success, when I had friends and family who were struggling. I felt guilty for buying a car. For my gifts and talents. I had found a reason to feel guilty about almost anything good in my life.

But why? How was the guilt causing me to shut down or experience exhaustion and other physical symptoms? And why was it particularly strong after experiencing a high degree of success, happiness or pleasure? Was I afraid of success? Incapable of being happy and feeling fulfilled?

Soon after turning my attention to this possibility, I came across a blog post on the "Psychology Today" website written by Mary Lamia, PhD titled "The Downside of Success: Guilt or Shame?" It referenced papers written by Dr. Sigmund Freud in which he explored the darker side of achievement. In the first, "Wrecked by Success," written in 1925, Freud noted the phenomenon of people becoming seriously ill after the fulfillment of a "long-cherished wish." He concluded that the illness had been induced by guilt following success.

In the second paper written 11 years later, he shared his own experience of visiting the Acropolis in Athens, Greece, an event in his life that he thought "too good to be true." Because it was something that his parents had never experienced, he felt disloyal to them. He concluded that this feeling of "filial piety," led to guilt.

My heart began to beat faster as I wrote the word *guilt* again, underlining it three times. And then I read Mary Lamia's words,

> *Survivor's guilt refers to the belief that fate has treated you better than others or that your favorable treatment was at someone else's expense.*

Tears rolled down my face as I read one of the concluding statements:

> *In moving beyond what was deemed possible, or in attaining one's ideals, a loyalty to parents, siblings, or peers can interfere with embracing accomplishment and even result in depression or anxiety.*

And then, as memory after memory flooded in, I saw the emotional whiplash so clearly. Driven with an innate desire to self-actualize, I was wired to learn, study, grow, achieve, and excel. To explore. To become better than I had been the day before. It was never about being better than anyone else; it was about being my absolute best. But I was also wired to feel guilty about the very thing that brought me pleasure and made me feel alive. Especially when it came to my family and, in particular, my dad.

I idolized my father. He was smart, loving, talented, witty and hilarious. He dressed up as Santa Claus every Christmas so children could climb onto his lap, look into his sparkly blue eyes and tell them their Christmas wishes.

But he was also in a tremendous amount of pain. His parents had divorced when he was 13, and he was never allowed to see his father again. His youngest brother Bobby was killed in a car accident when he was 19. And because the accident occurred on uncle Bobby's way home from Camp Lejeune, my father believed that my grandmother blamed him because he had encouraged his brother to join the Marines.

While my father was very talented with marine construction—building bridges and bulkheads and docks—his heart's desire when he was younger was to attend agricultural school and become a farmer. Instead, he ran his own construction company and had a wife and five children to support, a point that surfaced often during his angry rants.

It's my belief that he was volatile, emotionally abusive with us girls, physically abusive with my brother, and drank a lot because he was in excruciating pain and under a tremendous amount of pressure, and had no idea how to process any of it.

But his was a generation that had not yet made seeking help for emotional or mental health issues "okay" for people in general, let alone men. As time went by, especially during my high school and early college years, after my three older siblings had left home, my mother, my little sister Tanya and I bore the brunt of his tirades when his drinking was at its worst. Almost anything could set him off. Even an extremely well-behaved young woman who excelled in the classroom and on the athletic field. And so, I could totally buy into what Dr. Freud had seen so clearly almost a century before. Instead of shutting down my desire to excel, I had unconsciously chosen to feel guilty about my successes and for having access to opportunities that my father never did, and that he worked so hard to provide for us.

This, coupled with the unintentional conditioning, "Better stop that, or someone's going to end up crying" from my mother, had ingrained in me that it was inherently wrong or even dangerous to have success, to be happy, to have fun or to experience joy.

The irony in all of this is that I can remember so many hilariously fun times with my family. My father was hugely talented and well respected in his field. His friends adored him. "Do it the Waine Way," was one of his mantras, which to me simply meant "excellently and with a little pizzaz." Neither of my parents ever criticized my talents or abilities. My mother thought there wasn't a single thing I couldn't do or achieve. My dad bawled as he walked me down the aisle at my first wedding.

But the beautiful times were no match for the trauma of the emotional abuse, my empathetic absorption of his pain, and witnessing him punishing himself with overworking and over-drinking. What had started in my teenage years, and perhaps even earlier, had carried over into the rest of my life.

This particular shutdown wasn't occurring before an event as I had originally thought. It was occurring after 60 days of incredible personal and professional success. A time during which I had quietly achieved more than I thought humanly possible. Everything was going famously until I started celebrating and sharing my progress with others. True to form, I spiraled quickly, landing flat on my face in the abyss of paralyzing depression and anxiety.

It didn't matter that both of my parents were deceased. Or that I was surrounded by hundreds of people who loved me, believed in me, and wanted nothing more than for me to follow my heart and live a life of joy and happiness. I had been living a life of apology without even knowing it. But now I knew it. And now that I knew it, I could do something about it.

I came out of the spin two weeks before the writers' conference. A byproduct of the intense personal journey of exploration that occurred in the kitchen cubby was that I found another "porch." I didn't have the green tree-cloistered, cocooned feeling of the backyard courtyard in Braselton. Or the cardinal. But I did have majestic mountains, sparkling blue water, a town of activity, and a magpie.

In a bittersweet moment, I realized that the back porch may not be where I wanted or needed to be any longer. It had been a haven for me, and magic happened every time I was there. But I no longer wanted to face backward; I wanted to look ahead. To look outward. The evergreen trees that once provided a cloak of comfort, sentries standing guard against the grief and pain, now seemed more like captors. I wanted to bask in the sun streaming into the kitchen and gaze out into a blue sky of possibility.

No doubt I was in a season of change. The shutdown I had just experienced, while extremely painful and frustrating, was also one of the most liberating ones. I felt a renewed spirit. So much so that one day, a short time before leaving for the conference, I found myself checking the Weather Channel once again. But this time, instead of fretting about the destruction of a Category 5 hurricane, I was simply planning a workday.

The forecast promised that the rain would stop, the clouds would clear, and the sun would come out late in the day. It looked like that would be the last of the sun for the foreseeable future.

So, I booked five one-hour calls with thirty minutes in between, and staged them to take advantage of the five different time zones involved. I was interviewing candidates for the lead financial role in Sitka and, if all went according to plan, I would wrap up by 6:00 p.m. Alaska time.

As I talked my way across the country, I kept an eye on the gray day. I hit the road after my last call and was rewarded with an incredible fall evening.

The previous afternoon, I had also taken a drive and had pulled over at Potter Marsh, just outside of town, when I saw people gathered on the side of the road, many with cameras and lenses the sizes of which I had never seen. I had only my phone camera that evening and knew the zoom wasn't strong enough to capture the beauty.

Equipped with a much better camera the next evening, I was hoping that Mother Nature would give me a "two for one." And she did: a beautiful evening and swans.

As I looked at the pictures later that night, I was struck by how the colors changed as the sun dropped lower and lower, and by how many colors there were.

Eventually, I was the only one left out there. The brilliant sunset had turned the sky into cotton candy that reflected in the waters of Potter Marsh and on the snowy white feathers of the graceful trumpeter swans.

They were the last of the migratory birds to be seen around town. All the other ones had flown the coop. The swans would soon as well.

Fall doesn't last long in Alaska. Almost overnight, the lush green of summer turns into fiery fall color before the dance of floating leaves begins—sometimes hastened along by the first, light breath of old man winter.

There was a time when I wouldn't have planned a drive to see swans, much less considered it a priority. But just like the green leaves of summer, some things are meant to change.

The swans already know that. At the exact right moment, they will head south because they know instinctively that, while Potter Marsh was perfect for a pre-migratory pit stop, it's not where they are meant to be during the next season of their lives. If they stay, they will probably perish.

We have instincts about change as well. And even when we know it's time to migrate, we hesitate. We tell ourselves that winter isn't coming. We stockpile food and build ourselves a refuge. We convince ourselves that it's really not going to be that cold, and that we will be safe. But we really won't be safe because the canvas will remain blank, the chapter unwritten, the song unsung, the life unchanged. The cold of winter freezes us in our tracks.

I used to say that if losing Harry wasn't enough to jolt me into following my heart, I wasn't sure what would. And yet there I was, three and a half years later, huddled up and shivering in the Dungeon in my winter parka.

Well, at least that was what I had been telling myself.

But the trumpeter swans of Potter Marsh helped me realize that I had been transitioning to a new season all along. Lulled into thinking that reality was only what I could see and feel on the surface, I was failing to give myself credit for what had been happening beneath the surface. I *had* been making progress. Despite the grief. Despite the resistance. Despite the anxiety.

As a result, and like the swans, I was about to fly south. Literally. The writers' conference and a new season in my life were just two weeks away. Although I had come out of the spin, I was going to have to make a mad dash to climb a mountain of client work before departing. I was already emotionally exhausted and knew that I would be physically exhausted by then as well. But I took comfort in the fact that once I arrived in Florida, I would be able to relax into learning mode, get some rest, and enjoy some anonymity as I took the idea of being a writer for a test drive.

Two weeks later, I landed in Florida and quickly found out that my expectations had been off the mark. The sessions were emotionally charged, there was very little time for rest, and my cloak of anonymity didn't last long. Perhaps the biggest revelation was that there was no need to take the idea of being a writer for a test drive. For just as the Potter Marsh swans had taught me two weeks earlier, I had actually been paddling in a new direction all along.

Chapter 19

It was the third day in a row that Ted Capshaw made me cry. The first two times, I was sitting in the crowd of several hundred attendees, listening to his inspirational remarks. This time, I was sitting across the breakfast table from him.

After staring for what felt like an eternity, and knowing there could only be one answer for me to give, I smiled slightly, nodded and said with a trembling voice, "I think that would be fine."

A short time later, he excused himself. I stayed and chit-chatted with some new friends before heading to the first session of the day.

On the short stroll to the conference, I was long on thought. I couldn't believe what had transpired since I arrived, and was so thankful to have signed up for the conference in July—as a birthday present to myself—to celebrate my "birth" as a writer.

I had joined the AWAI—the American Writers and Artists Institute—the prior spring. At one point, I ordered some of their training materials, none of which I'd ever accessed online. I attended one webinar and then applied absolutely nothing that I had learned. But as I flew across the country a few days earlier, I finally decided to take a look at the agenda for the conference.

At first I thought, *What have I done?! I've signed up for a boot-camp for copywriters! The people who write junk mail! The ones responsible for that late-night Tony Robbins infomercial purchase I made 20 years ago! What was I thinking?!*

Part of my reaction, I'm certain, was that I was feeling nervous. And that newfound nemesis, guilt, was rearing its ugly head. Even though I had planned well in advance, and it was a strategy for taking steps in the direction of a new career, I was feeling unentitled to take a step away from my "day job."

But I quickly recovered as I reminded myself that there was a lot more to copywriting than authoring junk mail letters. And besides, the Tony Robbins course I'd bought actually had done me a world of good back then.

I also reminded myself that the content of the conference didn't matter. What mattered was that I was taking action, sending my "inner doubter" a message. And while I arrived at Bootcamp feeling woefully unprepared—having done nothing except board two Alaska Airlines flights and review the agenda—I still felt there was an important reason for me to be there.

For three and a half days, I sat in that ballroom with hundreds of people from 7:00 a.m. to 9:00 p.m. and listened to some of the most interesting and entertaining speakers I'd ever heard. Some were the best copywriters in the business, some were members of the institute, and others were the leaders of the AWAI.

And then . . . there was Ted, the emcee for the event. When I heard his voice for the first time and felt his presence emanating from the stage, I was mesmerized. That first evening, Ted brought me to tears with his words of wisdom about self-doubt as he shared his own vulnerability on that topic.

After the session, I had the good fortune of seeing him before he was swarmed by other attendees. I said hello, introduced myself, and told him how inspiring his session had been.

"You made me cry," I said, gently admonishing him. He glanced at my badge, called me by name, shook my hand and then looked harder at my badge.

"Anchorage, Alaska? Why is it that I detect a Southern drawl?"

I gave a brief explanation, stopping short of teasing that my real name was Cynthimo, and concluded with letting him know I looked forward to talking with him again sometime.

"I'll be here," he said as he gave my hand another shake.

The next day, he made me cry for the second time, as he talked about "taking things to the next level," and spoke about losing his father at the age of 24.

At one point he became very emotional as he said, "He. Was. My. Man."

I thought, *Yeah, I had a guy one time, too.*

Not willing to talk about what losing his dad had done "to" him at the time, he focused instead on what it had done "for" him, eventually. He pleaded with us to not wait for tragedy to strike before following our dreams or being true to our gifts. To stare down our fears and inner doubt.

He said that he'd spent a lot of years thinking that losing his father had been the worst thing that ever happened to him. And then he walked up to the front of the stage, and raw with emotion, said it turned out that losing his dad had been the best thing that ever happened to him. It snapped him out of the half-life he had been living and motivated him to build a life of meaning.

After hearing him utter those words, I realized *that* was the decision I made the night Harry died. I had never allowed myself to verbalize it, because how in the world could losing Harry become the best thing that ever happened to me? But Ted said it with such conviction that, instead of recoiling at the thought, I felt completely understood by this man I didn't even know. It was the framework under which I had been operating without being totally conscious of it. It was the only thing that had made each new day possible—to turn Harry's death into the best thing that had ever happened to me. It was my plan for survival.

I was in tears again, but I didn't care. I was beginning to understand that being at the conference had less to do with writing (of any kind), and so much more to do with living.

Not to legitimize my plan to survive, but to spur me into a plan to thrive.

I felt as if a truth, buried deep inside of me, had found its way to the surface—sailing out into the open on the wave of each hot and salty tear. I made no move to wipe them away; to do so would mean they weren't welcome.

I knew that it was no mistake I had signed up for that conference, and I wanted Ted to know that his willingness to share his vulnerabilities had been very healing for me.

That night, I sent him a message through LinkedIn, along with one of my posts that I thought he'd relate to. Exhausted, I fell asleep with my clothes on, and the alarm . . . not on.

When I woke up, I immediately reached for my phone, worried that I had slept through the first few sessions. As I peeled one eye open, I could see that it was 5:55 a.m.

When I got the second eye open, I could also see that I had an email.

Thirty minutes later, I walked off the elevator and right into a hug from Ted. During our breakfast discussion, he asked if he could read my post to kick off Bootcamp that morning.

A short time later, he announced to the crowd in the room and those watching the live feed that he was calling an audible. He explained that instead of delivering the remarks he'd planned, he was going to read a piece of writing he'd received the night before. He encouraged everyone to listen carefully, as he suspected they would find it as powerful as he did.

It was surreal to listen to Ted read words I had written three years before. To see the body language of people responding. Heads nodding. Tears wiped away. Smiles. A laugh or two.

During those five minutes, when I had the benefit of listening and watching anonymously, I thought about my decision to attend the conference, how "at home" I had felt—a stark contrast to the feelings of disconnection I had experienced at the technology conference in Vegas the year before, or any of the accounting conferences I had ever attended.

After kickoff that morning, a friend I made during the first hour of the conference gave me a big hug and a knowing look as she pressed her card into my hand. "We so need to talk about heaven. I lost my dad when I was 14, and not a day goes by that I don't want to know he's still with me."

By the end of the week, my reality had become what others had promised: that when we are on the path that is right for us, we will receive affirmations and encouragement. People will appear. Events will unfold. Opportunities will arise. We'll feel purposeful and incredibly alive.

That's when we can trust that it's okay to be happy, and that no one's going to end up crying—and that sometimes an ending may actually be a beautiful beginning.

Chapter 20

I returned to Alaska with more certainty than ever that I was on the right track, but not quite believing what had happened. I shared the incredible experience with my online friends and thanked them for being part of "the voice" that inspired me to reach out to Ted.

It didn't take long for The Duber to comment. *Probably one of the finest pieces of self-introspection ever written, by you or anyone else.* Then she lovingly reminded me I was not getting any younger. She finished with, *This book you're destined to write, and promised to write, is ready.*

The Duber's words, and comments from many other friends, fueled my desire to develop a more specific game plan. My newfound sense of direction also seemed to fuel my professional work.

Though it seemed nearly impossible just one week earlier, both client audits went off without a hitch, and I helped hire not one, but two resources for the hospital. I was monitoring my mood to ensure another shutdown didn't happen. Things lined up for me to break away from client work in December to focus on my personal to-do list. But I felt a strong call to do more than just check things off the list. I wanted to have a strategy. I needed to get specific, not just about my writing, but also about my entire life and what I wanted it to look like.

I'm still not sure whether it was the Universe delivering the way it delivers, or Facebook algorithms picking it up from my recently written post, but soon after I "blamed" copywriters for my purchase of a Tony Robbins product more than twenty years before, he started appearing in my Facebook feed. Two weeks later, I was on my way back to South Florida.

The product I joked about having purchased over twenty years before actually helped me turn my life around. It jump-started my thirst for personal development and put me on the path to inviting Harry into my life. So, when I realized I needed a road map for my life, and almost immediately Tony Robbins invited me on a "Date with Destiny," I thought I couldn't and shouldn't refuse. Besides, I was already scheduled to be out of the office that week, and I was fresh off an amazing Bootcamp. I'd always believed that riding a wave of momentum was important, and I now had one, for the first time in quite a while. So, I bought a ticket, booked my flights, and snagged a hotel room within walking distance. I envisioned attending the event by day and pampering myself at night with leisurely dinners, facials and writing. The thought of returning to Alaska with my life's roadmap in hand was very exciting.

As it turned out, I did pamper myself, but it had nothing at all to do with dining, writing or skin care. It had to do with dancing, hugging, and crying, and feeling totally energized and alive. Yes, I had been lured in by the copywriters again, but this time it wasn't a cassette-based program that I listened to on my Walkman. This time it was a live rock concert for my soul. When I got on the plane to leave a week later, I did indeed have a roadmap for my life.

I also had a lighter heart and a deeper connection to my own spirituality than I thought possible. The lighter heart came from a significant release of guilt and grief. In a meditation during the first evening, we were asked to imagine the worst thing that ever happened to us.

To really put ourselves there. This was interesting for me because I wasn't "there" when the worst thing happened. But that night, as beautifully healing music played, I let myself imagine, from the little details I had ever been brave enough to hear, that I was there watching when Harry collapsed at the restaurant, during his ride in the ambulance, and as he died in the emergency room.

Just as the emotion of that experience became almost too much to bear, I heard the words, "Now imagine that your Creator is also right there, and that everything happened perfectly." At that moment, an avalanche of grief slid off my heavy heart. Over the years, I had told myself countless times that "things happen for a reason." But I had never envisioned God being "right there," or that the moment was anywhere near perfect.

Suddenly I felt a burst of love and light in my heart that spread quickly throughout my entire body. I felt as expansive as the Universe, and as tiny as a grain of sand, simultaneously. It was the same feeling I had the first time I saw the cardinal, and during all the other countless times when I knew I'd made a connection to all that is.

In the same meditation, we were asked to think of a coincidence that had changed our lives. Suddenly, I saw myself sitting with Phillip in Las Vegas while David was on the phone with us. Since that coincidental meeting on Leap Day 2016, the twins had become an important part of my life. My heart filled again with love as I thought about all the smiles and laughter we had shared. How David had helped me out of the abyss after Vegas. Our hilarious "conference calls" and their use of middle names to blame the mischievous, trouble-making side of their personalities. And how my very own "Cecilia" made appearances when they least expected it.

At the end of the mediation, I felt totally connected to my heart. I looked at my "buddy" for the day who was sitting to my right, and smiled. The music changed and my smile disappeared instantly.

"What is it?" he asked, slightly concerned.

As I listened to the song that had played such a prominent role in Harry's memorial service and in my healing, I explained why it was so remarkable that "Here Comes the Sun" was the first song played after the meditation.

I was certain it was a message. But if I had any doubt, the second song wiped it away. When "Cecilia" began to play, I turned back to my buddy with my mouth and eyes wide open. "Oh my God!" I exclaimed. I told him about the cameo appearance of my "evil" twin Cecilia in the meditation, and he showed me the chill bumps on his arms.

As I walked back to my hotel well after midnight, I was deep in thought. The rock concert environment was a little overwhelming for me. I was well outside of my comfort zone. But then, elbow to elbow with 5,000 other people, one of the most healing moments of my life had occurred. Before I went to sleep, I made a deal with myself, as I always did with any book I read or conference I attended: I would take what worked for me and leave the rest.

As I had intended, when I boarded my flight a few days later, I had a roadmap for my life. It was summarized on a rolled-up poster that I placed into the overhead bin. The precious cargo included my mission statement, my list of values, and three big goals for the next year.

I nestled into my seat and was fast asleep before we even pushed back from the gate. When I woke up, I began to contemplate my next steps. I had cleared my calendar for a couple of days after the event to allow myself to get home, process what I had learned, celebrate Harry's birthday, and to complete any immediate follow-ups that were in order. I was still pretty exhausted, but I wanted to make good use of the time on the plane. So, I began to jot some of my "afterthoughts" down on paper. Before I knew it, I was in the middle of one of the biggest breakthroughs of the entire week.

As I stared at the words *Change your blueprint* on the page in front of me, a photo from my youth flashed in my mind and all the dots of the universe connected. My father's yearning to be a farmer. My yearning to be a teacher and a writer. His construction business. My consulting firm. Talented in his field. Talented in mine. His joy in playing the accordion. My joy in singing. Our desire to learn the piano. His addictions to alcohol and work. My addictions to crisis and work. His abuse of others. My abuse of myself. His rage. My anxiety.

Two months before, in the kitchen cubby, I realized that I went into shutdown in order to avoid the survivor's guilt of living a life better than others—particularly my father's.

Flying along at 36,000 feet that December night, I realized that I had designed my life to never be better than my father's. In fact, I had designed my life to be *exactly* like my father's. I had been living my father's blueprint. I had watched and learned from him, and then I did exactly the same thing.

I was overwhelmed with empathy for him as I imagined him toiling in the heat or the cold during the week to build big, beautiful things, while his heart longed to be on a tractor plowing green fields and growing vegetables. His need to express himself through farming was so strong that he never rested. On the weekends, after working incredibly long weekdays, he would pack us up and head out on the hour's drive to our "farm," where we did indeed plow the fields and grow vegetables.

Bittersweet tears streamed down my face as I thought about how happy he had become when he finally shifted gears from construction to more creative endeavors. How he stopped drinking, and bought an old piano.

I thought about the night he passed away as I sat by his side, with my sister Tanya just outside the hospital room door. I pressed cool towels to his face and applied balm to his lips. When the morphine dose didn't keep him out of pain, I asked for an increase. I knew he was getting close.

Eight years before, just as he and my mother were about to move to "the farm," the emergency room doctor who diagnosed his colon cancer said he had six months to live. It was Thanksgiving Day. I had insisted that we switch hospitals and doctors, and thankfully the family agreed. Surgery was successful, and chemo was added as a precaution.

A month after my father's surgery, on Christmas Eve, my mother fell and broke her hip and wrist while she and I were doing some last-minute shopping. After they convalesced together, my parents moved to the farm, and lived the best eight years of their lives together. Creating a sanctuary for them, my dad dug a pond, planted fruit and dogwood trees, built a beautiful one-room cabin, and edged the property with a white rail fence. When my mother told him a cabin without a bathroom wasn't going to do, he put a manufactured home on the property until he could build a house.

He was in the hospital for testing when we learned that his cancer had returned. After the doctors informed him that there was nothing that they could do but keep him comfortable, my dad said he wanted to go home. He was only there for a few days before he declined and we took him back to the hospital. During those few days at home, he often stood at his bedroom window or the front door, looking out. It's always been my hope that as he stood there, he felt the peace of fulfillment and not the pain of regret.

It was only two weeks from the time he went into the hospital for tests and the night I sat by his side. During that time, he had profusely thanked the family for taking care of him, and kept asking if he was being a good patient.

Sitting by his side that night, I realized that he had ever only wanted to get it right. I leaned in and whispered to him, "You've done everything just right. We'll take good care of Momma. It's okay for you to go when you are ready. And we'll catch up with you later." I kissed his forehead, and within ten minutes, he took his last, labored breath.

As I sat on the plane that night, eighteen years later, I cried in the comforting darkness of the cabin as I watched it all in my mind's eye, felt it in my heart, and saw that amazing photo come back into focus. I am in his construction office, sitting in front of a drafting table with him leaning in beside me. My dad is looking with keen interest at what I am enthusiastically pointing out on the set of plans unfurled in front of us.

Suddenly I heard my own voice in my head: *Look Daddy! It's our new blueprint!*

And he replied, *Well, I'll be damned.*

The moments that I described as "life-changing" had grown exponentially in the years since Harry had passed. This was one of them. Something healed instantly. And I mean, instantly. I was also dumbfounded. What was it about that scene, 34 years before, that prompted my mother or sister to take a photo? Was it one of the rare moments, during that time in our lives, when there were smiles instead of tears? And how had I miraculously summoned it up 34 years later, at the most perfect time possible? I may not have known the answers to the questions that night, but I did know one thing.

It was time to change the blueprint. For me, and for my dad. Once and for all.

I knew that to change the blueprint, I would need to focus constantly on the mission statement I had just developed: *To bring a smile to the world.* In order to do that, I had to bring one to myself first. A real one, inside and out. I had a lot of work to do.

During the Tony Robbins event, I learned how important it was to have coaches, mentors and role models. I identified the need and desire to expand my circle to include others who had similar goals and interests. A few weeks later, I received a promotional email from Jack Canfield:

Join me at my private retreat in Hilton Head, SC!

Co-creator of the *Chicken Soup for the Soul* book brand, Jack Canfield is also an author of many other books on success and motivation, including his best-seller *The Success Principles*. My heart beat faster as I evaluated the offerings of the retreat. While it looked perfect for a time when I had at least a book draft in hand, the event was only three months away. I saw that there was another option for October in Santa Barbara, California. After further research, I learned that Jack Canfield also offered a training program that he conducted himself. Upon completion, I would have two certifications: one in the content of *The Success Principles*, and one for "The Canfield Methodology," his proven framework for delivering world-class seminars, workshops, and keynote speeches.

I applied to both programs. When they called to confirm that I really wanted to do both in the same year, something they rarely encountered, I explained the method to my madness. After their review of the extensive written applications, I was scheduled for interviews. By the end of the week, I was accepted to both programs.

One of my big goals for the next year had been set in motion—to immerse myself in learning. I was going to be learning from one of the best. I had perused the training program content and knew that the coursework would be transforming. Not only would I improve my presenting and speaking skills, the Success Principles were going to provide a framework for my continued healing and professional development. The retreat was going to help me devise a strategy to implement my mission: to bring a smile to the world. The Canfield training and future attendance at Tony Robbins events would constitute my "Master's Degree in Life."

As I headed back to Sitka a few weeks later, I was traveling lighter. I had not packed my usual sense of dread. It appeared that as I began to really follow my heart, it suddenly had the capacity to love even those things that only a short time before seemed unbearable. I couldn't wait to see how much more capacity it had at the end of the coming year—a year I suspected would be one of the most exciting and pivotal ones of my life.

Chapter 21

Shortly after midnight, the tsunami warning sounded. I had just returned to Sitka after spending the first few weeks of the new year in Braselton, working remotely and handling personal affairs. Exhausted from the emotional strain of the cross-country trip that started on the anniversary of Harry's death, I was sound asleep in the Loft when the first alert sounded on my phone. Shortly thereafter, I heard the town's siren wailing in the night. A 7.9-magnitude earthquake had struck in the Gulf of Alaska, and residents were ordered to evacuate to higher ground.

The Loft was about 150 yards from Crescent Harbor, which opens quickly to the Sitka Sound and again quickly to the Gulf of Alaska—the portion of the Pacific Ocean that tucks into the curved coast of south and southeast Alaska. Despite my geographic location and awareness of the devastation that tsunamis could bring, I felt an immediate sense of calm. I was very focused. I checked my phone for Sitka's evacuation protocol, and I looked outside for activity.

Houses behind me had come alive. One car was already pointed out of the driveway, its headlights illuminating the snow and slush of the cold Alaskan night. Following suit, I quickly gathered essentials and within minutes was headed to higher ground.

I spent the next several hours at the high school, where hundreds of people had gathered. It felt more like a community get-together than a waiting room for disaster. Lively conversation filled the air from our round tables of ten, while kids played or quietly asked each other, "Is this your first tsunami?" While occasionally checking news updates, I reviewed and edited the materials for a budget training I was conducting the next day.

In the wee hours of the morning, we received the all-clear, and I returned to the Loft for a couple of hours' sleep. But sleep did not come easily as I tossed and turned with thoughts of how differently things could have turned out. The map I had sent to friends showing my location probably didn't help. I couldn't get the image of it out of my head. There I was, a tiny blue dot, thousands of miles away from family and most all of my friends, with the powerful Pacific Ocean on one side and the frozen expanse of Alaska on the other. I had not felt such isolation and vulnerability since the night Harry died.

I had started the new year with joyful anticipation of what lay ahead. A middle-of-the-night tsunami evacuation and feelings of isolation and vulnerability were not what I'd had in mind. But I had some new tools in my emotional toolkit, so I drifted off to sleep with a powerful question on my mind—*What else could this mean?*

Ultimately, it meant that I deferred the budget training. Not only was I not feeling on my game after being up all night, I knew my attendees wouldn't be at their best either. The CEO and the managers had been eagerly awaiting the training. I wanted the conditions to be optimal.

I finished reading *The Success Principles* the night before the first rescheduled session. My heart began beating wildly as I realized that the tsunami evacuation delay had provided a perfect opportunity for me to take Canfield's principles for a real-life spin. Even though I had not started the coursework on how to teach the principles, I knew I had to do it, and that meant I had to change the training materials quickly. And so, I did what any consultant would do after making that decision at midnight before an early-morning presentation the next day.

I promptly went to bed.

The next morning, after I selected a handful of Success Principles from the 67 listed in the table of contents, I realized I didn't need to change the presentation at all. I would simply use Slide 6, which said, "Why Are We Here?" I would then guide the session from a focus on the mechanics of preparing a budget to a discussion on how a budget could be used as a roadmap for organizational success.

When I got to Slide 6 during the first session, my apprehension about teaching the content slipped away. Energy and engagement were high. The CEO was beaming after the first session and stayed until after we covered the Success Principles in the second one. When I got back to the Loft on the evening after the second session, I finally took time to think about what had happened. I replayed the sessions in my mind. I saw the smiles and thoughtful expressions.

Someone left an anonymous notecard on my desk after session two. The front of the card included a quote from *Here and Now* by Henri Nouwen:

We have to choose joy and keep choosing it every day.

Handwritten on the back was a simple but very meaningful,

Thank you for today, Cynthia.

To say I was humbled by the experience would be an understatement. Once again, I had taken just a few steps in the direction of my heart. The universe had responded with a resounding "yes," and even threw in a tsunami evacuation to help get the party started. The feelings of isolation and vulnerability that overwhelmed me the week before had slipped away and were replaced by feelings of connectedness and confidence. I had helped bring new meaning to budgets and financial management, topics dreaded by most. And I was energized by the enthusiastic and emotional responses. I was now eagerly anticipating a day that I might bring new meaning to other dreaded topics through writing, teaching and speaking.

I was so excited that I shared the experience through a post in the online Canfield community. The response was a beautiful mixed bag of kudos and thank you's. As I read the comments from several people I would eventually meet in person, and a few who have now become dear friends, I realized that my willingness to share had opened the door for others. It had also provided a real-life example for those who may have been struggling to see the work in action.

One of the comments was written by a group administrator. I read the glowing remarks with interest, and then my eyes welled up as I read the last sentence: *Keep posting and definitely KEEP WRITING!*

A few months later, at the first week of our live training, I found myself standing in front of the same group administrator. Patty Aubery had been Jack Canfield's right hand for decades, and was the business mastermind behind the *Chicken Soup for the Soul* success. She was there to support the live training, so I wanted to ask a question about one of their other offerings—a writers' retreat taking place later in the year—and to thank her for commenting on my post.

Patty was as approachable as she had promised when introducing herself from the stage earlier in the day. When I asked about the difference between the private retreat and the writers' retreat, she asked how far along I was with my book. I explained I had not yet started, but had a collection of social media posts written over the prior four years that I thought would provide the basis for one.

"Do you have any of them with you?" she asked.

"Not at this moment, but I do have some on my laptop upstairs. I could bring them to you in the morning."

"How about this afternoon? And I'll give you feedback tomorrow."

I was stunned. Obviously, I had not planned to share my writing with anyone there, or I would have been carrying it with me. I realized that an incredible opportunity had just presented itself. So, I agreed to provide the content during our lunch break.

As luck would have it, the normal hour-long lunch was only 40 minutes that day. After racing upstairs, I realized that most of my writing was on an old laptop in Alaska. Now firmly inside my own *Mission Impossible*, I worked quickly to extract some posts from Facebook, careful to include a few of the cardinal stories. I added some introductory and background information, and saved it all on a thumb drive. I dashed back downstairs, printed the document, handed it off to Patty, and slipped into my chair just before Jack started the afternoon session.

The next morning, I was talking with fellow attendees during a break when Patty pulled me aside. She told me she loved what she'd read, that I could help a lot a people, and encouraged me to pursue my writing. My classmates, overhearing the conversation, smiled and gave me knowing looks. I couldn't believe the feedback. And yet, I didn't feel as excited as I should have. A part of me immediately began to downplay it. *Don't get too excited*, it seemed to say. It was that part of me that didn't trust that good things could happen without someone ending up crying.

But another part of me *was* a tad excited. After all, I had just received encouragement to pursue my writing by a woman who was an accomplished writer and had been the mastermind of one of the most successful book brands of our time. I couldn't imagine it getting any better than that. Until it did.

On the last night of training, we were having a "Come as You'll Be Party." The only requirement was that when we walked through the

doors to the party, we had to act as if it were five years later and the
dreams and goals we had visioned during our training had indeed
come true. We were encouraged to dress the part, use props, or do
anything else that transported us into the reality of our sure-to-be
new future.

It sounded like huge fun, but before I left Sitka, I had been so
immersed in client work and preparing for the training that I didn't
think I had time to plan for "dress up and pretend." Looking back,
I think I was also afraid of having fun. So, I had decided that my
"Come as You'll Be" experience would be a state of mind. I didn't
need fancy clothes or a prop.

Before I left for California, I had a change of heart. I had committed to giving it my all if I were accepted to the program. So, in
May 2018, I sauntered into 2023 with two of my best-sellers in hand.

"Hi Jack! So great to see you! I've just got to tell you . . . After I saw
you five years ago at this very hotel, the floodgates opened. I started
writing and haven't stopped. I made a run at your record of seven
books on the *New York Times* best-seller list, but fell short—having
only three make the list in 2019, and one per year since then."

"Well, that's nothing to sneeze at!" Jack replied. "Let me see what
you have there." He reached for the "books" in my hand, *Song of the
Cardinal* and *After Midnight*.

He looked at each cover and when he finished, I guided him to
the final paragraph of the inside flap of *After Midnight*. It was part
of the book summary I had crafted before leaving Vegas over two
years before. To my surprise, he read it out loud to the small group
that had gathered around us. After he finished, one person joined in
the fun, saying that her sister had been reading my books and loved
them. Another said she had seen my Oprah interview on TV, and
that I had knocked it out of the park. Jack then reviewed the "also
by" titles I had handwritten on the blank back cover of the book and
commented on how catchy they were.

As he handed the books back, he noted, "That's some graphic artist you have," referring to the cover of *After Midnight*.

"I'd tell you who the artist is, but then I'd have to kill you," I said with a smile. The truth was, I couldn't remember the artist's name.

In the wee hours of a morning just before traveling to California, I was scouring the internet in search of the perfect picture for one of the book covers Jarrell, a high school friend, had created for me. When I came up empty on the typical photo sites, I cast a wider net, Googling phrases that might call up a careening carriage racing off into midnight. I had scrolled through countless pages, and was just about to call it a night around 2:00 a.m. when I saw it.

The picture was hauntingly beautiful, with hues of black and deep blue. The castle sat in the upper left corner of the background, illuminated by a moon peeking out from behind a cluster of clouds. In the foreground, four horses raced away from the distant castle with a carriage in tow and no driver in sight. Their muscles bulged. Their eyes were filled with fierce determination. I could hear the pounding of their hooves.

There couldn't have been a more perfect picture to cover a book about a real-life and determined "princess" who snatches the reins from the hands of grief, and drives her carriage straight into the hours after midnight.

I downloaded the image and sent it to Jarrell. When I saw the revised cover the next morning, it took my breath away. Since I was just using it for a prop, I felt safe to do so without permission. But I saved the link to the photo, anticipating that I might need it in the future.

After Jack's comment, I felt remiss that I didn't at least have the artist's name top of mind. I was still bothered by that when I woke up the next morning, and it was still on my mind when I learned that plans for lunch were foiled by a water issue at the hotel restaurant. So, I sat down at the desk, flipped open my laptop and located the document titled *Permission Requests*.

I clicked on the link and found the artist's website. I was surprised to see that he had a California address. *California is kind of big, though*, I cautioned myself as I clicked on the map. My heart started beating faster when I saw that his studio was only an hour away from my hotel.

One of the last things that Jack advised us in our closing session the afternoon before was how important it was to "take inspired action." To act on the messages we get from our little voice. So, I called the phone number even though it was Sunday, and the online hours listed the business as closed.

"Hello, this is John . . . ."

I was so surprised to hear a voice and the first name of the artist that I hung up on the voicemail message. *That was way too easy*, I thought suspiciously. But I couldn't ignore how fast my heart was beating. I called back. After the beep, I left my name and started into a message, explaining that I had found his art online while "researching a project." I said that I lived in Alaska, but was in Newport Beach on business. As I started to say I was hoping to arrange a time to visit his studio, he picked up.

An hour later, I was sitting in the home studio of John Rowe, the artist of the painting I had been flashing around on my fake book cover the night before. I met his wife, saw a project he was working on for Disney, another painting for which he had just won an award, and a collection of paintings he had done for a book series. I also learned that, a few years before, the publishers of Walter Farley's *The Black Stallion* commissioned John for over twenty new paintings to cover the reissued classic series. It was easy to understand why the horses on the cover of *After Midnight* were so lifelike.

I showed him my props and explained how they came about. We marveled at the geographical coincidence that resulted in a Sunday afternoon chat in his studio. And at how perfectly his artwork brought to life the words on the inside jacket of my fake book.

"You know, that painting has been around for quite a while," John shared. "It was on a Disney cruise ship for the longest time, and is now at a studio in Orlando. I don't understand why it never sold."

Before I could stop myself, I smiled and said with quiet confidence, "Maybe it never sold because it was waiting for me."

After that day in John's studio, the painting continued to make the rounds. It survived two potential sales at the Orlando studio before John secured its release. After a flight to Alaska and a pit stop in a climate-controlled storage unit next to Papa Jack's, it finally landed where it was always meant to be: on the wall of my office.

After I hung up with John that Sunday afternoon in my Newport Beach hotel room, my hands shook, and it felt as if my heart were going to beat out of my chest. At one point, I had to sit down on the bed to catch my breath.

Before that moment, I didn't think the week could get any better. I had learned so much and felt such a deep connection to every person in the room. I had received incredible feedback on my writing from Patty Aubery and had bantered with Jack Canfield. But then along came a grand finale, on top of the extraordinary events that had already occurred. The cumulative effect was so powerful and so beautiful that it left me shaking and breathless. It felt as if I had received my very own, booming message from the Wizard of Oz and that my intended path had been divinely confirmed.

Feeling a sense of urgency as I made my way back to Alaska, I concluded that there was only one way forward. I would complete my Canfield training, attend the retreat, and wrap up my client work by November 30. In December, I would tackle my personal to-do list and begin 2019 working on my first book. Oz had spoken, and I was ready.

Chapter 22

With a renewed sense of purpose, I returned to Alaska and dove headlong into the plan I'd developed on the flight home. The four months between the first and last weeks of Canfield training were intense. My pain increased. A nickel-size red circle that appeared on my leg just before my birthday trip to Italy had grown as large as a baseball, and other red circles were popping up everywhere. And the controller, hired to fill Ida's position at the Sitka hospital, resigned.

Having learned a lesson when the controller retired at the same unfortunate time of the year two years before, I worked out a game plan with the client that would provide an opportunity for me to be of service, while also remaining true to my goals and game plan. The Canfield events remained on my schedule, as did the transition date of November 30.

During the last live week of training, we were required to teach and present in a variety of settings—one on one, small groups and, finally, on the stage with our classmates and the Canfield leadership as our audience. I experienced high anxiety leading up to each presentation, but it disappeared as soon as I started speaking. By the time I received my framed "diploma" in a commencement ceremony at the end of that week, I was convinced that I was finally on course.

I had been through two other "graduations" in my life—high school and college. Each time, I had graduated at the tip-top of my class. Yet neither of those graduations had provided the sense of accomplishment and excitement that came with receiving my Canfield diploma. Later, as I contemplated why this one felt so different, I realized that those earlier graduations had provided external recognition for accomplishments achieved on a path of least resistance. This graduation recognized an internal journey of healing and transformation on a path to joy and fulfillment—a path more aligned with my vision and values, and which I had consciously chosen. I had not felt so accomplished or happy in a very long time.

The retreat, which followed about two weeks later, was ideal reinforcement for the training I had just completed, and a perfectly placed precursor to my imminent professional transition. It also provided unexpected moments of healing, one of which centered on the pervasive feelings of guilt I had not yet managed to release completely.

I was grouped with four or five attendees, all of whom were, or were aspiring to be, authors. We each had an opportunity to interact directly with Jack, while the others watched and learned. Not long into my session, I found myself unable to speak for the tears. When Jack asked me what prompted them, the first word that popped into my head was "guilt." After I shared the reasons for my guilt, Jack homed in on the very one that had been quietly gnawing away at me for nearly five years. "Cynthia, would you have returned to Alaska if you knew that Harry was going to die?"

It was a question amazingly simple to answer. In doing so, I saw the perfection in it. I'm certain that I had discussed my regret over returning to Alaska against my better judgment with several people over the years. All of them had wisely advised that I not beat myself up about it. But no one asked the question that Jack did. Would I have gone if I had known? In answering the question, I had to acknowledge that I had acted based on the best information available at the time.

During the meditation the prior December, I had experienced profound healing when I accepted that Harry's creator had been with him at the time of his passing. Almost a year later, I experienced profound healing when I accepted that I was not.

I had often wondered if Harry was upset with me for not being there. Even though I felt like I was a satellite dish for his messages, I rarely saw him in a dream. When I did, he almost always had his back to me. I had only clearly seen his face once in nearly five years.

Later in the Canfield retreat, Jack was leading the entire group through a guided meditation in which we were ultimately asked to imagine a divine being presenting us with a gift that represented our mission in life. I was cranky when the meditation started, because it had not gone well for me when we did it during the training program weeks before. I couldn't concentrate; I never saw a divine being. At the end, I simply guessed that I had seen a big, gold, antique-looking key, like one that would have opened the medieval garden door in Florence.

But that afternoon at the retreat, I immediately saw a divine being with a familiar smile and mischievous eyes. His skin was as tan as ever, making the contrast of his white robe and wings that much more dramatic and beautiful. I took in every single detail of his handsome face, as I felt nothing but love emanating from him. And then I saw his large, strong, elegant hands holding a beautiful box, and heard the familiar words, *Here Punkin, I wrapped it myself.* This time, there was no ugly wrapping paper, shipping tape or exposed corners. The box, covered in intricate scrolling designs, was shining a brilliant gold. When I lifted the lid and peeked inside, a starfish, in matching gold, glowed back at me.

No longer concerned that Harry was upset with me, I shared my meditation experience during the open discussion afterward. I concluded with, "I would never have guessed that Harry would look so dashing in all white, and sporting a pair of wings to match!"

That day, I decided that the five points of the starfish represented five ways in which I would fulfill my mission. Two years later, I created Starfish Publishing, a company under which I planned to write and distribute messages of healing and renewal, and to encourage others to trust that the storms of life do indeed leave treasures of starfish in the sand.

As my heart opened more and more during the retreat, I became less interested in my goal to leave with a well-organized EXCEL spreadsheet of action items and due dates. Instead, I wanted to leave with nothing to do but stop the merry-go-round. So, I departed with a notebook full of wisdom, healing, and certainty that taking the month of December to rest and reset was the best strategy of all. I would redirect my time and attention from client work to fully envisioning what I wanted my life to look like. After creating a clear picture of that, I would then prepare the detailed plan. And then, I would get busy with implementing it.

Wisely, I had built a buffer into my schedule to allow a few extra days for reflection before returning to Sitka. I thought that such reflection would be perfect during a drive along the PCH—the Pacific Coast Highway. So, on the day after the retreat, I headed for the coast and an overnight stay in Cambria.

Cambria was one of Paolo's favorite stops on an epic trip that he, Harry, and another dearly departed friend, Kirk, had taken on a break between industry trade shows in Vegas many years before. They rented a van, drove through Death Valley to the coast, and then made their way up and down the PCH, visiting many attractions and even more wineries before returning to Vegas.

The seaside town was as charming as Paolo had promised. After dinner at a popular restaurant, I spent a memorable evening on the back patio of my room listening to the surf crash and chatting with the gentlemen who were staying on either side of me, as if we had been neighbors for years.

The next day, I set off early. Any concerns that the California coast wouldn't compare to the majesty of Alaska dissipated immediately. From the beginning, the scenery was breathtaking. By the time the day ended, it had been unexpectedly life-changing.

I started grinning from ear to ear when it came into view. A day that was already perfect had just gotten even better.

As I slowed down, I thought, *What trip along the Pacific Coast Highway is complete without an old, classic VW van?* I was traveling north. The van was facing south, parked in a cut-out across the busy road from me. I'm not sure what year it was, but it was a "hippie van" with obvious vintage, a sky-blue paint job and a chrome luggage rack on top.

I got a photo from the front and then pulled slowly forward until I was perfectly parallel. Framed by the rocky and rugged topography of the California coast and matching blue sky that turned white before disappearing into the equally blue sea, the old van whispered "possibility." Its clear windows, tinted with the horizon that stretched out beyond them, seemed an invitation to dream.

I drove away, thinking about trips with no beginning or ending, and only adventure in between. I stopped looking at my watch. I stopped checking for a cell signal. I took photos and explored— amazingly without feeling an ounce of pain. Somewhere along the way, on one of those exploratory stops, I dug a headband out of my suitcase. No doubt, my inner hippie had emerged.

Later, I would laugh at the selfies I took that day as I noted my most groovy selection for a shirt that morning. It was a head-band-matching gray painted with crazy lines of many colors. The huge silver heart dangling from my necklace may as well have been a peace sign, since it felt as if a "peace" of me had magically slipped into place.

That afternoon, I succumbed to the allure of Carmel by the Sea. Lingering longer than I planned resulted in a perfectly timed arrival at Pebble Beach and a most spectacular sunset. Afterward, I sat on a seaside park bench, not wanting to leave, while the waves crashed below me. For sure, I didn't want the magical day to end, and yet I was excited and eager for the next one to begin. I smiled into the darkness as I thought, *And this is just the beginning.*

It was not unlike the feeling I had experienced three years before, in Italy. That Cynthia, who fearlessly jumped on the damn train, was the same one who had donned the headband and driven the California coast on an afternoon of life without limits. In my heart, I knew that was the real Cynthia. And I knew that was how life was supposed to feel, how I wanted my life to feel.

It was late by the time I reached Santa Cruz on the last leg of my journey, so I pulled over to contemplate my options. I decided to press on to the San Francisco airport, but was no longer on the PCH when I returned to the road.

Instead, I found myself on a very dark, curvy road that seemed to be going in the opposite direction of my destination. I didn't go far before pulling over to verify that I was really headed toward the airport. Both the car's navigation system and my phone showed the same route. I was headed in the right direction, but I had the distinct feeling that I wasn't. Rather than listen to my little voice that was clearly in dispute with the GPS, I pulled back onto the road and continued.

About an hour later, I collapsed on the bed in an airport hotel. The drive had been terrifying, which is saying a lot because I love to drive. The road had two extra-narrow lanes going in each direction, separated by a concrete median. Sheer mountainsides rose abruptly from both sides of the road, with frequent switchbacks that twisted and turned, dipped and peaked. The headlights and taillights from the bumper-to-bumper traffic on both sides were a sea of distraction. Scared to even think about changing lanes and with white knuckles glowing from the steering wheel, I held on tight. Periodic rain only made it worse. I felt trapped—swept along with no control and no options.

As I lay there recovering from the terror of the drive, I couldn't stop thinking about it and what a stark contrast it was to the serenity of the Pacific Coast Highway. It was like nothing I had ever experienced. *Where the hell was I?* I thought as I looked at Google Maps. And then it made sense. I actually had not been very far from hell.

Because I was driving on it.

California Route 17, which runs between Santa Cruz and San Jose, is considered one of the most dangerous roads in the country due to its blind curves, sharp turns and speed limit changes. As I read about the route I had just traveled, I burst out laughing. It suddenly seemed hilarious that my beautifully, magical day had ended with me holding on for dear life as I sped through the night on a road also known as "Killer 17" and "Blood Alley."

Eventually, I realized that the ending of the day had been no laughing matter. The Universe had served up a timely learning experience for me. When I was aligned with my heart and soul, the road was smooth, the sky was blue, and I felt as joyful and carefree as an old hippie van. But when I went against my intuition, the road became dangerous, the sky darkened, and I felt trapped and full of fear. I had traveled that dark road before, but it wasn't the 26 miles or more of Blood Alley. It was the 26 years or more I had been traveling while not following my heart.

Energized by the California trip—and thankful for the lesson courtesy of "Killer 17"—I returned to Alaska for the final countdown to November 30, the last day of my client engagement. After a two-week stop in Sitka, I returned to Anchorage for the month of November and the home stretch. I almost couldn't believe that it was finally happening. I had been working toward this moment my entire adult life.

With laser-like focus, I cranked out client work during the day and worked on my own to-dos at night. I recorded my progress on a large whiteboard easel in the corner of the living room. Each night before I went to bed, I added a sticky note to the board that listed five things I had done related to my new goals and aspirations.

About a week into the month, the pain that disappeared on the magical California drive returned with a vengeance. The rash was spreading like wildfire, and I'd also developed a general sense of unease. I felt something ominous stirring.

Worried that I may be subconsciously trying to sabotage my transition, I scheduled a call with Bedford. It had been nearly a year since I checked in; we were long overdue.

"How much time do we have today?" I asked. I loved Bedford's willingness to do extended sessions.

"I'm glad to be your advice-giving, head-shrinking, blame-it-on-your-parents therapist. I'm at your disposal," he had responded. "And I'm so eager to hear what Harry's been up to!" Like most people, Bedford had fallen in love with Harry, and had found his messaging system fascinating and entertaining.

By the time we finished nearly two hours later, I had brought him up to speed on Ted Capshaw and the writers' conference, my year of Jack Canfield, and everything in between. He was amazed and ecstatic about it all, especially the upcoming date of November 30.

When I told him about the pain, the rash and the general sense of unease, he said without hesitation, "Cynthia! Of course, your body is rebelling! You have a book inside of you, and it needs to come out!" Then he told me about another client, with permission of course, whose debilitating pain disappeared after finishing a book he had long desired to write. "It's making you sick, girl! Time to get it out of there!"

I always felt better after a session with Bedford, and that day was no different. But over the course of the next couple of weeks, the general feeling of unease turned into an ominous feeling of doom. I continued to knock out client work, and every night a new Post-it of personal accomplishment went onto the whiteboard. But no matter how hard I tried, I couldn't shake the feeling of being in danger. Fire trucks seemed to blare past whenever the thoughts broke through. Evacuation routes glared at me from grocery store doors. A house two blocks away burned to the ground.

By the time Thanksgiving arrived, I had almost come unraveled. I told myself, *It's not just my body that's rebelling. Now my mind is getting in on the act.* It seemed that a part of me was so terrified of the unknown of a new life, it was doing everything possible to scare me back into the old one.

On Thanksgiving night, I was nearly desperate. So, I checked in with someone who always seemed to have the answers.

I turned on Fire Face and sat down on the sofa. "Okay, H. Cough it up. What in the world is going on?"

Not expecting a reply, I grabbed the small throw on the back of the sofa and started to lie down. Just before my head hit the pillow, I heard it. It wasn't Harry's voice "out loud," but it sounded like him in my head.

Leave the condo, Punkin.

I sat up straight and listened for more, but there wasn't more. I replied out loud, "Could you be more specific, please? Do you mean . . . like . . . tonight? Next week? Next year?"

Based upon the way I had been feeling, it's surprising that I didn't immediately bolt. Instead, I went to the kitchen and availed myself of another Thanksgiving champagne. Before I went to bed that night, I defiantly put another Post-it of five completed to-dos on the whiteboard.

The instruction to leave the condo had unnerved me. It was particularly upsetting, because calling Anchorage home was foundational to my plan. I didn't know what or who was trying to derail me, but I decided that I wasn't going to succumb. I completed the client work with days to spare, and on the night of November 29, I went to bed after triumphantly putting the 29th Post-it on the whiteboard.

With client work finished, the long-awaited November 30 was all mine. I was going to spend the entire day planning the month of December—the first month of the rest of my life.

The next morning, I was awake but still in bed when it hit.

"I *KNEW* it!" I exclaimed as I threw back the covers. Barely able to stand, I staggered to the foot of the bed, steadied myself with the footboard, and then fought my way through the narrow hallway that led out of the bedroom, in what felt like the worst kind of carnival ride ever. A nuclear-sounding alarm shrieked with ear-splitting intensity, while an oddly calm voice repeated: "A fire event has been reported. Please leave the building immediately."

I braced myself in the doorway between the hallway and the living room as the building bucked and shook violently. Steel grinded and groaned. Much too calmly, I stared at the chandelier, rattling over the entryway as I considered my fate.

So . . . this is how it ends.

When the building finally stopped shaking, I stepped to the door and peered through the peep-hole. The fire door across the elevator lobby was closed. *Well, I'm screwed if that door doesn't budge.* I had to clear the fire door in order to reach one of the stairwells on either side of the building.

I pulled my long winter parka off the hanger. A gift from Harry, it was the same parka I'd used to cushion his ashes on the ride home from the funeral home nearly six years before. "You'll laugh at the cold in this one, Punkin!" he had promised as he helped me slip it on. I was hoping he would be right one more time.

I sat down in a chair to put on my boots, another gift from Harry. I was quite aware that a small stretch of living room and a wall of windows was the only thing separating me from L Street, nine stories down. I assumed I had just experienced a massive earthquake, and that there could also be a fire in the building. I donned a hat and gloves and collected my cell phone, a charger, and my keys. I put them all in my pocketbook, also a gift from Harry, and draped it over my head and one shoulder. The building lurched again violently, which meant that I wasn't going to grab another single thing. Not even a pair of pants.

I stepped out of the condo, cleared the fire door, and headed for the stairwell. I checked on the neighbor next door. She was terrified.

As calmly as I could, I told her, "I'm not sure what we are dealing with here. Either the earthquake caused a fire or just triggered the alarm. I'm going down the stairs. Would you like to come with me?" She nodded and began repeating that everything was broken. Not wanting to waste a minute more, I interrupted. With a knowing look, I simply said, "We should go."

The stairwell was eerily quiet, and there wasn't another soul in sight. For a split second I thought, *Maybe we should stay put.* But then the calm I felt earlier grew even stronger. I thought about the message, *Leave the condo, Punkin.* And so, with deep faith and armored by gifts from Harry, I did just that—pantless in a parka.

By the time we exited the building, a large crowd had gathered across the street in the dark, 28-degree morning. It didn't take long to learn that a 7.1-magnitude earthquake had struck, followed closely by a 5.7 aftershock.

I was on high alert, paying attention to everything and everyone around me. When I noticed the building manager go back into the lobby of our building, I followed him and asked about the underground parking garage. He was going down to open the doors, and said that we would have to enter from the outside. A small group had gathered in the lobby, so I notified them of the plan. One man, also a resident, was expressing concern about making the trek around to the back of the building. He was wearing a coat, sweater and bright yellow running shorts.

"Trust me, you have on way more than I do!" I teased.

"Oh really?! Can we see?" he taunted.

"I think we've had enough excitement for one morning, don't you think?" I said, not caring that my hair was askew and my legs peeked out occasionally—pale against the black of my boots and thankfully very long parka. The small group erupted in laughter. It was a light moment in an otherwise dark morning.

First out of the parking garage, I drove right to the nearest gas station to fill up. I then went across the street and parked in the middle of the grocery store parking lot, out of the reach of any falling street lights or utility poles.

I wanted to get to my vehicle because it had plug-in power, Wi-Fi, several cases of bottled water, and hopefully, pants.

The twins were the first to call me.

"So, what's shakin'?" Phillip began. His tone was jovial, with an undercurrent of concern. I received my first intel on damage that day from my dear friend in Georgia. The on-ramp to a major roadway just a mile from me had collapsed.

David called next.

"Please tell me you found pants," he said dryly when I answered. I had posted about being *pantless in a parka* to let everyone know I was safe. I concluded the post with *Pray for pants!* Thankfully, my car also had a suitcase of clothes, not yet removed after my last flight from Sitka. So, not long after my call with David, I added a selfie to the post. Peeking out from the large hood of my parka with a big smile on my face, I was holding the prized possession, folded and hanging neatly on a hanger.

Donnie G called shortly thereafter. He was across town when it struck. "I was scared shitless, and I'm not scared of anything!" he growled. "I thought the earth was going to open up and swallow me whole!"

No doubt, it was a ferocious quake. The aftershocks were happening with alarming frequency and intensity. Because of the spot I chose in the parking lot, I felt relatively safe, unless Donnie G's scenario played out. I spent most of the day in my car, fielding phone calls, checking for hotel openings, and watching the aftermath appear on news across the world.

My dear friend Brian called in the late morning to say hello. He had not yet heard about the quake. He was very concerned and strongly suggested that I get on a plane and leave. Admittedly, I had contemplated that already. A hotel room in Seattle sounded pretty good to me.

I didn't realize it until that moment, but something had stirred in me as I sat in my car, feeling the rolls and rumbles of the aftershocks. I had just declared that Anchorage was going to be my home, and I wasn't going to let an earthquake or a voice in my head convince me otherwise.

"I can appreciate your concern. And I had considered that." My voice started to crack for the first time that day. "But I've been trying to find home for years. I've just decided that this is it." I explained that I had planned for December to be a pivotal time for me, and that leaving would disrupt everything I had been working toward. "If I leave, I want to do so with intention, because I'm moving toward something, not because I'm running away."

That first evening, I walked into a fully booked Courtyard Marriott at the very moment they received a cancelation. Feeling a need for human interaction and food, I sauntered into the bar, and ended the evening by drowning my sorrows in chicken pot pie and prosecco. I crawled into bed with my clothes on and laid as far away from a large wall unit as I could. My backpack leaned against the door, ready to go if need be. I barely slept as the building trembled over and over, each aftershock bringing another wave of fear.

I had thought about the souls of 9/11 that morning when I started down the stairwell of my building. That night, I thought about people who live in war-torn cities. Who never know when the next bomb will land or missile will strike. I knew it wasn't the same thing at all; they were at the mercy of enemies trying to kill them. I was at the mercy of Mother Nature just doing her thing. But I did feel for them in a new way.

The next day, I returned to the condo to assess the damage. Anchorage had implemented the strictest of building codes after a 1964 Good Friday quake. That 9.2M earthquake, which is still the largest in US history, liquified the earth, causing portions of town to slip into the Cook Inlet. The rest of the town suffered catastrophic damage, and over one hundred people died. Amazingly, the 2018 quake caused relatively little building damage and no loss of lives. The hardest hit had been roads and freeways. Donnie G told me that Peterson Tower, constructed a few years after the historic quake, was built like a tank. Even so, I was pretty nervous about returning. And I was expecting the condo to look like a disaster.

I was surprised to find it in pretty good shape despite the violent shaking and the horrifying sounds from 24 hours before. I stood in the very spot where I had contemplated the end of my life. My eyes welled with tears as I realized that the terrifying grinding and groaning the morning before had not been sounds of the building falling apart, but rather the sounds of it fighting to stay together. Something that I could relate to entirely.

I cleaned up the condo, and then sat down at my desk to restart my game plan. But the aftershocks continued. As the short Alaska winter day turned to night, I went back to the hotel, once again drowning my sorrows in pot pie and prosecco. Once again sleeping with my clothes on, my backpack by the door.

I was in the bathroom at the condo the next morning when another big aftershock hit. I walked out of the bathroom, packed up my scanner and a few boxes of materials, and returned to the hotel. Using the office equipment from Sitka which was still in the car, I set up shop in my hotel room.

By December 3, 170 aftershocks measuring 3.0 or higher had occurred. They were expected to continue for 300 days or more. After another week of aftershocks, I knew I was done in the condo. It was beautiful, I loved my office setup, the kitchen cubby had become my "porch," and I loved its location. But, being totally honest with myself, I had never slept well there, even when Harry was with me. Since the master bedroom was at the end of a long hallway which made me feel trapped, it didn't help that I was in the bedroom when the quake hit. And it certainly didn't help that Harry had offered his recommendation to "leave the condo."

In the first half of December, I took myself through an evaluation and decision-making process. I had to find a new place to call home. At night, I journaled while spending hours at Simon & Seafort's or in the hotel bar—taking solace in the fact that if another big quake hit, I would at least be with other people. I kept eating, and I kept drinking. The aftershocks kept coming. Everyone was on edge; the entire town seemed to have PTSD.

Shortly into my decision-making process, I realized it was time to leave Anchorage. I had done some research after Harry passed away. I knew there wasn't anywhere else in town I wanted to live. More importantly, I wanted to focus my attention on all the exciting things in front of me—not on trying to overcome a fear of staying in a condo in which I had never been wholly comfortable.

One day, as I was chatting with God about my plans to move, I heard the words loud and clear in my head: *I have assembled a team to love, support, encourage and help you. They are waiting for you there.* It wasn't hard to believe. The cardinal had signaled it the year before, and my tenants had moved out a few months later. So, from my hotel room "office," I began to mobilize. In addition to the exciting events planned for the year, I now had something else to run toward. Savannah was waiting. It was time to go home.

A couple of days later, I went for a drive along the Turnagain Arm to clear my head. I was listening to beautiful Christmas music, thinking about how quickly life had changed, when I felt a sudden sense of urgency. I wanted to get on with a beautiful life, and I didn't want to wait another minute to do it. I drove back to the hotel, where I had slept for the previous 22 nights. It was time to check out of the hotel and check back into life.

I went straight to Savannah. Even though I had made a solid decision to move back, my intuition told me to go there to audit my thinking. Without telling anyone, I returned to the house where Harry and I started our life together, where Wise Old Al and I experienced the incredible cardinal event the year before. Where I would start the next phase of my life. I just wanted to be there by myself, in the quiet. To see how it felt.

The cardinal was waiting for me on the front of a magazine left on the garage stairs. I walked through the empty house, my steps on the hardwood floors echoing off the bare walls that Harry and I had joyfully decorated together. I climbed the stairs, not an easy endeavor given the pain and weakness in my body. I felt sad as I looked into the room that had been Harry's office, imagining it as mine. I returned to the kitchen, a well-used room we had made our own with paint, new appliances and a little remodeling.

I walked outside and sat down on the steps leading from the deck into the backyard. I listened and waited. No doubt, I loved the location. The tan stucco home backed up to a golf course and sat across the street from vacant land where no homes would ever be built. Just around the circle there was a deep-water marina, with boardwalks leading to lovely walking trails along palm-lined marshes and shaded with majestic oak trees. The island community had a plethora of dining and recreational facilities, and nonstop social events. It would be a nearly perfect place for me to be.

Nevertheless, I wasn't feeling the conviction I had when analyzing it on paper. I wondered if it were because of the memories. Or that, on some level, moving back to Savannah seemed like undoing or erasing everything that had taken place over the 15 years I had been gone. A few years before, both of those might have been valid considerations. But the last year of intense personal work assured me that wasn't the case at all. I was a different person. When I acknowledged that, a question popped into my head.

Would I buy this house again today? I felt a weight lift from my shoulders as I answered, *No, I would not.* It seemed that I had applied the lesson I learned from Blood Alley. My intuition had been to go to Savannah to "try on" the house. By doing so, I had taken another step forward in crafting a life of intention, rather than choosing the path of least resistance. Though I still felt Savannah was my landing spot, I knew that this house was not.

The year had started with a tsunami evacuation in Sitka, and ended with a soul-shaking earthquake in Anchorage and my decision to sell the Savannah house. In between, I had begun to follow my heart, and received confirmation along the way that my path was sure and true.

During those days and nights in the Anchorage Courtyard Marriott, while relentless aftershocks shook my resolve as much as they shook the building, I continued working toward my dream. I assembled every bit of writing I had completed over the past five years, and made plans to visit my mentor and dear friend in January. For years, she had been badgering me about writing a book. Now I was heading south because I couldn't think of anyone better than The Duber to help me get started.

Chapter 23

"It's not good, kiddo. They believe it's cancer."

My entire body froze, except for my heart. It was pounding wildly inside my chest. I had only ever known The Duber as tough, tenacious and resilient. But she had called me at 1:41 a.m. I knew she was scared. I was too.

I had gotten back to my hotel room less than an hour earlier. In West Palm Beach at a business event, I was heading to Orlando the next morning to start my week with The Duber. I smiled when I checked my phone to see that I had three missed calls from her. I assumed she was excited about my impending arrival and wanted to let me know that she was well-stocked with red pens.

But her voicemails told a different story. She had been admitted to the hospital, and was having some tests done. Due to the late hour when I got the messages, I immediately texted instead of calling. I let her know that if she woke up in the middle of the night and wanted to talk, to please call me, no matter the time.

Less than an hour later, she took me up on the offer. Sadly, red pens were the last thing on her mind.

I took a deep breath and replied, "As usual, you are right. This is not good." She wasn't one to sugarcoat things, and I wasn't going to offend her by doing so. I followed up with an assurance that more information may shine a brighter light on the news, and that

I would see her the next day. We ended our call as we always did, with "Love ya."

After hanging up, I tried to find something positive on which to focus. There was still a lot we didn't know, so there was a lot of room for good news. I also took great solace that, as luck or divine intervention would have it, I was just a couple of hours down the street, instead of half a world away in Alaska. The next day, I headed to Orlando.

Ours was a unique connection. While I could count on one hand the times we had connected in person over the 30-plus years since high school, and a few more times than that on the phone, the bond between us ran deep. I still had the two handwritten letters from her during those in-between years. She still had papers I wrote in the eighth grade. It had always been important for me to "get the A" from Carol Duberstein. As a result, she had been ever-present in my life.

She was pretty tuckered out by the time I arrived the next day, so I visited with her briefly. She didn't seem nervous or afraid. Just extra tired, disappointed, and apologetic that her being in the hospital was an inconvenience.

The following day, I had her all to myself. Her oldest daughter Shani was on her way from out of town, and her youngest daughter Nanci had a prior commitment that The Duber insisted she keep.

We spent a good part of the day at a nearby diagnostic center. She was scheduled for a test to confirm the preliminary diagnosis and determine the extent of disease, in order to determine a treatment protocol. She continually thanked me for being there with her. I continually thanked the Universe that I was.

Shani arrived the next day in time for the diagnosis. It was worse than we could have imagined. The advanced, rapidly spreading small cell lung cancer had already gained the upper hand. I was horrified. And yet, an overwhelming sense of purpose in being there infused me with an aura of calm. I visited twice a day—once in the morning when her daughters were there, and later in the day to give them a break. A couple of days after the diagnosis, she informed me that she had decided against any treatment. She did not want to spend the precious little time she had left on treatments that were certain to leave her depleted, with no guarantee to help.

I knew better than to argue with her. In fact, I couldn't even make an argument against her logic. I would have likely decided the same thing if I were in her position. But with every ounce of me, I wanted to beg her, "Please don't give up! You're The Duber! You are my fearless hero. Just please . . . don't go."

But the truth was, The Duber was dying, and no amount of begging was going to change that. So, I focused on bringing as much light to the darkness as possible. With her permission, I posted on Facebook, and asked her Savannah students to send their comments and favorite memories. I sat by her bed, reading the beautiful messages coming from students, and kept her in good supply of milkshakes, the only thing she felt like eating.

When she told me she wanted the sign of her after-death presence to be, "You know . . . the insect with wings that buzzes around," I asked, "A bumble bee?"

"No! Bigger wings," she said, without opening her eyes.

"A dragonfly?"

"Yes! A dragonfly."

"A dragonfly it is!"

It wasn't long after our dragonfly chat that I decided to leave. Shani and Nanci were planning the funeral. They asked if I would share some remarks and also be a pallbearer. I was honored to do both, and I couldn't have been more appreciative that they were including me. I knew that time was short, and I wanted them to have the most time they could with their mother. I felt the need for some quiet time, and to begin thinking about how I could pay tribute to The Duber.

I decided to drive north to Savannah and meet with Wise Old Al about prepping the house for sale. And then I would head up to Braselton and get some work done. We had been told that The

Duber did not have much longer, and I wanted to be ready to return for the funeral.

On the afternoon I left, only she and I were in the room. She had been sleeping a lot, and appeared to be doing so at the time.

"Are you sleeping?" I asked.

"No," she replied. Again, without opening her eyes.

I leaned in closer. "I'm going to leave for a couple of days, so I want to tell you a few things before I go."

"Why? In case I croak?"

If my heart weren't so broken, I would have burst out laughing. Even at death's door, she was quintessentially The Duber. Again, I dispensed with the idea of sugarcoating it.

"Yes. In case you croak."

"Okay," she said in a tone that I'll never forget. It was a sing-song "Okay," halfway between neutral and excited, and with a hint of relief.

She never opened her eyes while I held her hand and poured my heart out to her. I used my time wisely. While I had a tremendous longing for all the things we would never do, it was eclipsed by a gratitude for things we *had* done. The bond we had shared. The love that had run so deeply, even without constant nurturing. It was a love and connection that had always been and would always be. Needing nothing at all to keep it intact, it simply was.

I had managed not to cry, but my voice cracked near the end as I promised her I would write the book. And that I would do great things.

It was only then that she opened her eyes and looked at me. For a moment, it was the old Duber, seemingly beyond the reach of cancer. Her voice was strong and true.

"Oh, I know. Of that I have no doubt."

I kissed her on the forehead. "Love ya, Duber."

Her eyes were closed again. "Love ya, kiddo."

I started to lean back in my chair.

"You'll be back in a couple of days?"

"I'll be back in a couple of days," I promised. "Try to behave yourself until then."

"Okay," she said with that same sing-song tone as before.

I walked out of the hospital, crawled into the rental car, put my head on the steering wheel, and sobbed until I couldn't breathe. Finally, I drove to Daytona Beach to meet Brian. He had driven up from South Florida to have dinner with me. After he left to go home, I returned to my hotel room and sat on the oceanfront balcony, listening to the waves, well into the night.

I had traveled to Florida to start working on the book with The Duber. Instead, I was now going to speak at her funeral and help carry her casket. The Duber was supposed to see her grandsons graduate from high school and college, and build more memories with her beautiful and brilliant daughters. Somehow it seemed worse because we were finally going to crank out a book called *Song of the Cardinal*. We had more memories to make, too, on a trip to France and an Alaska cruise. I went to bed feeling that life wasn't fair. Despite all of the crises I had faced in my life, it was the first time I could remember ever feeling that way.

By morning, those feelings had dissipated a bit, but I felt unusually fragile and vulnerable. Thankfully, I had a session already scheduled with Bedford that day. We started our call when I hit St. Augustine and finished as I drove onto Skidaway Island in Savannah, three hours later. Feelings of overwhelm, anger and sadness bubbled up as I crossed the St. John's Bridge in Jacksonville. My sister Tanya and I, as little kids, tried to hold our breath from one end of the bridge to the other on our way to our grandparents' house. Ironically, Bedford's response to my sobbing was, "There you go, Cynthia. Just keep breathing." And so, I did.

And so did The Duber. By Valentine's Day, two weeks after the diagnosis, the family had moved her to a hospice facility. I was in my office in Braselton, working on the review work I had committed to for the hospital in Sitka, when I saw Nanci's latest update. Her medical team didn't think that she would make it through the night.

Suddenly, I heard her sleepy question, *You'll be back in a couple of days?*

And then, out of nowhere came the words from one of the many Facebook comments she had left for me over the years. It was in response to the post I had written in tribute to my Eskimo friend named Edna.

I hope, and feel sure that if there is time, you'll come say goodbye to me. I hope many years from now.

I looked at my watch, did some quick math, packed up and headed south. I drove eight hours, with only a 15-minute pit stop at the Georgia/Florida line.

At about 10:30 p.m., I walked into her room.

"That's it!" Nanci exclaimed. "I bet she's been waiting for you. Can you please do something? She's been like this for days!"

It was hard for me to see one of my first heroes laying lifelessly in the bed. I felt too young to recognize the breathing pattern. I knew she was close.

I immediately had a "public" chat with her, as Nanci had pleaded. A short while later, I sat by The Duber's side and had a private chat with someone else.

With my eyes closed and one hand on hers, I appealed to my greatest love. *If you are there, please, please come get The Duber and give her a Very Harry welcome to heaven.*

I smiled as I heard his familiar reply, *Of course, my princess! My feet have wings!*

Fifteen minutes later, she was gone, just before midnight on Valentine's Day.

The funeral happened within days. Shani and Nanci put together an incredible service with beautiful passages and photos, a captivating tribute video, and a eulogy they crafted and Shani delivered. It all perfectly captured the adventuresome and loving spirit of Carol Duberstein. She would have been so very proud of her girls.

At the end, when it came time for others to share stories and comments, the officiant advised us to "keep it short." As a few people stepped forward, I found myself in a quandary. There was nothing short about the remarks I had planned to deliver. I had lived a life of following the rules. Fortunately and unfortunately, I'd had a lot of experience over a short period with the finality of death. I knew there was no chance for a do-over. Suddenly, I became fiercely determined to deliver the message I had for The Duber's family, while letting every person in the room, and those who were watching from above, know just how special I thought she was, and how far and wide her influence had spread.

As I stepped behind the podium, I decided that if I were going to break the rules, I may as well be honest about it. I started out by advising my captive audience that I understood we were to be brief, but that I had a lot to say, and they were stuck with me until I was done. When laughter rippled through the room and I noted two beautiful faces smiling their approval back at me from the front row, I knew that I had chosen well.

I have always believed that we leave an imprint on every person we encounter. Sometimes that imprint is as light as a gentle breeze. Some imprints are deep and profound. They "leave a mark." They change a life.

On the eight-hour Valentine's Day drive to Orlando, I had plenty of time to think about The Duber's mark on me. And that is how I started my remarks.

I had been instantly drawn to her as an eighth grader. There was something so familiar about the new teacher who had sauntered into our classroom from New York. I thought it might have been because my dad was born and raised in New York, but as the years went on, I came to understand that the connection went far deeper than that.

It was a connection that meant those phone calls and messages, though few and far between, were always delivered at the perfect moment, when either of us needed them the most. It was a connection that explained how I, living in Alaska, came to be in Florida at the very moment she was diagnosed with cancer. And why I was able to be there during the last two weeks of her life.

For five of my 12 years in school—eighth through twelfth grade—I had The Duber every single year. English, French, creative writing, and journalism. But I learned far more from her than one would ever find within the four walls of a classroom. When Hancock was sold near the end of our first year together, I was thrilled to learn that she was going to be teaching at the school to which I was transferring. Just as she had done at Hancock, she won over her Memorial Day School students immediately. One of them, Sandy, wrote a beautiful tribute, describing her perfectly:

> *Carol was energetic, passionate, direct, and well … 'bossy.' And it was all perfect. The Duber stands out as the one that made writing fun and cool. And being a late bloomer, I finally made the connection that journalism wasn't English or writing or science or any prescribed methodology. It was capturing history as it happened. It was honest and direct and noble. Just like The Duber.*

It wasn't hard to connect the dots between what I was reading from my classmates and what I had heard from her firsthand. I had sought her wise counsel after applying for a teaching job in 1990. Even then, nearly thirty years before, I was trying to transition out of a career in accounting. And while I didn't get the job, I had seen teaching accounting at a vocational school as a stepping stone to a different professional focus. In one of those two handwritten letters, she provided me with the principles that clearly guided her as an educator, and which were showing up so vividly in comments from her students.

> *Expect each student's best, and be satisfied with no less. A 'C' from some students is better than a 'B' from others. And a 'B' from some, if it represents less than his/her best, is not acceptable. Push each to his limit. Aim high. Love your students. Be honest with them.*

I had been mesmerized by her. She was hard-charging but gentle. Smart, funny without trying, decisive and bold. In many ways, she was everything I either needed in my life, or wanted to be myself. She pushed me relentlessly, so much so, that even when we were out of touch for years, I felt her influence and expectation.

When it came time for this Star Student to select her Star Teacher in my last year of high school, there was really no choice to be made.

I may have been the Star Student in her classroom, but Shani and Nanci were the Star Students of her life. That was clear in what I witnessed over those last two weeks. She was trying to protect them. Didn't want to be a burden. Never once complaining, she faced the knowledge that she had so little time left with amazing grace and dignity.

They were both there for her in her greatest time of need. Stepping in and stepping up—caring for their mother with a strength and resilience that was beautiful to see and experience. I am thankful beyond measure that they allowed me to play a small role.

They had grown into such beautiful women, on the outside and inside. And while I could see and take delight in their unique personalities, I also saw so much of their mother in each one of them. During those last dark days, when they chose laughter over sorrow, I could also see those angelic little-girl smiles I remembered from photos always proudly displayed on The Duber's classroom desk.

As I wrapped up my remarks, I expressed my greatest wish for them: that their journeys out of the darkness of loss and into the light would be swift, and that their hearts would quickly fill with beautiful memories and the certainty that they were the best part of their mother's life. Her pride and joy. Her why.

Later in the day, at the post-burial reception, while I waited for Nanci and Shani to sit down for a moment, I gazed at the gift bags on the table and thought about the moments right after The Duber took her last breath.

Nanci was closest to the bedside, and her expression of sorrow was immediate and intense. Shani and I were standing near the foot of the bed. Shani stood quietly for just a moment, before her shoulders started shaking and tears began to fall. She leaned into me, and I simply held her as she cried.

And then, she stopped. I continued to hold her. She sniffled. And then, with her head still burrowed into me, she said, "You smell good."

I laughed softly, and gently held her away from me. Still holding her by the arms, I looked into her red and swollen eyes and smiled. I glanced over at Nanci to make sure she was tuned in.

"Well, guess what it is?" I asked.

They both just stared at me.

"Eternity."

Shani went right back into a hug with me as Nanci exclaimed, "Oh my God! You were *so* supposed to be here with us!"

And so tucked inside a gift bag for each of them was a bottle of Eternity, a small, red journal, and a heart-shaped coin purse. I bought a set for me as well, so we'd all have something to memorialize the time during which we became sisters, and reluctantly but lovingly sent The Duber on her way. To eternity, with love, on Valentine's Day.

The next morning, I was having breakfast and reflecting on the prior day. Glad to have broken the rules of "keeping it short," I was hoping The Duber was happy with my remarks. I picked up my phone, and was drawn to one of my "memories" on Facebook for that day. I started reading the comments when my heart nearly stopped. I stared at one of them in disbelief.

You can never take the teacher out of me, so here goes: Your use of onomatopoeia was just perfect, and I thought your similes/ metaphors were just wonderful. Yes my dear—A+. Harry and I are very proud of you.

I have no way of knowing for sure what took place in that hospice room on Valentine's night. But based upon a four-year-old comment that "coincidentally" surfaced the morning after her funeral, it appeared The Duber was indeed proud. It also seemed that two of my greatest loved ones *were* together, and wanted me to know that The Duber was happily stocked with red pens in heaven, and Harry's size 14 feet did indeed have wings.

Chapter 24

Even though I received a divine message of comfort and assurance the day after her funeral, The Duber's death was the proverbial straw that broke this camel's back, though it would take a few more months for it to snap.

When I flew out of Sitka on October 31 of the prior year, I had grand plans. To finish a book, to start a year of immersion in Tony Robbins training, to get into tip-top shape, and to figure out where home was. Instead, I thought I was going to die in a 7.1 earthquake, and my precious Duber *did* die. I'd made little progress on the book, was mostly living in a hotel, and had gained 25 pounds.

The earthquake and The Duber's death had delivered a one-two punch that sent me reeling. Rather than give myself time to recover completely, I simply got back on my feet and ran right into the comfortable arms of discomfort. I re-engaged with the hospital in Sitka and took on a new client in Petersburg. My client-less calendar had barely survived two months.

The Sitka engagement was very project-oriented, and the Petersburg project was teaching and coaching only, not sliding numbers into boxes. Both engagements had definitive end dates. I justified them both as being more closely aligned to the new career I had in mind. The truth was that I found it nearly impossible to say "no" to someone in need. Unless that someone was me.

I suspected that this pattern of mine, plus PTSD from the earth-quake and unresolved grief over The Duber's death, were manifesting physically. The pain in my legs, hip and feet had become debilitating. Flight attendants were asking if I needed a wheelchair when they saw me struggle to stand. During a conference in Whistler, British Columbia, I declined an opportunity to bobsled, certain that if I somehow managed to get into the sled, it would take the Jaws of Life to get me out.

After the Whistler trip, I canceled all travel for the spring except for trips directly related to my client work. When my landlord decided that she wanted to move back into her condo, I scrambled to relocate. Even though I had anticipated my next move to be Savannah, my house had not yet sold. My client commitments didn't provide me with time to move anywhere but Anchorage. So, I rented a little cottage on the park strip just a few blocks from the condo. I could barely walk around once everything was in. As a result, I mostly used it as my office, slept at the Courtyard Marriott when I was in town, and promised myself that I would be out before the snow started falling in October.

The first trip on the roster after the spring break in travel was a Tony Robbins business conference in Amsterdam. I planned to have both client engagements well in hand by then and hoped that a lot of rest would have helped with the pain.

The day after I arrived in Amsterdam, I set out for the convention center and event registration. I did fairly well on the walk over, but by the time I got back to the hotel, it felt like I was walking on rocks. I crawled into bed and cried, "What was I thinking? How in the world am I going to do a five-day Tony Robbins event?" I had grown so accustomed to "playing through the pain" that I'd just assumed I would adapt and overcome. But my feet had never hurt the way they did on the walk back.

The next morning, I made my way to the event as slowly and delicately as I could. Despite the pain, I had started the day with a quiet determination to power through. But as the day wore on, my determination faded.

Through it all, I had been a good sport. I had acknowledged that growth came from pain. I had committed to turning Harry's death from the worst thing that ever happened to me, into the best thing. I had poured my heart and soul into my client work, even when my heart and soul cried for something else. I had constantly focused on the light instead of the ever-present darkness. I kept smiling even when I was crying inside. And, especially during the previous year, I had worked extra hard to turn my professional career in a different direction—to turn my dreams into reality.

I had been rewarded with death, pain and frustration. Anxiety and overwhelm. And it was happening again, half a world away, and at the very time I had expected things to be getting better. It seemed that the more I moved the needle toward my heart's desire, the more challenges I faced. And not just ordinary challenges: delivering eulogies and carrying caskets. Food addictions and too much alcohol. Weight gained and confidence lost. I felt done with it all. But then I heard the words that I most needed to hear.

"You can't take people to places you haven't gone. You can't influence someone, if you can't influence yourself. You can't lead people when you haven't led yourself through your own fear, at the same level. And if you learn how to do that and execute effectively, you'll reach and touch more lives than ever before."

There's a video of this moment on YouTube. I saw it a day or two later. Tony Robbins was doing an intervention. I could see a woman, in a blue jacket, standing in the background. Then I saw her sit down, and I knew she was writing what she had just heard. I knew that because the woman was me, writing what I knew was one of the reasons I had traveled across the world: to hear that there was purpose in my pain. All of it. To receive a promise that if I could get to the other side of it, I could use it to help others. I could make the world more beautiful.

Shortly after this realization, I decided there could be no higher priority than to get to the other side of the pain. That meant I needed to take care of myself. With the words of wisdom I so needed to hear scratched down in my notebook, I packed up my things and left. It took me nearly 30 minutes to make the five-minute walk back to the hotel. I crawled into bed as soon as I got there and fell sound asleep.

I knew I wasn't going back to the event, at least for a few days. I was going to get as much rest as possible. I slept a lot and cried even more, but the feelings of angst intensified. With feverish determination, I wrote about anything and everything that surfaced for me emotionally. And then I came across an educational session on Ho'oponopono, a Hawaiian prayer and practice of forgiveness:

> *I'm sorry.*
> *Please forgive me.*
> *Thank you.*
> *I love you.*

I said the prayer out loud, and then I said it again. And again. Over and over again. I knew that the person who most needed to be on the other side of that prayer, was me. I'm not sure how many times I said it, or for how long. But I do know that something broke free inside. Suddenly I was writing my own detailed version:

> *I'm sorry that*
> *I have abused you*
> *I have abandoned you*
> *I have ignored your needs and wants*
> *I have run you into the ground*
> *I have not put you first*
> *I have let so much get in the way of you being happy*
> *I have not cleared a path for you to express your gifts*
> *I have not trusted you*
>
> *Please forgive me*

I never intended to hurt you or limit you in any way. I was simply caught in patterns that I learned as a child, watching how your parents reacted to you. It was, however, the very best they could do with what they had and who they were. Like you, they loved you and meant no harm. And while they are no longer here to physically take care of you, you know deep inside they are indeed still with you, and can now be those ideal parents that you wanted and needed. They ARE those ideal parents now.

Thank you
For not giving up
For continuing to believe
For keeping your sense of humor
For being brave
For refusing to settle
For your faith
For your determination
For wanting to help others
For loving me
I love you, Cynthia.

When I started writing, I felt shame and embarrassment. By the time I finished, I only felt love.

Things seemed to change after that. I was successful in scheduling my first session with a new coach while in Amsterdam. Then I received a text from Tony's personal manual therapist who was available for sessions during the event. I had heard amazing things about James's ability to resolve chronic issues, and thought he might be able to help me. He had an opening during one of the last days of the event, and I took it.

The call with my new coach Tanya was exactly what I needed. We had barely started when she asked in a voice that sounded amazingly like Oprah's, "So why do you hate yourself?" Considering I had just written a page full of abuses, it was a valid question. I had treated strangers better than I had been treating myself. She knew I was in crisis a world away from home, and her question, though rather brutal, did the trick of redirecting my focus from crisis to extreme self-care. She had me identify things I could do each day to take care of myself, and she concurred that an appointment with James was part of it.

The next day, I took a cab to downtown Amsterdam. I walked into the hotel as if walking on rocks and walked out as if walking on a cloud. My feet didn't hurt for the first time in nearly a year. "Do not go and walk five miles, Cynthia," James had advised. "I know how you super-achievers are. But take it easy."

When I asked James what he did, he told me that he had used integrative neurosomatic therapy and fascial counterstrain techniques. I decided to simply call it "magic." Before I left, he agreed to another session at the next event, which was coming up in Dallas.

I was in Amsterdam for 10 days. The first several days were among the lowest I'd ever had. But by the time I left, I had finished a client project, organized my writing files, completed paperwork for my Canfield certifications, had a session with my wonderful new coach, and captured pages and pages of creative ideas. I had also taken a baby step toward self-love with the apology and thank-you notes I had written to myself. I expected to be taking even more baby steps in that direction, especially since I was heading home with happy feet.

Some would have categorized my trip to Amsterdam as a total waste, maybe even concluding it was a mistake for me to leave the event. I felt that way initially. I was also very concerned that maybe I was wrong about following my heart, and that to do so was only going to end in heartbreak and havoc.

But I was humbled by what took place. I decided to do what I thought was best for me, regardless of what others might think. As a result, it felt as if the Universe stepped in with words from Tony to inspire me, hotel staff to comfort me, my new coach Tanya to guide me, and James to heal me. And perhaps most importantly, for Cynthia to love me. Yes, I had paid to be in the room at the event. But I would have paid more had I not left, and what took place outside of the room was priceless.

I had reached a low point while in Amsterdam. Early on, I was angry that I had been hit with struggle and strife for years. The more I followed my heart, the more intense the struggle became. For the first time ever, I wasn't sure that I was up to the challenge. I was tired of constantly overcoming. I didn't want to be the warrior anymore. I was exhausted. I hurt all over and inside. I felt defeated.

I cried heavy tears the last night I was there. They were cleansing, as I felt an extreme sadness for how close I had come to giving up on a better life, and an extreme gratitude that I had not. As I made my way through the airport the next day, the absence of pain in my feet made me realize just how much I had been suffering. As we waited to board, no one asked if I needed a wheelchair, and I didn't avail myself of early boarding "for those needing extra time or assistance." I knew I wasn't completely out of the woods, but I was a lot closer than when I'd arrived.

The trip to Amsterdam was a turning point, no doubt. In general, things seemed better afterward. But by the time a trip to Maui came around in October, I had run out of gas again. Traveling to more events, and to my clients in Sitka and Petersburg, had taken its toll. I was still sleeping in a hotel in Anchorage and working most every single minute that I wasn't in the air. And though my body had felt good from the treatments from James, I continued to gain weight, the rash continued to spread, and my anxiety reached an all-time high.

I decided to skip the Maui trip. The subject matter of the event was "relationship," and I thought it would be extremely painful for me. But oddly enough, I packed a bag the night before my scheduled flight. The next morning, I woke up at 4:15 a.m. without setting an alarm. I still felt very undecided. I was frustrated and asked myself out loud, "Why wouldn't you want to go?" That's when I realized my indecision was actually fear, and I was tired of it. Trusting that there was tremendous healing on the other side of the fear and pain, and because I was so close to the airport, I threw back the covers at 4:20 a.m. When the jet took off at 5:30 a.m., I was on board.

I attended all sessions for the first couple of days. Interestingly, I saw my relationship with Harry in most everything being taught. Surprisingly, it didn't make me feel sad. It simply validated what I already knew to be true—that ours had been a gold standard kind of love.

One afternoon, in the middle of a session, I closed my notebook, picked up my backpack, and left the room. I wasn't injured. I wasn't sick.

I was ready. I knew that what I needed was not "inside the room" that day. It was inside of me.

It took two days, but when I was through, I had nine goals and two action items for each one: an action I could take immediately, and one when I got home. During the process, I committed to slow down. To take myself off the road and out of the air. To be in one place. One of my goals was a personal sanctuary where I could heal physically and emotionally. Another was optimal health and vitality. Achieving other goals would free things up financially so I could focus exclusively on a new career.

I returned to the event on the last day. While helping others write vow renewals for a ceremony that night, I found myself filled with gratitude for having stepped through my fears. As I made my way to the airport the next day, I was eager to get home and build upon the action I had already taken. Every time I'd had a serious goal-setting session, my life took a dramatic turn for the better. But even I was surprised at how beautifully and quickly things unfolded.

Chapter 25

The Savannah house sold within weeks of my leaving Maui. I found a beautiful brand-new apartment in Anchorage, and a doctor to partner with me on my goal to achieve optimal health and vitality.

I began moving into my new abode on January 31. From then until late February, I worked on setting up my personal sanctuary. But I dreaded shopping for furniture. The Peterson Towers condo had been mostly furnished except for our bedroom and my office. On the last stop of a long day with no luck in finding anything of interest, I was drawn to a pale pink button-tufted set the moment I saw it through the showroom windows. I cannot explain why the sofa, oversized armless chair, and princess-looking lounger seemed so familiar to me, but I knew it was mine before I even walked through the door.

The dreaded shopping spree turned into a festive occasion as I added a four-chair pub top dining set. I knew right away that the table and two chairs would be ideal next to one of the large windows, and two chairs would be perfect at the kitchen island.

But the night before the move and the same day the furniture was being delivered, I woke up in the Courtyard Marriott with high anxiety. I felt nowhere near ready. In a panic, I texted Rudy who had moved me to the cottage only a few months earlier. Citing that I wasn't ready, I asked if we could defer.

Rudy wrote back, assuring that everything would be okay. He advised me to relax and suggested, "Let us help you, Cynthia." His message should have made me feel better, but it didn't. And that's when I realized it wasn't about the move.

"Oh my God. I bought *pink furniture*! What have I *done*?!"

Suddenly I had a fear that the traditional-looking furniture would be out of place in the sleek, modern apartment. But it wasn't really about the style of furniture or its color. I was overwhelmed with anxiety because I had chosen. For me. It started when I told the owners of the building that I was interested in one unit, and one unit only. Then I bought unique furniture for it. Tasteful, but almost whimsical. Somehow it seemed all wrong. Deep down, I must have known that moving into the new apartment was another acknowledgment that I was living a life without Harry.

As I began nesting, I put pictures of us and some of just him in the usual places. On the nightstand, in the living room, on my desk, and even on a kitchen shelf. And then I found myself making little decisions based on what Harry would have done or wanted. That caught my attention. I wasn't making it my own place after all. And so, one afternoon, I gathered up the photos and put them in a drawer. *This is only for now, my love. I need to make it my own.*

The sense of peace I felt in my new home was amazing. Unending displays of ever-changing sky, icy blue waters, moonrises and sunsets, appeared in the picture windows featured in every room. No longer living above a busy downtown street, I relaxed in the peace and quiet.

I couldn't think of a better place to ride out the COVID lockdown, and was so glad that I found the apartment and moved in before it began. I felt more than a little guilty that the virus ravaging the world was creating the very scenario I envisioned in my Maui goal-setting exercise—being off the road and in one place.

For a while, I sank into sadness, seeing the death and despair while watching organizations like my hospital clients fight to protect their community and save lives. Supporting them from afar became a priority for me. I also made a conscious decision to make the best of the lockdown for myself.

I had long since dispatched with the idea that meditation required sitting cross-legged and chanting while incense burned in the background. In fact, I knew I'd often been in meditative states when I took walks, went on long drives, or wrote in my journal. Some of my most healing moments occurred in the guided meditations during my training events over the prior two years. So, I incorporated meditation into my daily routine. On most days, that meant I simply sat quietly by the fire with my eyes closed, on the beautiful pink sofa that looked perfect in my new abode.

I also continued to practice self-care, unpack from the move, and organize my office. When I saw the lockdown coming, I did something that had been on the back burner of my life for far too long. After stocking up on groceries the day before lockdown, I stopped by the local music store and picked up a piano keyboard.

The box was huge and heavy, and I still had a lot to unpack and put away to make room for it. I knew it would be safe and warm in the heated garage, so I left it in the car.

I had been doing well with Alaska's version of shelter in place, which we called "hunkering down." It was nice to have my feet on the ground for more than a few days and sleep in the same bed, especially since it had a cozy new mattress. I got some much-needed rest and handled a lot of my own personal to-dos. I gained some traction with my new doctor, lost ten pounds, and continued to serve my clients.

And I wrote. A lot.

But the keyboard stayed in the car. And it didn't take long for my energy to dip. My mood followed shortly behind it. Nights turned sleepless. Suddenly, the peaceful emotional sanctuary seemed to have slipped away. The best I could do was to wait it out. In bed. Exhausted. It wasn't lost on me that this came on just after allowing

myself dedicated time to do something I loved: four solid days working on a book. I had great fun, and as usual, someone ended up crying.

On Mother's Day afternoon, I woke up from yet another nap.
For a delightful nanosecond, I forgot that my mother had passed
away, even though she had done so four years before. The spark of
happiness compelled me to throw back the covers and give the rest
of the day a whirl. I was pleasantly surprised to feel a boost in mood
and energy.

I still had Momma on my mind as I padded into the kitchen. The
feeling had lingered, almost like a "Hilda hug" which always stayed
with me long after her three short and surprisingly strong squeezes. It
was a beautiful, blue-sky afternoon in Anchorage. From the kitchen
window I could see many people in the park strip—the west end
of what used to be a runway that ran through the middle of town.
Children were flying kites, adults were walking dogs, others were
roller-blading on the sidewalk, and some were just lounging, six feet
apart, enjoying the afternoon sunshine. I smiled, noting the grass had
turned green while I slept.

Why not? I thought as I reached for the teapot. Filling it with
double the usual amount of water, I continued defiantly, *Little girls
have tea parties all the time with their imaginary friends. Maybe a
spot of tea with Hildie is just what Little Cynthee needs today.*

By the time the kettle whistled, I had prepared our "crumpets"—
an assortment of strawberries, blueberries, and half a navel orange
each. I thought them a nice complement to the blueberry tea I was
going to serve.

"Flowers! Momma also loved flowers," I said as I grabbed the
hydrangea arrangement from my desk and placed it on the table.
While the tea steeped in our cups, I turned on the TV for some
beautiful background music. But instead of the Soundscapes channel
I listened to during my recent writing fiesta, I found a blue screen
message of a "Civil Authority" test alert from two days before. No
matter what I tried, I couldn't get the blue screen to go away.

I put down the remote and slipped into my chair. And there was
my beautiful mother, smiling back at me over a cup of blueberry tea.

If the whole idea weren't creepy enough, I had printed an 11 x 17 photo of her—that favorite triumphant one I had taken two months before her death. I taped it to the chair opposite me—the one with the view of the water. The best seat in the house.

"Sorry, Hildie. I was hoping we would have a backdrop of beautiful music. But looks like it's just me and you, kid," I said. My eyes watered as I faltered for a second. *How crazy is THIS? Maybe hunkering down HAS finally gotten to me.* And then I saw that smile and heard the giggle.

Oh Cynthee. Don't be silly. I AM right here. Cheers!

As we had countless times, whether with tea, coffee or anything in between, we clinked our cups. "Cheers, Momma!" I toasted out loud.

As I dished berries onto her plate, she commented on how different the milk seemed. When I confessed it was Milkadamia—an alternative made from macadamia nuts—she nodded, took another sip and smiled. *Oh, it's delicious, Cynthee. Thank you!*

When I asked her about heaven, she told me it was even more beautiful than I'd suggested during our night at the hospice house. *You wouldn't believe the colors, Cynthee. It's more magical than I could ever describe. And the flowers! Oh my!*

She told me how great she felt, how happy she was, and affirmed that she had been reunited with Daddy—that they went dancing every day. She'd been with her sisters and parents, and had run into some of my dearly departed friends.

"And Harry?" I asked.

Oh yes, she said with a smile. *He's very busy keeping an eye on you, you know.* And then she giggled. *We still call each other H.*

Halfway through our time together, I realized how peaceful I felt. My Fitbit told me that my resting heart rate, which had been rather high for weeks, had decreased by 50 percent since I sat down to have tea with Hildie.

We covered a lot of territory during that hour. I was amazed and comforted by Momma's words of wisdom. She had been my first and biggest fan. I was her "Little Rose Bud." Even though she had not been to school past the eighth grade, I never submitted a paper or project that didn't have her stamp of approval.

That day, she had a confidence and sense of authority that, though unfamiliar to me, was very welcomed. She advised me that my team of angels was going to help me get to where my heart and soul wanted to go.

And because I know you are going to ask . . . Yes, Harry will be with you every step of the way. He has never left your side, Cynthia. All the signs. All the messages. The cardinal. The sun. The songs. I wish you could see how happy he is when you pick up on the messages. As you know, he's pretty crafty with some of them. He loves it when you connect the dots!

She told me to get a notebook because she had some "homework" for me. For about 15 minutes, she laid out a plan. As she filled me in on who was going to help me do what, she reminded me I had a team of angels "on the ground," as well. She looked at me with quiet determination and said, *Follow your dream, Cynthee. It's time.*

The woman who joined me for tea that day was the Hilda I always knew was there, buried somewhere deep inside. I had seen the glamorous photos of her when she was younger, posing like a model, and I often wondered where that woman went as I watched her cover her face and hide from the camera. She had let the day-to-day struggle of life and my father's anger smother her strong, adventurous, authentic self. I was sure she had appeared that day to advise that I not let anything do the same to me.

"You'd better eat everything on your plate, young lady!" I had teased just before our time together was over.

But alas, she didn't. I sat for a while, not caring how crazy the last hour had been. There was no mistaking the peace in my heart. And I had a Fitbit reading to prove it.

As I relished the experience, I felt compelled to try the music again. Within minutes I executed the "unplug the cable box" solution. As the Soundscapes channel came back to life, I slipped into my chair to finish the tea party by myself.

An unusually beautiful song began to play. Most all music on Soundscapes is instrumental only. This one had vocals. I grabbed my phone, slid off the chair and walked over to the TV to capture the song information with a photo. When I returned, I looked across at the regal woman smiling back at me as I listened to the hauntingly beautiful music of the song, "If a Rose Could Speak." The lyrics seemed to be saying exactly what I needed to hear from my mother.

So there I sat, Hilda's Little Rose Bud, amid the remnants of our imaginary tea party, with tears streaming down my face as I looked across at the photo of my beautiful mother, with a triumphant look on her face, and a rose in her hand.

I felt the familiar rush while thinking, *The rose could speak!* And it was speaking the very words of encouragement that I most needed to hear.

I then noticed that the sun had set. I was happy that I had given Momma the best seat in the house. I was also happy that I'd decided to have my little girl's tea party. For an hour that afternoon, it was like old times: me and Hildie, talking and laughing. Her listening to my dreams and assuring me anything was possible. Only this time, she didn't just assure me anything was possible; she showed me by appearing as her limitless, authentic self.

Although the tea party seemed outrageous and make-believe at first, the beautiful, impeccably timed and perfectly titled song, reassured me that my little party was absolutely, positively, tea for two.

I finished the last of the brew and gazed at the photo of my beautiful Hildie. How wrong I had been: no amount of Alaskan blue sky or golden sunset could have topped *my* view. I'd had the best seat in the house.

I went to bed that night, thankful that a silly idea led to an amazing experience—a few stolen moments with the beautiful woman who carried me for nine months and loved me for a lifetime, and even longer than that, it seemed. Before I fell asleep, I wished her a happy Mother's Day, thanked her for being the perfect mother for me, and assured her she was and always would be my cup of tea.

Chapter 26

After the tea party with my mother, I shared the experience on social media. I could tell by the responses that people wanted to talk about the possibility of connection, and to believe it was true.

Harry had felt ever-present since the night he passed away. While I couldn't know for a fact that he was still tagging along, the frequency and intensity of the experiences had left me convinced that he was. That belief had been one of the most unexpected and powerful antidotes to my grief.

In 2018, during my Canfield training and with starting a book on my mind, I succumbed to my curiosity. At first, I read online articles about messages from heaven. Then I read books and watched movies. Eventually, I had a medium reading.

I had been thinking about it for months. The Duber had been encouraging me to try it, and other people that I also highly respected had experienced great healing from their readings. In the end, I approached it as entertaining research. At best, Harry would materialize and give me a hug; at worst, I would have a fun story to tell. So, in June 2018, during a trip from Anchorage to Braselton, I took a clandestine detour through California.

I had found Susan Grau during online research. She was located fairly close to where I had attended Canfield training, so I was familiar with the area. More importantly, I liked the fact that, in addition to being a professional medium and life path intuitive, she was also a certified grief counselor, an energy healer and had a host of other specialties and certifications. Along the way she also earned a Doctorate in Divinity. Even so, I was fairly nervous and "on guard."

However, the atmosphere couldn't have been more professional, completely erasing any concerns of coming face to face with Cher's "Dark Lady." After a brief introduction and some instructions, we began.

The facts and observations that she relayed to me were stunning. But what really brought them to life was that, as she shared what she was "hearing," she also communicated what she was feeling in terms of personality. If I wanted to believe that Harry was there, she gave me every reason to believe that he was. One minute I was laughing; the next minute I had tears streaming down my face.

We were about halfway through the hour, when she suddenly asked, "Is there a Bryan?"

Until then, the session had been remarkable, yet I was still skeptical. But there's no way that Susan could have known about Bryan. As I listened to her describe the twins' older brother, and my first serious boyfriend, I felt like I was inside my own little miracle.

She told me Harry was still there, and then asked him if he minded that Bryan was also still there. She laughed as she "listened" to his response and then said, "Harry is a very confident man, isn't he?" I burst out laughing as I agreed that indeed he was.

There were other amazing revelations, such as the fact that our wedding vows were "different" and that I couldn't find them. Harry chimed in for me to call the "tribal people in Hawaii." I laughed because we got married on Little Palm Island in the Florida Keys. Maybe he got his islands confused. But I made a note to myself to call Little Palm Island.

Of course, there were some things that didn't make sense. Like Susan hearing "single white flower" over and over again. So, she advised I tuck that away in my memory, because Harry was possibly referring to something yet to come.

I nearly stumbled out of her office that day. Based on the spiritual stalking that I had experienced over the prior four and a half years, I wasn't surprised that Harry showed up in such a big way. I put my head on the steering wheel of the rental car and laughed. I couldn't believe that I walked in not quite knowing what to expect, and walked out having had a spiritual threesome with my first boyfriend and last husband. By the time I boarded my flight to Atlanta, I felt as if I *had* gotten that hug from Harry, and also had quite a story to tell.

My trip to Atlanta had a nearly singular purpose: for me to meet The Bud Man at the house in Braselton. I had been working diligently on my to-dos, and tending to some much-needed repairs at the house was one of them. I had also been working on my ability to ask for help, which was why the repairs were long overdue in the first place. Killing two birds with one stone, I asked for Bud's help with the house. He had stayed in close contact with me over the years, and we had connected in person a few times along the way. I knew he would be thrilled to help me assess what needed to be done, and it didn't hurt that he had inspected the house with Harry while it was being built.

I arrived a day or two before The Bud Man. As had been the case on the last few trips back, the house seemed to have lost some of its magic. The backyard, which had been my sanctuary, was showing some of the same signs. The evergreen trees were turning a burnt orange and dying a slow death. The poolside dolphin fountain was covered with spidery cracks. The flower bed, a gently sloped mound behind the pool, was barren, with only some monkey grass and a few stray weeds to its credit. Long gone were the days when Harry made sure it was filled with my favorite flowers—"stinky vinca" as he'd called them.

On the afternoon that The Bud Man arrived, I stepped onto the small back deck on my way to check on him. He was in the utility room under the house. I took one step toward the stairs and stopped dead in my tracks when I saw it—one of the most precious sights I had ever seen.

A single white flower.

The vinca had come up in the center of the weed-filled bed. I scurried down the stairs to take a closer look. The plant had several buds, but only one flower had bloomed.

Surprise! I could hear Harry bellow. *A single white stinky vinca for the Punkin!*

I was tempted to pinch the flower off to preserve the memory forever, but I also wanted to enjoy that barren bed adorned by its single white flower for a day or two more. A couple of mornings later and much to my dismay, I found that the white flower had fallen off and was shriveled beyond repair.

No doubt, I was disappointed and chastised myself for not treating it with more care. But I need not have worried because by the very next morning, another single white flower had burst into bloom. This time, I waited only a day before pinching off the flower and pressing it into a book.

The next morning, a third single white flower had emerged from one of the remaining buds. This time, and because I was leaving the following day, I pulled up the entire plant and laid it between two sheets of computer paper before pressing it between the pages of the heaviest book I could find. The next day I departed for Alaska with both versions of the single white flower nestled in my briefcase, and a feeling of indescribable enchantment in my heart and soul.

As I flew back to Alaska, I contemplated what had happened and what lay before me. I had only told a couple of people that I was doing the medium reading. I decided that I was going to keep it that way, even though the results had been beyond amazing. It was one thing to write about visits from cardinals and tea parties with my dead mother. It was another to confess a trip to see a medium, a spiritual threesome, and a bouquet of single white flowers, promised and delivered, by Harry. Besides, I had a professional job and reputation. Even though I was in the process of transitioning to a career in which sharing such an experience would be more mainstream, I wasn't there yet.

The following year, when I left The Duber so that she and her daughters could be together before she passed, I arrived in Braselton to find another appointment with Susan on my calendar. I had forgotten about it, having purchased it months before when she was running a special. The consummate bargain shopper, I had snagged two of them, and then promptly forgot about them.

As expected, Harry showed up. But he was not the first one to. As Susan described a woman who could only be The Duber, I instantly assumed she had passed while I drove north. When I explained this, Susan suggested that The Duber was likely in the middle of transitioning. She had felt her presence behind me the minute we connected via teleconference, and picked up that this person felt close to me like family, but was not family. Her direct personality came through as she sent a message for me: "Enough is enough. Get it together. Get it done." She had endearing messages for her daughters and wanted us all to know that we were "enough." Then Susan asked why she was seeing an eagle. I smiled and said that it was the mascot for Hancock Academy, one of The Duber's most cherished teaching venues, and the school where we met.

Over nine years after Harry passed, I had another reading. This time it was by a medium who had been recommended by a mentor, and it was in downtown Savannah, a stop on his east coast tour. My first hour was a private reading. Then, to take full advantage of a local "research" opportunity, I participated in a two-hour group reading with seven others.

The private reading left me reeling. For an hour, he rattled off names and facts he couldn't possibly have known. During the group reading, I felt like I was in my own version of *Midnight in the Garden of Good and Evil.*

Two attendees, who clearly had hit the adult "punch" in the lobby a few times before we started, insisted the rest of us join them as they delivered little plastic cups of cheer around the table. As the medium delivered messages, attendees laughed, gasped in amazement and broke down in tears. Eventually, the two "enthusiastic" attendees became raucous enough that the medium asked for "the room" to settle down.

Afterward, while waiting for dinner to arrive at the hotel restaurant, I canceled a trip scheduled for the next day. I was emotionally drained and physically exhausted. As I sipped on my sparkling water, words from the night replayed in my head and soothed my heart and soul.

"Who's Harry?"

"I'm feeling a term of endearment. Why am I seeing pumpkins?"

"There's been a healing between Harry and his mother. Jean, correct?" That one made me cry. Harry's relationship with his mother Jean had been one of those deep sources of pain I knew about.

"Your father wants you to know that he's very sorry about the alcohol and the anger. And this was Richard, correct?"

And then there was the grand finale . . .

"Your aura is filled with cardinals."

After each medium experience, it became harder and harder to discount the signs and messages I had been receiving for years. The readings fascinated me. Even so, I wasn't sure that I would ever tell anyone about them, and I still wasn't sure what it all meant. But I *did* know that I healed a little more each time, and I felt even more convinced that our deceased loved ones are closer than we could possibly imagine. Of course, I couldn't possibly know if this was true, but after each reading, the same question echoed in my mind.

Wouldn't it be cool if it were?

Chapter 27

COVID hit just over a month after I moved into the new apartment in Anchorage. Initially, I felt a lot of pressure to dive into projects related to a new career. Some of the pressure was self-imposed. Some came from those who were eager to see me get rolling in a different direction.

I pushed back. I didn't want to rush into projects when I was just slowing down and seeing a glimmer of my authentic self. The meditation was impacting me more than I'd ever expected. My days had finally become quiet and calm. I was sleeping better than I ever had. My journal had become my constant companion, and a lot was spilling onto the page. I knew it wasn't just about what I decided to do, but what I decided not to do.

I continued to support my clients, and reveled in watching my trainees bloom and blossom. That summer, as the controller for the Petersburg hospital presented the annual budget to the Board of Directors, I wrote in my notebook, *I couldn't be more proud right now*. At that moment, I realized how satisfying it was to be the teacher in the background instead of the performer out front. For once, I didn't need or want the applause, the approval, or the adrenaline. There was an inherent serenity in being the guide rather than the hero. And it meant that my services could naturally taper off over the coming months.

Not long after my Mother's Day tea party, I read two books by Kyle Cease, a former stand-up comedian turned transformation coach. My first experience with Kyle had been the previous fall, when I stumbled across one of his online videos. I was drawn in by his voice, his sense of humor and his words of wisdom. It didn't hurt that he was using a shiny black grand piano as a prop.

I first read *I Hope I Screw This Up.* Laughing and underlining my way through the book, I couldn't help but feel that I had found a manual for the rest of my life. Immediately after finishing it, I moved on to *The Illusion of Money.* I was lying on the pink princess lounge when I read Kyle's words, *Your love will catch you.* Those five little words spoke volumes to me as I thought about the leaps I wanted to take. *How could I ever not land softly?* I once again felt the surrender of jumping on the damn train, and I knew that letting go of what I had allowed to weigh me down was going to be easier from that moment forward. That night, I took a selfie of a smiling Cynthia with the late-night Alaskan sun shining on my face and glistening eyes. I posted it with a short statement that had been a long time coming.

> *When you finally surrender to the whispers of your heart and soul, the sun will smile upon you with golden rays of joy. Even at midnight.*

One week later, my birthday arrived along with what would have been my and Harry's 15th wedding anniversary. The celebration started the night before with a happy birthday wish from a Canfield classmate and friend, living in Hong Kong, who had made it to July 1 before me. As we chatted online, I remembered we had a birthday connection. "Isn't your birthday close to mine?" I asked.

"December twelfth," he responded.

I smiled as I thought, *Well it didn't take you long, did it, H?* December 12 was also the day of Harry's birth. I initially thought that was the gift in my friend's birthday wish. But the ultimate gift was his recommendation that I read Michael Singer's book, *The Surrender Experiment*. That book and his *The Untethered Soul* turned out to be the perfect follow-ups to Kyle's books, and instrumental in my continued journey to surrender to my authentic self, and let go of anything that didn't align with it.

Later in the day, while perusing his website, I came across an opportunity to work one-on-one with Kyle. I immediately filled out the intake questionnaire. For once, I wasn't trying to answer "correctly" or how I thought I should. I was honest and direct. I didn't even re-read my responses before I hit "submit" with a "Happy birthday to me!"

Within the hour, my application had been accepted, and I was scheduled for a session with Kyle for the very next day. It was the only slot available for several weeks. I was skeptical that anyone had actually reviewed my application until a few days later, when Kyle's right-hand person Mary told me she normally wouldn't have looked at emails that late in the day. But a little voice nudged her, and after reading my application, she approved me immediately because she knew Kyle and I would be a good fit. My heart felt so overflowing with love and generosity of spirit, it seemed unlikely that my birthday could get any better. Until it did.

By making the apartment my own, I had taken a big step toward making my life my own. But I had missed seeing Harry's smiling face on my desk, and knew I would no longer feel that his "presence" was a deterrent from making my own decisions. It was time for Harry to come out of the drawer, and I had a treat for him.

After the medium reading in 2018, when he suggested I call "the tribal people in Hawaii" to locate our wedding vows, I tried to track down our wedding officiant in the Florida Keys. It was tricky because Little Palm Island was still closed after devastating hurricane damage. But I kept trying, and I finally found her on Facebook. She responded that she'd used the "Apache Wedding Song" for our vows. Harry had been partially right. Tribal, yes. Hawaiian, no.

So, for our fifteenth anniversary that year, I retrieved the vows and popped open some champagne. With a photo from our glorious wedding day and one of my favorites of Harry looking on, I read the song in a vow renewal ceremony as the midnight sun sank low on the horizon.

My voice cracked as I read the line about making a life together in our "dwelling." When I finished, I smiled at Harry. He smiled back as I lifted my glass and said, "Welcome home, my love."

From that day forward, I became both a student and practitioner of surrendering and letting go. By the end of the year, I had moved my things out of the Loft in Sitka, sold the house in Braselton, and moved the houseful of furniture and personal effects into a rental home on Skidaway Island in Savannah, just around the corner from the house I'd sold the prior year. I kept the apartment in Anchorage for the time being. Admittedly, I wanted a little time to ensure that I felt comfortable before I put all of my eggs into the Savannah basket.

With the work in Sitka concluded and the Petersburg engagement back into maintenance mode after helping them with COVID-related tracking and reporting, I had ample time to settle into the Savannah house. Because it was just a short-term stop on the way to a more permanent address, I named it "The Middle."

Although it was only temporary, and Anchorage was still my primary residence, I set about nesting to make the most used areas feel like home. Carol Albert, the pianist who played at Harry's memorial service, accompanied my every day as her "Morning Music" album of beautiful music elicited feelings of promise and possibility. I also organized my writing content, and when my client needed assistance, I responded. About once a week, I'd glance up to see Wise Old Al swaggering around the yard, making sure the house and yard were okay. Almost always, I fixed coffee, and we sat outside, six feet apart, and visited while he checked to make sure I was okay as well.

After my first session with Kyle, I signed up for more. Now I had another weekly visitor who showed up on my computer screen. It's fair to say that some of the sessions were brutal. Not because Kyle was anything but gentle and kind, but he wasn't interested in hearing about circumstances, goals, and plans. Time after time, he brought me back, kicking and screaming, to the very present moment. He held space for me. He suggested that there could be a higher version of myself than I had ever been able to imagine. During every single session, I cried something out.

In one of our early sessions, while I was still in Anchorage, I decided I wanted to talk about *Song of the Cardinal*—what had happened, and what it meant.

Before our session, I made a run to the post office. But instead of returning right away, I felt an impulse to make the scenic loop out to Point Woronzof. On my way back, I was rehearsing my chat with Kyle about the book, when I noticed a Jeep in the distance. As I continued to rehearse, the Jeep suddenly came into sharper focus. I sped up to get a closer look. My heart beating wildly, I grabbed my phone. While trying to maintain speed and not rear-end the Jeep, I got even closer and snapped a photo.

They say that hindsight is 20/20. I had spent considerable time in my life ruminating about what I could have or should have done in many situations. Before the pandemic, I was more focused on the future, looking forward to 2020 as the year in which everything would turn around.

In the end, at least for me, 2020 became the year in which envisioning the future took a back seat to the "now." It was a year in which I came to appreciate what was right in front of me, in each beautiful present moment. The large cardinal on the wheel-covering of the Jeep that came into focus when I was rehearsing my *Song of the Cardinal* conversation with Kyle had reminded me of that.

For seven years, I had felt his presence as a spiritual messenger, assuring me that Harry was close. But I also felt his guidance and inspiration for many changes in my life. As Harry had done so well, the cardinal had become a GPS of sorts. I had followed him from Georgia to Juneau, where I found him perched in the break room cabinet, and then on to Sitka, where he landed on the radiology window just before my arrival. But now it seemed the Anchorage cardinal, driving away from me on a Jeep, was beckoning me instead of welcoming me.

Let's go, Punkin! It's time to head home!"

This time, it really was.

Chapter 28

I'd often said that "Home is where Harry is." When he passed away, the concept of home became much more complicated for me. In the years that followed, I craved a home where I could feel safe, comfortable, and inspired to pursue my creative interests. I also craved an emotional home of peace, love and joy, and a professional one better aligned with my heart.

It was a tall order, and there were plenty of challenges on all fronts. But I had never subscribed to the philosophy that life on earth was meant to be filled with struggle and strife. Although I had experienced my fair share, I also experienced many moments of grace. Gradually, I recognized that the beautiful moments appeared when I was quiet, contemplative, and totally present with the world around me.

The decision to set up Savannah as a part-time residence and the continued sheltering in place due to COVID provided me with an opportunity to build on the practices that I'd developed in Anchorage to create more quiet in my life. I also learned about Julia Cameron's writing practice called "Morning Pages," which are three handwritten pages a day, first thing in the morning. Any topic. Any style. I had been journaling almost every day for years. So, I shifted my writing time to the morning and called mine "Morning Magic." I continued to read books on the practice of surrendering, and eventually heard about David Hawkins's book, *Letting Go*. The timing couldn't have been more perfect. Reading and journaling my way through that book each morning, and continuing my one-on-ones with Kyle, had been transformational beyond measure.

My client work continued to taper off, which provided me with optimal time to dig into my writing projects. It also gave me an opportunity to start a project that never got off the ground in Anchorage.

It started when his piano instructor played during one of Kyle's weekly online events. After seeing the instructor's information in the chat, I emailed him before he finished playing. Two days later, we met via Zoom.

Soon after Robin started talking, I knew that his mindfulness approach to piano instruction was exactly what I needed. Since I was planning to return to Alaska and my newly purchased keyboard in two weeks, I suggested we wait until then to get started.

I felt it the minute I said it. Before I left Anchorage, I had retrieved the keyboard from the car and bought a self-study online course. But that's where it stopped. As usual, I let other things get in the way. I was about to do it again.

A lifetime of putting myself on hold hovered in that tiny sliver of time.

"Or . . . . I could just buy another keyboard," I said.

"You could!"

"And we can start Monday, and do a lesson every day next week?"

"Absolutely! I have a slot at ten a.m. your time. Will that work?"

"That's perfect!"

By the time the call ended, I was in tears. Happy, giddy tears. I had not only said "yes" to piano lessons; I had said "yes" to joy. I had said "yes" to me. So, with little-girl excitement, I grabbed my purse, fired up the Cop Car, and headed for Portman's Music. I bought a keyboard in record time that day. Just before 10 a.m. on

Monday, January 18, I climbed the stairs to find it waiting for me, along with a dedicated laptop and dining room chair, doubling as my piano bench.

My homework from the intro call had been to pick a song, so I had chosen "My Heart Will Go On." Our lesson started with Robin finding a suitable beginner arrangement, and ended with me playing a few notes.

After the lesson, I stayed at the keyboard and practiced for a while before heading back downstairs. It had been a beautiful morning. A walk at sunrise, Morning Magic, and piano with my new favorite instructor. As I walked into my office, I knew the beautiful mornings I craved in Italy were now mine. *This is how every day WILL start*, I thought.

For weeks, that *is* how most every day started. After writing, I headed to the piano room, excited about what would unfold in the 60 minutes awaiting me at the top of the stairs. Most days, we began with a chat about my practice or the lessons I was learning that went far beyond the 88 keys on the piano. Every day we started with a hearty "Buongiorno!" as we raised our mugs in a toast, having discovered a mutual love for Italy (and coffee). Eventually I headed back down the stairs, counting my blessings and the minutes until it was time to head back up again.

Ten days into my lessons, I wrote in my journal,

Whew . . . just finished my lesson with Robin. I'm so emotional. Have tears. My heart is just totally open right now, and I feel like I've come home.

In the middle of learning a new part of the first song, I played a series of notes with both hands. It was the most beautiful sound I had ever heard. I felt it all over, in my body, heart and soul. I stopped playing and started crying. It would not be the last time that playing the piano unlocked something deeply emotional in me. As Robin observed many months later, the piano was like a long-lost lover to me.

The learning was totally pleasurable, and my progress was swift. There was no agenda, except to revel in the learning and the discovery. There were no lofty goals. No awards to win. No money to be made. No recital ahead. Sometimes I pushed myself with a marathon practice session, but it wasn't to achieve anything. My inner work and Robin's genius approach to instruction turned learning the piano from a technical endeavor into a spiritual practice. I simply could not get enough of it.

I had picked a song in tribute to Harry, to let him know I knew his heart had gone on. But after crying at the keyboard, I saw that the song was actually for both us. Learning to play the piano was allowing me to see, and most importantly to feel, that my heart was going on as well.

I cried constantly during those first few months back in Savannah, but this time, they were happy tears. I was overwhelmed by my peacefulness of spirit and astounded by my feelings of letting go. It felt so incredible that I named those first few months "Magic in The Middle." Life was not without challenges, but as I continued the practice of letting go, I no longer felt the need for others to understand me. I didn't have to be right. I didn't have to win—and that's really when my life seemed to change.

Making very conscious decisions about where I allowed my energy and focus to go, I was able to navigate several challenging situations, including the unexpected resignation of the Petersburg controller and the need to move from The Middle sooner than I had planned.

I wasn't just observing life through rose-colored glasses or avoiding confrontation. Every day, I was becoming clearer about what was important to me. I could have chosen to be upset about moving sooner than expected, and I was for a while. I almost couldn't believe that once again I was living in a hotel. But I knew that something important was happening. I was seeing blessings in everything. Had it not been for the issues at The Middle, I might never have learned that Robin was one of two perfect people to help me launch full-steam ahead into writing my first book. And I may not have found the absolute perfect home in which to do it.

It started a few weeks into my lessons when I shared about my writing goals. "I feel like I have eight or nine books in me!" I gushed.

Robin laughed and wisely advised, "I think it would be good for you to finish *one* of them."

When we found ourselves with a week of piano lessons scheduled, but no access to my keyboard because of repairs scheduled at The Middle, Robin suggested we use our sessions for the book. He had long been interested in coaching artists on creative projects, and asked me to be his guinea pig for a week. It was a no-brainer for me. I'd had a lot of teachers and coaches in my life, and Robin was one of the best I'd ever had. And now he was viewing me as an "artist." He had made me an offer I couldn't refuse!

It didn't take me long to realize that his creative genius extended well beyond music. I shouldn't have been surprised. He is an extremely talented musician, an accomplished songwriter, and a composer of musical theater. So, when he responded with a "Holy shit, Cynthia!" after I read him the back cover of one of my "fake" books, it was almost like getting an A+ from The Duber. His enthusiasm and interest in the story were motivating, and he recommended I hire a coach.

I'm not sure why I hadn't thought of that myself. I had built my own "A-Team" of coaches and advisors, and yet I didn't have one for writing. I'd just attended a writer's workshop, so I reached out to the featured literary agency. After a wonderful discussion with Donna, the matchmaker for authors and resources, she paired me with Barry.

With an incredibly diverse background in all things literary, Barry was a self-described journalist, lyricist and interviewer who loved to tell a story. He had a Grammy nomination to his credit, had written for several well-known newspapers and magazines, and even co-wrote the song "In Between Dances," which became a hit for country music star Pam Tillis. I engaged Barry to provide draft support services. His primary role was to read the draft as I wrote it, two chapters at a time, and provide feedback and encouragement to assist me in writing the next two.

During our initial call to confirm that we were a "match," I was drawn in by his gentle demeanor and thought-provoking questions. I knew that we could work well together. My challenge was determining which story to tell first and when we could start, since my schedule had developed a wrinkle with needing to move out of The Middle.

And I had one seemingly insurmountable problem: I had nowhere to go.

I had decided against buying until I knew the move to Savannah had been a good one and there wasn't a single suitable house for lease on Skidaway Island. Believing that everything was working in my favor, I refused to panic. I considered other areas in town and checked out other cities. Ultimately, I reconfirmed that Skidaway Island was where I wanted to be, for all the reasons I'd outlined in my post-earthquake decision just over two years before. That's when I got resourceful. And then I got lucky.

I had a feeling it was "the" house, the moment I pulled into the driveway. I could hear the cardinal singing loudly before I even opened the car door. When I walked inside, I noted the same pale-yellow walls as the house in Braselton. Same fit and finish, even the same cabinets in the kitchen. And windows everywhere. When I walked onto the veranda off the kitchen, I noted the breathtaking view of lagoons teeming with wildlife. My heart swelled as a gentle sea breeze blew in and whispered, *This is where you will write the book.* As the realtor and I walked to our cars, she said, "The cardinals are singing so loud today, aren't they?"

Thirty years before, I had done the accounting for her real estate company. When I saw that she had a home listed that had been on the market for a while, I contacted her to see if the owners might be interested in renting. That was me being resourceful. Though they were not interested in leasing, she had friends with a house who were. And that's when I got lucky.

I moved in 30 days later. Over the next few months, my inner artist emerged more and more as I spent my days playing piano, writing, and decorating. In the mornings and late evenings, I hung art, unpacked boxes, and set up my office. During the Alaska daytime hours, I supported my client as needed. When I decided that the best room in the house for my office was the master bedroom, I called the movers to rearrange accordingly.

I slept marvelously, lost weight, and the rash that had exploded on my legs and arms began to fade away. I was able to spend quality time with my sister Tanya. During our Friday-night slumber parties, I always followed her upstairs to rock her to sleep with a piano lullaby.

Wise Old Al continued to check on me, often dropping by on Sunday mornings to have coffee on the veranda. On the night before I returned to Alaska for the first time since I had moved from Braselton, he and his wife Nanette came over to have dinner and see me off. It was a good thing I had not waited to start piano until I went back to Anchorage, because I had remained in Savannah for months, not weeks as originally planned.

I continued to see blessings in everything. The house repairs led to my first book sessions with Robin, which led me to Barry. It also led me to the beautiful house, which happened to be right around the corner from where I started my life with Harry, in my favorite area of Skidaway Island. I had come full circle, only it felt more like an upward spiral. I may have landed in the same place geographically, but I was nowhere near the same person who'd left Savannah fifteen years before.

By the time my birthday arrived that year, I felt incredible. I went to my favorite club on the island for dinner. When I came home, I walked upstairs to the piano room and played "The Entertainer" better than I ever had. It was the second of three songs I had learned in the five months since I started lessons. I turned on Zoom and recorded myself, playing it again, better than the first. Much to my surprise, I decided to post the video for all my Facebook world to see. Sharing that moment with my friends led to pure, unapologetic, unbridled joy.

But the joy wasn't really about playing the song better than I ever had. In fact, it wasn't even about me at all. It was about what came through me to spark laughter and make people smile. When I saw the comments, I felt a connection to my friends like never before. It was as if we were triumphantly claiming a collective victory, no matter our trials and tribulations. No matter the odds. That we were laughing and celebrating because we realized that:

We made it through.

It's never too late.

Life is beautiful.

Even when it's not.

I've played "The Entertainer" every time I've sat at the keyboard since. Not once have I come close to playing it the way I did that night. I've been okay with that, because now every time I sit down on that bench, I know that, between the unknown that precedes the first note and the known that follows the last one, lies an exhilarating, infinite realm of possibility of what could happen in between. It was a veritable Magic in The Middle that had followed me to the new house.

Yes, there is always the possibility of stumbling and falling. But there is also always the possibility that I will simply disappear so that something can emerge—something so beautiful and magical, no human could ever create it.

I've always believed that is how life is supposed to be—going through each day with little-kid excitement about what may be around the next corner. Learning piano had taught me to revel in that unknown again, and as a result, my life was changing in ways I could never have imagined. I was waking up with a song in my heart and walking into the rest of the day with a spring in my step. My feelings of joy inspired me to launch into writing with energy and inspiration. Peacefulness permeated each day. But then, without warning, I suddenly felt as if I were in the doghouse. Again.

The birthday piano party had been exhilarating. The amazing reaction from so many people had been intoxicating. But within days and despite everything going so right, I suddenly felt so wrong.

I quickly determined that some of it was work-related. Just when my engagement was winding down to leave a lot of room for creative endeavors, I offered to extend for five months. The controller had resigned in the spring, and they were heading into one of the busiest and challenging times that a client of mine had ever faced. On top of the annual audit and typical regulatory requirements, they also had extensive and complex COVID reporting to complete. And they were going through a complete overhaul of their clinical and financial systems. I loved my client and knew the challenges they faced. I didn't want to abandon them.

By my birthday, I realized that five months might get them through the deadlines, but they would likely need more of my time beyond that, as they searched for a controller and a CFO.

No doubt some of it also related to the huge fun I had with my birthday. Old patterns do not die easily. I had shown my friends that I was having fun. I let them see my joy, and now I was terrified that "I was going to end up crying."

I had just come downstairs from a piano session with Robin, when it hit me like a ton of bricks—harder than it ever had before. It was so dark and heavy, like a dreaded disease. In the past, I would have immediately gone into evasive actions like overworking, overeating, or descending into a shutdown.

But this time I didn't evade. I let myself feel the emotion. It was hot-coal anger. The life I'd designed felt more wonderful and well-fitting than I could have imagined. I had finally let my guard down and let others in. I was being vulnerable at the keyboard with Robin, sharing my book ideas with Barry, and letting the world see my delight in learning something new. I felt more aligned than ever with my heart and soul. I was living in a beautiful home. I felt safe and inspired.

I did not want it to be wrong to live like that.

I wasn't mad at my client. I was mad at myself. After all I had learned and worked toward, I had done it again. My desire to help others had won out over my desire for a different life. I had broken my own heart. Again.

Not only that, but it felt as if something sinister was trying to derail me after having had all the birthday fun.

I'd finally had enough.

I grabbed my pocketbook, fired up the Cop Car, and drove to the north end of the island. Still seething, I eased into the parking lot to gather myself, but I didn't stay there long. I backed out, drove slowly to the exit, and pulled onto the long, and hopefully deserted, McWhorter Road.

That's when I started screaming. In the split second before, I wasn't even sure that I knew how. But driving slowly, I unleashed the first one. And then a second one. And then the volcano erupted. The protective adult in me, vigilant and calm at the wheel, observed the primeval release as the unexpressed scream the night Harry died, and every other suppressed desire and unexpressed pain I had ever experienced, found their voices inside the cocoon of the Cop Car. I don't know what I would have done had the road not ended.

A person can only scream for so long.

A week later, my face exploded with acne and burned as if it were on fire. It raged for nearly five months, leaving me very thankful for makeup and Zoom with its "enhance your appearance" function.

I'll never know if the violence of the screaming triggered the acne, but I believed it did—the boils and whelps representing the emotional toxins I had been carrying inside for far too long.

Shortly thereafter, my rash disappeared completely, I stopped overeating, cut back on alcohol, and lost weight. I supported my client in every way possible, while also being true to my heart.

That fall, I had planned to return to Alaska for onsite work at my client in Petersburg. As my departure date approached, COVID spiked again and client deadlines had grown tighter. Not wanting to risk travel exposure to COVID or lose momentum on my client projects, I deferred travel until late November. This decision also provided me with an opportunity to settle in more in Savannah and socialize, something I had not done since moving the household from Braselton the prior year.

One evening, I went to see a dear friend who had recently lost her husband. We talked a lot about grief, and I had shared one of Robin's video posts in which he talked about grief and played the piano.

It was 2:30 a.m. when I left. I turned up my phone to full volume, pressed "play," and put it on the dash. As Robin's video post played again, I headed toward Skidaway Island, deep in thought about the visit with my friend.

I won't soon forget how it felt—not another car on the road, in the wee hours of the Savannah morning, crossing Johnny Mercer's "Moon River" while Robin's soulfully jazzy version of "Georgia on My Mind" played from the dashboard of the Cop Car.

It was a stark contrast to the screaming drive I had taken just a few months before. And that's when I knew Georgia had not only been on my mind, it had been on my heart as well.

I am exactly where I'm supposed to be right now: emotionally, spiritually, creatively, and geographically.

Forty-five days later, while on a Zoom call with Robin and Barry, that thought echoed again. *I'm exactly where I'm supposed to be.* And then I said out loud, "So, I guess the next step is for me to start writing!"

For the next fourteen months, I wrote the first draft of *Song of the Cardinal* in between debits, credits, client deadlines, and work weeks that averaged 60 to 80 hours. I wrote on the veranda and in my office in Savannah, in a picturesque waterfront cottage in Petersburg, in Anchorage with my pink furniture looking on, and on planes as I traveled between Anchorage and southeast Alaska, and back and forth across the country. After a December 2022 meeting in Santa Barbara, California, I decided I wasn't getting back on a plane until I finished the first draft. So, I holed up in my hotel room and wrote the final four chapters, finishing the last one on Harry's birthday.

The next morning, I woke wanting to share the news with Donna at the literary agency. And then I thought, *Wait . . . doesn't Donna live in California?*

The next afternoon, I arrived early to the Los Olivos Wine Merchant & Café. I was looking forward to meeting Donna and amazed that, much like the artist John Rowe years before, we were "coincidentally" just down the street from one another. Since I was in California's central coast wine country, I decided to check out the restaurant's selection as I waited.

I was gazing at the wall of wine that ran the length of the dining room, when something made me look down into the trough of wine that also ran the length of the room. The label on the wine bottle staring back at me had only two things on it: a picture of an old barn, and the word *cardinal* in simple, red lettering in the upper left-hand corner. As I lifted the bottle from the trough, I thought, *I hope Donna likes red!*

We had seemed to connect from the very first phone call eighteen months before. Meeting Donna in person only confirmed what we both already knew: that an inexplicable bond ran between us. That night, as we drank cardinal wine and feasted on appetizers and pasta, we meandered back and forth between personal and professional with the ease of longtime friends and colleagues.

Eventually, our conversation turned to the topic of grief, and I launched into a passionate diatribe. Just as Bedford had said to me all those years before, the expectation seemed to be: stuff it into a box, cram a lid on top of it, and shove it into the back of a dark closet. That's where it stays, festering and wreaking havoc on us. People who continue to talk about their loved ones are often labeled as "stuck" and "unable to move on."

But why is that? We didn't stop listening to Elvis when he died. We didn't stop taking delight in the Mona Lisa, even though Leonardo da Vinci lived long before any of us. So, why are we encouraged to rip off the band-aid of grief, get on with our lives, and stop talking about and celebrating people we loved with all our hearts? Especially when we don't do that with people we never even knew?

It had certainly helped me to believe that Harry was still with me in spirit. I wished that for others—to give themselves permission to believe that their loved ones were closer than they could possibly imagine.

Eventually, Donna shared that her twenty-year-old grandson had passed away unexpectedly and that her grief was deep, dark and unresolved. She had been trying to find ways to honor him and feel connected.

That we were sharing on such a deep and intimate level seemed comforting to both of us. Though we didn't want the night to end, we had forty-five-minute drives in opposite directions and it was getting late. We donned our coats and were discussing the timeline for our next connection when I felt the nudge.

"Donna, do you mind me asking . . . on what date did Daniel pass?"

I could barely hear her response, as the table next to us erupted in laughter.

"I'm sorry, what was it?"

"January twenty-first."

I stared, not believing what I'd heard. Louder, she repeated it, thinking I'd missed it again.

"January twenty-first."

"Donna. Harry passed. On January twenty-first."

Not saying a word, we stared at each other. A fast-forward movie played in my mind as I saw all of the events falling into place to land us in that moment—a beautifully, affirming moment that something or someone had orchestrated our meeting.

As I drove back to Santa Barbara, I continued to think about our enchanted evening, including what I observed within myself during the discussion about grief. I sensed a disparity between my passion and the one-sentence summary of the book I shared with Donna—a summary that focused on my transformation from accountant to artist.

Toni Morrison, one of America's greatest authors, once said, "If there's a book that you want to read, but it hasn't been written yet, then you must write it." Over dinner with Donna, I experienced my first inkling that the ten-pound, three-ring binder in my hotel room was not the book that I wanted to read, or the book I wanted to write for the grieving Donnas, Paolos, and Cynthias of the world.

Over the next two months, as I talked to more people about the book, and read it myself for the first time since finishing the draft, I *knew* it wasn't. It was, however, the book I needed to write in order to effect a professional transformation. I'll always believe that, with the first draft, I wrote my way out of my accounting career.

I chose to first write about a career transformation because I thought it was easier. Safer. More acceptable. In the end, it was none of that, because I was refusing to honor what my heart was begging to say. In the end, there was really only one first story to tell. I had given it a title just a few months after Harry passed away. But it had taken almost ten years to unfold completely, and for me to become brave enough to tell the story, as I had felt called to tell it.

In mid-January 2023, I set the book aside temporarily and put all of my efforts into concluding the Petersburg engagement as quickly and gracefully as possible from my home office in Savannah. Afterward, I would devote my full time and attention to the book.

Just after the anniversary of Harry's death on January 21, I learned that Juli, who rescued me from Vegas, was not doing well. She had been battling cancer for years. When we spoke in December, she told me, "Status quo." I promised to visit in early February since I was traveling for the first two weeks of January and then had client deadlines at the end of the month.

After receiving a message from Juli's husband Jody that my dear friend wasn't doing well, I immediately traveled to Braselton and stayed at a nearby hotel. For ten days, I came and went like a family member, dropping by numerous times a day when not working on client deadlines in my hotel room. Many mornings started with love and hugs at Papa Jack's; an occasional evening included happy hour with Broughton and Paula.

I made a number of shorter visits during the next couple of months as my friend continued to decline. One morning, after visiting Juli and with no client meetings that day, I decided to go shopping.

Knowing that one of my closest friends was about to die had triggered in me an urgency to live. That day, living meant ditching the keyboard and buying a piano. I had been looking without success in Savannah. But now I was in the Atlanta area, and felt sure "my" piano was waiting for me in the myriad of used and new piano stores: a petite baby grand, shiny black, with a built-in player.

By the time I made the last stop, my enthusiasm and interest had waned. I knew that I was reacting emotionally to the impending death of my friend and the winding down of my Petersburg engagement. Even though I was eager to focus on the book full time, I loved my client and I loved Alaska. And I loved Juli even more. Anticipatory grief had set in.

I returned to Savannah, resolute that buying a piano could wait. I would treat myself to one after the book was finished. That plan was working pretty well until, one day, it seemed Harry stepped in and said, *Not so fast, Punkin'!*

"I'll buy the piano on one condition. You have to help me find a mover, and be at my house when it's delivered."

"Done."

"And one more thing. I'm currently writing a book. When it's published, you and Bekah have to buy a copy."

"We can do that! What's the book about?"

Before I got very far with my answer, Larry cut me off, his eyes wide with excitement.

I listened as he explained that, just days before, he was standing by the kitchen window while his sister Bekah sat nearby.

"Is that the hawk?" she asked, after noting raucous singing from the backyard while she read messages on her phone.

"No, it's the cardinal."

And then Bekah continued, "She's writing about the piano, again."

Despite swearing off the purchase of a piano after I got back from Braselton, a week or two later, one showed up in my Facebook feed. It was exactly what I had envisioned. I sent an initial inquiry with questions. And then I sent a follow-up. To Bekah.

I stared in amazement as I realized that the "she" Bekah was referring to was "me."

Larry continued, "Can you believe that?! The cardinal was singing its head off to us, at the very moment Bekah got your second message about the piano!"

"Welcome to my world! And now you and Bekah are part of the story!"

The next day Larry texted a photo of the cardinal, in the tree again, with a message. *I think Harry wants me to play him a concert!* A few days later, I welcomed the piano home: a petite baby grand, shiny black, with a built-in player. As promised, Larry had secured the services of an excellent piano mover, was there to supervise its arrival, and test to make sure the player was working after its cross-town trip.

It's the first thing I see in the morning, and the last thing I see at night. It has made my heart feel more complete, and the house feel more like a home. Robin was right: a piano *does* seem like a long-lost lover. But this one, having made its way to me in a most divine way, seems like so much more.

Chapter 29

The cardinal also seemed like "so much more" when he flew into my life with red-feathered promises of eternal connection. The moment I saw him gazing at me from the crabapple tree in Braselton, I knew something remarkable was happening.

Since then, I've learned about the spiritual "folklore" that cardinals represent visitors from heaven. The word itself derives from the Latin word *cardinalis* or *cardo*—which means hinge. Thus, a cardinal is known as the hinge on the door that swings between heaven and earth, allowing messages to pass back and forth.

I'd certainly had my fair share of heavenly messages. At first, they felt like words of comfort from Harry. *I'm still here, Punkin!* As time went by, the cardinal seemed to be guiding me as it sang its song of comfort, guidance and hope. It was waiting for me in Juneau when I returned after Harry's death, and in Sitka shortly thereafter. Eventually, it led me back to Georgia, and even to a shiny, black piano.

It also led me to this story.

I started writing it in October 2021. Just days before, I was on the veranda having coffee, listening to Soundscapes, my favorite Music Choice channel. I was contemplating the journey ahead. I had written a lot over the years after Harry's death, usually in bursts of one or two thousand words as events unfolded and emotions were high. But I had never written a book. I was curious how it would go.

Robin and Barry had sent me off with words of encouragement, reminding me that the story was already written; I just needed to let it come through me. Bedford had told me that the book, trapped inside me, was making me sick.

That morning, Michelangelo joined in. When I glanced at my phone, the perfect Soundscapes quote was waiting:

I saw the angel in the marble and carved until I set him free.

Barely able to contain my excitement, I took a screenshot to share later with Barry and Robin. And then I thought about my mantra the night of Harry's service: *I just need to get to the podium.* This time I thought, *I just need to start writing.*

Even so, I was nervous. Though the first draft's major theme was a career transformation, it contained a lot of "cardinal." I felt a deep calling to tell *that* story also. But I couldn't possibly say with authority what it all meant.

I picked up my phone to look at the Michelangelo quote, captured moments before. I stared at the screen. Michelangelo was nowhere to be found. In the split second before I took the screenshot, Joan Walsh Anglund joined the party with her own beautifully timed, even more perfect words of wisdom.

Though it would take fourteen months and dinner with Donna to admit it, I knew that morning the Universe was telling me to write *Song of the Cardinal* as it was meant to be written. I didn't have to prove anything; I only had to tell the story.

I was determined to do just that—to write the story that I so desperately needed to read in the days, weeks, months and years after Harry passed away.

I didn't want instruction. I didn't want exercises to do. I didn't want answers. I wanted to see someone experience grief differently, and trust that the messages from heaven were real. I needed to watch someone drink champagne during the cremation, spray cologne on his pillow, and cry so hard it hurt. To realize that the first time she cut his hair was the last time his hair was cut.

But then . . .

To smear on the war paint
To face each day
To find the good
To believe the sun was still shining even on the darkest day

Mostly, I wanted to see someone remain connected to their loved one—not to stay mired in the past, but to thrive going forward. To trust that their hearts do go on, and that one day they *will* find them above the chimney tops.

But I couldn't write that book until I'd lived it. Until I'd experienced firsthand something that was bigger, and more magical and powerful and loving, than I'd thought possible. I will always believe that Harry has been with me from the moment he left his body, constantly nudging me to look here and listen there. To be my mission control and personal GPS. To send me assurances on the wings of a red bird. I don't have the answers of how; I just believe it to be true. This knowledge, rather than keeping me rooted in the past, helps me to live more fully in the present.

I was never supposed to write a book full of answers. As if to prove that point, I was first sent a songbird, then two accomplished songwriters, and then Joan Walsh Anglund's perfectly timed quote to clarify the mission:

A bird does not sing
     because he has an answer.
He sings
     because he has a song.

As I write the last words of this song, my friend Mary Beth is taking her last breaths. Six years ago, she traveled to Alaska to convince me to leave the accounting profession, return to the East Coast, and pursue a writing career. "All I'm saying is, find a way to make it happen," she'd said before she left.

Mary Beth and I were the friends who didn't need constant contact. We had known each other for nearly 20 years, and often went very long stretches without talking. For the last two years, I had assumed she was busy enjoying her retirement, while I was busy with client work and writing the book. I didn't know that she wasn't busy with retirement. She was busy fighting cancer, again. Paralyzed from the waist down, she had moved into an assisted living facility, and was under hospice care.

When I found out, I was horrified. And mad. I was mad at myself for not staying in touch. And I was a little mad at her for not telling me.

Tears rolled down my face as she shared the details. When she finished, I squeaked out, "Can I come see you?"

"Oh, absolutely!" she responded in the same high-pitched, enthusiastic voice that had always been quintessentially Mary Beth.

My anger didn't last long. In fact, it disappeared almost immediately as I asked myself the question, *What else could this mean?* I didn't know the answer to the question, but as I boarded my flight to Baltimore, I trusted that my visit with Mary Beth would somehow be perfect.

When I walked into her room, I was surprised at how amazing she looked. Each night, I returned to my hotel room exhausted from the nonstop conversation, the champagne and the laughter. With a smile on my face I thought, *Mary Beth is wearing me out!*

One afternoon, I had the honor and pleasure of meeting three of her best friends who brought a delicious home-cooked meal. We picnicked in the room and laughed the afternoon away, ending it with a beautiful photo of smiles, Mary Beth in the center of us all.

During our four days together, she was energetic and in high spirits. In fact, it was hard for me to believe that she was dying. She got emotional once—when I pulled the wooden cardinal from my backpack. For years, it sat in my office, keeping an eye on me. "Now he can keep an eye on you," I said as I placed it where she asked me to—on a table where she could easily see it from her bed.

Her voice cracked as she confessed greeting Harry each morning on her way to work as a cardinal always flew in front of her car. She called on him to watch over her during the many surgeries she'd had in recent years. "He's been my angel," she said.

When I noted how well she seemed to be doing, she told me that others asked how she could be so upbeat when facing death. At 68, she was still very young, and the cancer had tragically returned just as she retired.

"It definitely sucks, but I can't do anything about it. I've lived a beautiful life!" she said, without an ounce of false bravado. "I've had this for 20 years and was lucky to hang around as long as I did. I have amazing friends and family. I've traveled and had a ball!" Then she smiled and said, "Now I'll get to see Harry. I can't wait to tell him what his girl's been up to!"

When I left Mary Beth, I expected to see her again before the end of the year. Barely a week later, on the day after Thanksgiving, I got a call from her dear friend Donna. Things had changed quickly and dramatically. Just as my emotions got the best of me, the beautiful question drifted in again:

What else could this mean?

Mary Beth had been on my mind a lot, even before I knew she was dying. I wanted her to visit me in Savannah. Hang out for a week. Keep me company while I finished the book. I was on the third draft and having trouble with the final chapter. I thought her presence might help me push it over the goal line. Besides, she had been to every place I lived after I married Harry. It was time for her to christen the newest abode in Savannah.

After I hung up with Donna, I knew the answer to question. *Mary Beth is going to keep me company after all.*

I turned on Peter Kater's *Wings of Love*. It was my favorite album of piano music and had been playing in the background for almost every writing session the last two years. I edited all day and well into the evening. When I went to bed, I left the music playing on all speakers in the house.

When Donna texted the next morning that they expected Mary Beth to pass that day, I doubled my efforts, stopping to cry several times, while noting the total calm that blanketed me. I was still at my desk late that night when Donna texted, *Our girl is still hanging on.*

During my Sunday Morning Magic on the veranda, I wrote:

Nothing hurts this morning. I woke with such a feeling of peace and calm. Like all of my systems are in alignment. Like the struggle is over.

I wondered if it had anything to do with Mary Beth.

My game plan for the day was to dive into the final chapter after coffee and writing time. But while pouring a refill in the kitchen, the phrase "last words, last breaths" came through like someone had whispered them in my ear. I returned to the veranda and wrote most of this last chapter in thirty minutes. Then I sat back in my chair, emotionally spent.

That's when it started. A gentle breeze. And a female cardinal, watching quietly from the crepe myrtle tree. I made a note of the time.

Just before noon, I was back at my desk when Donna called to let me know that Mary Beth passed that morning. After hanging up, I smiled as I looked at the notation in my journal.

Female cardinal in the tree when I wrote the last words.

Mary Beth was the fourth dear friend to pass away during the twelve months I was finalizing the book. First it was Donnie G in Anchorage. Then Tiffany, who helped orchestrate my Sitka birthday surprise in Italy. Then my dear Juli, followed by Mary Beth six months later. In the ten years after Harry died, my personal death toll had reached 13 close friends and family members. At 58, I felt too young to have experienced so much loss and grief.

I won't deny that sometimes I want to ask "why?" I want to rebel against reality. And always, I want them back. But now, more often than not, I accept that their journey on earth has ended, and that they are now providing love and support in ways not possible before.

That doesn't mean that I don't cry. Or miss them. I now have deep faith that they are still with me. As Harry once told me when I asked if he believed in God, "I think we all need something to believe in."

As for me, I believe the cardinal is singing all the time. Sometimes it's just the quiet presence of the red bird. Sometimes it's his staccato song. Or a movie. Or a smiley face. Maybe it's a conversation with a stranger. Or a timely question from a friend.

"Do you think that Harry's death has changed you?"

I took a sip of my sparkling water as I thought for a moment. And then I smiled at my friend Jennifer.

After Harry passed away, I often planned my travel to and from Alaska to include a layover at the Seattle Airport Marriott. Sometimes I arrived in time for a full evening of chatting with Jennifer as she managed the concierge room. Other times, I barely made it in before closing time. But every time, I left my friend feeling comforted by her and deep in thought as she invariably asked a profound question or made an astute observation about my journey.

This evening was no different.

"Harry understood that my world changed dramatically after we met. But he insisted that I wasn't 'changing.' I was simply evolving. I think his death put that journey on turbo. So, no, I don't think it has changed me. I'm still just becoming the person I was meant to be."

That person came alive the night that Harry died. When I hung up on Death. When I refused to let it "do me in." At one point, I thought my way to accomplish that was to turn the worst thing that ever happened to me into the best thing. But it wasn't. It was to turn it into the *only* thing possible. To turn it into a song. To take the messages and inspiration I received and sing them out into the world—by how I lived, how I laughed and how I loved.

I believe we all can do this. To listen. To sing. We just have to trust. To keep going when we think we can't.

To get to the podium.

To jump on the damn train.

To refuse letting Death do us in. Or Life.

To find our joy.

My joy didn't come from a piano or a house. It came from the inside and above. It started with a cardinal singing of eternal light and love. Of transformation and truth. Its song, a promise that life is beautiful, even when it's not. A song that guided me to do exactly what Mary Beth advised me to do: find a way to make it happen.

After finalizing the last of the accounting work this year, and as Robin wisely advised, I've finished *one* book. This book has been my cardinal hinge between heaven and earth. Between pain and healing. Between the known life as an accountant and the unknown as an artist. Between Alaska and Georgia. It has closed the door to limitation and opened the door to possibility. It has been a magic in the middle of life-changing transformation.

I am now splitting my time between Georgia and Alaska as I embark on a new career of writing, speaking and advising. But I miss my clients and colleagues. My professional frustration was never about not wanting to serve them; it was about knowing I could serve them even better, outside the box of accounting. I'm looking forward to how that may manifest in the months and years to come. I'm still popping champagne corks, still afraid to sing in front of others, and I have weight to lose. But progress is being made.

I periodically get the "Aaahhh . . . Buongiorno . . . ah?" phone calls from Italy, and I returned there to celebrate the 60th anniversary of Paolo's family business. I continue to banter with the twins, David and Phillip, on our festive "conference calls." Occasionally, I head to Braselton for hugs from Paula and Broughton, or all-you-can-eat love at Papa Jack's. Sometimes Juli's husband Jody, who is also a dear friend, now sits across from me in my favorite booth.

During the last year, my sessions with Bedford have morphed from therapy to celebrations. Susan Grau and I have become fellow authors and friends. She and Bedford are my spiritual "board of directors." And Tanya T., who coached me out of the darkness in Amsterdam, has been integral to the quantum leaps I've made with my career transition, writing this book and living joyfully.

The Duber's daughters, Shani and Nanci, as proxies for their mother, read the book and blessed it. Their input also helped me decide on the final cover design. Many of the other angels who appeared in my life at the right moment, have continued to come and go. They still seem to be perfectly synchronized.

Slumber parties with Tanya punctuate my weeks, as do visits from Wise Old Al, who's still swaggering around the yard, checking on the Cop Car, and having coffee with me on the veranda.

In addition to my weekly visitors, I have a daily one. No longer making dramatic appearances once in a while, he has become a constant companion. When I sit down to eat on the veranda, he is usually quick to appear on the feeder which hangs from the decorative pole that Harry and I bought for our first home almost 20 years ago. While writing, I often look up to find him sitting in the tree, quietly watching me, while the shiny black piano plays softly in the background.

Regular appearances of the cardinal seem to mirror the regular appearance of peace and joy in my daily life. They have taken up residence in my heart and soul, just as the cardinal has taken up residence in the backyard.

Max was right—doing something significant after Harry passed away didn't have to be my name in neon. My "significants" were peace and joy.

Certainly, I had to fight my way out of the claws of grief on more than one occasion. I felt pain I didn't think possible and lost an innocence that I'll never get back. But in its place, I found a connection to myself, to the world, and to the divine that I'll never give up. Grief was the portal to my authentic self. It was the ultimate gift, wrapped up just like those presents from Harry.

Ugly on the outside, beautiful on the inside.

The light that shines now is brighter than any amount of neon. Though I didn't know it at the time, when I turned my face to the sun on that dreary January morning in 2014 after taking off from Seattle, I was opening my heart to the possibility that there is light in the darkness. Today, ten years later, I *know* that there is. That light has illuminated my path every step of the way while the cardinal has looked on, singing at the top of his little-bird lungs.

Along the way, I've experienced eternal love, a spiritual awakening, and transformation in most areas of my life. The journey has left me assured that I was never alone, it wasn't too late to follow my dreams and that grace was waiting patiently for me on the other side of grief.

While I may not know exactly where the beautifully illuminated path will take me next, I do know that it will have challenges. But I also know that, despite those challenges, the path will be paved with miracles and magic.

I can't wait to see what happens next.

The Cardinal's Song

Hello my love, my darling
I know you need to cry
But know that I am with you
In the moon, the sun, the sky

I send you snowflake kisses
Swirling on the wind
And winks of shooting stars so that
Your broken heart will mend

But most of all, I send you love
Swift upon the wings
A bird so bold and oh so red
A bird that loves to sing

It's fun to see that smile of yours
When I have hit the mark
You know it's me without a doubt
And feel that timeless spark

Don't second guess the signs you see
Just let yourself feel loved
And know that I will always be
Watching from above

Our connection is eternal
Our love forever strong
So think of me and feel me close
When you hear the cardinal's song

—*Cynthia Waine Brandt*

A Message for You

M y Dear Reader,
Thank you so much for joining me on this journey! Of course, I express my gratitude with mixed emotions, suspecting that you likely picked up this book because you or someone you love is hurting.

It is my hope that *Song of the Cardinal* brought you comfort. That, on occasion, you saw yourself peering back from the pages. That you laughed. And, yes, that you cried, which sometimes is what we most need to do.

Early on, one of my mentors asked why anyone other than family and close friends would be interested in reading my memoir. "Unless you are famous, memoirs are a tough sell," he had said.

I knew he was testing my conviction, and I didn't flinch. I explained that I had long felt divinely called to tell the story, more for you, the reader, than for myself. I finished with, "And I believe that it will be *more* relatable because I'm *not* famous."

A year later, I opened an email from that mentor and found the words that you now see on the front cover and the first page of "Praise for *Song of the Cardinal*."

I stared at the email as my eyes misted with tears. I knew it was ready for you if Jack Canfield thought it was "one of the most beautiful and captivating books [he had] ever read."

You see, I thought of you often as I was writing. I even overruled my excellent editors more than once, believing I knew best what would be important to you. In many ways, I felt as if I knew you, before we even met!

In the end, it was the only place from which I could write the story. It was never just about me and Harry. As I declared at his memorial service, it was really about "all of us." That night, I didn't quite know what I meant by that. Only that I felt compelled to say it. Today, I have a better idea.

I believe we become inextricably connected to those we encounter along the way, especially those with whom we've shared a deeply emotional experience. I am humbled and honored to now share a bond with you, and I would welcome an opportunity to connect!

Of course, we can do so through social media. And I hope we do. But I also invite you to contact me directly and privately to share what's on your heart after reading *Song of the Cardinal*. It would be such an honor to open an email or reach into my mailbox and find a note from you!

There were many times that the road to completion became difficult. It was during those times that I relied heavily on the encouragement from so many amazing people in my life. But I also relied heavily on you . . . believing that I had been called to take the gifts I had been given and pass them along to you.

So, please keep believing that you are never alone, it's never too late to follow your dreams and that grace is waiting patiently for you on the other side of grief or anywhere else you happen to be.

With much love and gratitude,

Cynthia Waine Brandt
Author | Speaker | Advisor

cynthiabrandt@cynthiabrandt.com
www.cynthiabrandt.com
PO Box 190126
Anchorage, AK 99519

Connect with me on Facebook and Instagram:
Author Cynthia Waine Brandt

Please keep reading to see what's next and meet
the incredible team that helped me create this book for you!

What's YOUR Song of the Cardinal?
Do you have a story to tell?
Help me write another "Song!"

Song of the Cardinal: The Choir Sings
A collection of inspirational stories

And . . . Coming in 2026!

Song of the Cardinal: Second Verse

If you enjoyed *Song of the Cardinal*, you'll find plenty to love about the *Second Verse*. With untold cardinal stories and a deeper dive into my strategies for healing (including facing one of my biggest fears), it promises to be music to your ears and healing for your heart.

Ways to Work with Me
Mentoring & Coaching
Workshops
Speaking Engagements
Book Club Appearances

To Learn More About it All
Please Visit
CynthiaBrandt.com

Acknowledgments

There isn't a person in my life who didn't help get this story out of my heart and into your hands. With unbounded gratitude and appreciation, I acknowledge the following groups and individuals:

Song of the Cardinal cast of characters. No matter how small or large a role you played, your love, support, encouragement, and wisdom helped me weather the storm and bring this story to life. Thank you with all my heart.

Leslie Wells, editor. Even though your client list boasted such names as Michael J. Fox and Mitch Albom, you said "yes" to this first-time author. Wielding a red pen reminiscent of The Duber's, you provided big picture perspective and minutely detailed edits in a direct, but respectful way that was perfect for me. Thank you for making me a better writer and this book a better read.

Cate Hogan, editor. Thank you for a deep and thorough critique of Chapter One. Your keen insights helped hone the all-important start and provided me with invaluable guidance.

Kristen Hamilton, editor. Thank you for being a great "book-end," by delivering a first chapter critique and copy-editing services of the final manuscript. You are a consummate professional!

Tabitha Lahr, interior designer. Your eye for detail and design, a can-do attitude and amazing turn-around times transformed a raw manuscript into a real life book.

GSPH, 99designs.com. Thank you for a cover design that took my breath away and for turning around my requested edits in record time.

Beta Readers: Sandi Atkinson, Bedford Combs, Jarrell Dickey, Nanci Duberstein Warner, Shani Duberstein Magosky, Julie Doss, Ida Eliason, Mary Fast, Betty Heery, Kristen Jones Johnson, Donna Martineau, Jeanette Paxia and Sherry Spencer. A special thanks to you for giving up precious time to read the final draft. You willingly followed my request to color code your way through the book so that I could tell what made you laugh, cry, feel inspired or cringe. Your invaluable feedback helped make *Song of the Cardinal* the best it could possibly be. Your love, friendship, and encouragement have helped make *me* the best I could possibly be.

Sandi Atkinson and Carol Mangiero, proofreaders. Your eagle eyes and humorous commentary turned a tedious task into great fun.

Jarrell Dickey. Thank you for those first beautiful "fake" book covers, your insights, opinions, enthusiasm, record-breaking phone calls and afternoon meetings at Starbucks.

Cindy "Loo Hoo" Wheeler. Thank you for bantering with Harry during his last breakfast and for showering me with flowers, cardinal gifts and love every day since. Your calls "to check on me" helped me finish this book more than you know.

Charity Lindop, artist. Thank you for the late-night chats by text, the messages from Harry, your amazing art and for showing me what it looks like to take a risk and follow your heart.

Tanya Thomas Scott, my "Coachess." How amazing that our first session came during the darkness of Amsterdam, and we are now celebrating the publishing of this book, over five years later! Thank you for your gentle guidance, your tough love, and for always being in my corner. Not only are you a brilliant coach, but you are also a strong role model and dear friend. Thank you for "you."

Barry Alfonso, book mentor. Thank you for your thought-provoking questions and insightful feedback. Not once did you treat me like a first-time writer, and that made all the difference in the world to me.

Donna Galassi, marketing expert. You matched me with Barry before I wrote the first word and were there with a marketing plan after I wrote the last one. In between you encouraged me and became my friend. Thank you!

Robin Holloway, piano instructor and advisor. After teaching me piano for six months, you sat with me daily for six weeks, drawing the stories and insights out of me that became *Song of the Cardinal.* Then you provided wise counsel and friendship as I wrote my way through the first draft and worked myself out of a job. You were right: It was important for me to finish *one* book. I couldn't have done it without you.

Betty Heery. Thank you for coming into my life at the perfect time to push me across the finish line with friendship, wisdom, inspiration, love and...coffee. Your energy and enthusiasm were the rocket fuel I needed to finish. You are the youngest 94-year old I've ever known.

My Facebook Friends. It was only hours after Harry passed away that his sister Heidi alerted you to his passing. You immediately swooped in to wrap me in a warm blanket of comfort and love. In so many ways, you helped shape this book. You patiently listened as I poured my heart out, sharing the unbelievably beautiful things happening during the depth of my sorrow. And then you encouraged me to write a book about them. You reacted to and commented on the hundreds of posts I wrote over the last ten years, traveled with me virtually, sent me private messages of encouragement, and you never, ever let me forget that I promised to do this. Thank you for your love, support, encouragement and belief that I could. And thank you for pestering me until I did.

My Alaska clients and colleagues in Southeast Alaska. I was with you when Harry passed away and it was with you that I spent most of my time in the ten years afterwards. It was my honor to serve you, to work with you and to become your friend. Thank you for embracing me as your healthcare financial management professional and for encouraging me on my new endeavors.

My Chateau Elan Village family, including Paula and Broughton Caldwell, Debby and Grant Carlson, and Juli and Jody Butler: There was no greater feeling than sitting at your kitchen or dining room tables or on "The Porch," sharing Harry stories, great food and a bottle or two of Veuve. You believed in me, read my stories and helped me survive after Harry passed. Thank you. I love you.

Sandra Denton, MD. You practice medicine the way it was meant to be. During this last year, despite my two bouts of COVID and a fractured vertebra, you kept me going with the best medicine there is: LOVE. Thank you for believing in this message and for treating all of me (body, mind *and* spirit) so that "The Cardinal" could take flight.

David Herrin. You pulled me out of the abyss of Vegas and then put a journal and a hand-crafted wooden pen into my hands and told me to "get busy, missy." And then you taunted and teased, encouraged and loved . . . until I did. Thank you for making me laugh and inspiring me with your indomitable spirit.

Tanya Waine Herndon. You sent me the beautiful book, *The Right to Write* by Julia Cameron just months after Harry passed. It was the very first book I read about writing and planted the seed that this could one day be a reality. Thank you for the long chats, countless FedEx shipments, listening to my piano progress and all the beautiful cardinal photos you took. Most of all, thank you for a lifetime of love.

Brian Fried. You've cheered me on for most of my life and believed in me when I did not. Thank you for your loving guidance and gentle nudges to maintain a heading of "true north."

Bedford Combs, spiritual advisor. You sent me home from that first retreat 30 years ago with a note: "God has a remarkable plan for you." Twenty years later you answered a late-night email and, over the last ten years, watched as that remarkable plan unfolded. Thank you for your wise counsel, spiritual insights and endless enthusiasm.

Bill Mays and the Papa Jack's Country Kitchen crew. Thank you Bill for the early encouragement to write and to you and your crew for watching over me as I did, while in "my" booth, with abundant love and a never-ending cup of coffee to keep me company.

Patty Aubery. Canfield Training Group, CEO. Thank you for that first message to "KEEP WRITING" which inspired me over the years to do so.

Jack Canfield. Coauthor of the *Chicken Soup for the Soul*® Series. You mentored me through the final months of my transition from accountant to author with wisdom, insight and honesty, helping me create a vision for a new career and an amazing life. Our time together and your words of encouragement were priceless to me.

Ted Capshaw, transformational coach. Your decision to share my Facebook post with the 2017 AWAI bootcamp attendees sparked a fire in me to make this dream come true. Thank you for embracing the message from your father and encouraging me to "stay true."

Kyle Cease, transformational comedian. I laughed until I cried, cried until I laughed and finally accepted the truth: there truly is no time like the "present." You held a safe space for me as I moved toward a more authentic life. Thank you for your wisdom, generosity of spirit and love.

Paolo Mantovani. You rushed to my side when Harry died and have been there ever since, no matter the physical distance between us. Thank you for loving Harry as a brother, now me as a sister, and for sharing your beautiful family with me. At your kitchen table, with our angels looking on, is one of my favorite places to be.

Carol Duberstein. "The Duber." You always expected my best and you sent the Hancock-green dragonfly to my early writing sessions. You can now put your red pen down. We did it!

Richard and Hilda Waine. I can see so clearly today the perfection of you being my parents and how I have the best of both of you in me. Thank you for the love and sacrifices you made, for believing that I could do anything I dreamed of and for staying close to me in spirit while I did.

Denise Jue Marino. Within hours of the cardinal's first appearance, you sat across from me for the first time in 35 years and asked the question that seems to have set this story in motion. Since then, and as you have since we were little-girl playmates, you've quietly cheered me on. Thank you for our forever friendship.

To the rest of my friends, family and colleagues. Thank you for your love, friendship, encouragement and support. You've played an important role in bringing this book to fruition.

Harry
Thank You
For choosing me,
For making my life sparkle,
And for loving me.
Yesterday, today, and always.
I love you . . . more.

My Team of Angels

1999
Richard J. Waine *(Daddy)*

2007
Sebastiano Mantovani

2012
Bryan Scott Herrin

2014
Harry Charles Brandt (*My Love)*
Betty Lou Barnett Meyers

2015
Coach Tom Carlyle

2016
Hilda Slade Waine (*Momma)*
Jerry L. Atkinson, Sr. (*Pops)*
John F. Adkins, Jr.
Glenda Brannen Smith

2017
Edna Sue Karmen Oliver

2019
Carol M. Duberstein (*The Duber*)

2022
Don Guthrie (*Donnie G)*
Tiffany Jai Martin

2023
Julianne Reiner Butler (*Juli)*
Mary Beth Lepsom

2024
Franca Mantovani
Alberto Mantovani

Permissions

Much appreciation to the many publishers and individuals who provided permission to reprint copyrighted material in *Song of the Cardinal*.

"A bird doesn't sing..." from *A Cup of Sun* by Joan Walsh Anglund. Copyright © by Joan Walsh Anglund. Used by permission of HarperCollins Publishers (print) and the family of Joan Walsh Anglund (electronic).

Here Comes The Sun
Words and Music by George Harrison
Copyright © 1969 Harrisongs Ltd.
Copyright Renewed 1998 All Rights Reserved
Reprinted by Permission of Hal Leonard LLC

"I've heard you talk about Harry..." from a note of condolence by Kendall Gee. Reprinted with permission.

"I have never met anyone quite like Harry..." from a note of condolence by John Bioff. Reprinted with permission.

"Let me know what your intuition..." from an email by Bedford Combs. Reprinted with permission.

"There is no elevator to success...." Quote by Zig Ziglar. Reprinted with permission from Ziglar, Inc.

"A bridge of silver wings..." from *The River of Winged Dreams* by Aberjhani. Reprinted with permission.

Printed in Great Britain
by Amazon

a7c565fd-528c-4ca6-a151-01cbecac9463R02